BEFORE ONTARIO

McGill-Queen's Native and Northern Series
(In memory of Bruce G. Trigger)
Sarah Carter and Arthur J. Ray, Editors

Edited by
Marit K. Munson and Susan M. Jamieson

BEFORE ONTARIO
The
Archaeology
of a Province

McGill-Queen's University Press   Montreal & Kingston • London • Ithaca

ISBN 978-0-7735-4207-5 (cloth)
ISBN 978-0-7735-4208-2 (paper)
ISBN 978-0-7735-8919-3 (ePDF)
ISBN 978-0-7735-8920-9 (ePUB)

Legal deposit fourth quarter 2013
Bibliothèque nationale du Québec

Printed in Canada on acid-free paper

McGill-Queen's University Press acknowledges the support of the Canada Council for the Arts for our publishing program. We also acknowledge the financial support of the Government of Canada through the Canada Book Fund for our publishing activities.

Library and Archives Canada Cataloguing in Publication

Before Ontario : the archaeology of a province / edited by Marit K. Munson and Susan M. Jamieson.

(McGill-Queen's native and northern series ; 72)
Includes bibliographical references and index.
Issued in print and electronic formats.
ISBN 978-0-7735-4207-5 (bound).–ISBN 978-0-7735-4208-2 (pbk.).–
ISBN 978-0-7735-8919-3 (ePDF).–ISBN 978-0-7735-8920-9 (ePUB)

1. Ontario—Antiquities. I. Munson, Marit K, editor of compilation II. Jamieson, Susan M, editor of compilation
III. Series: McGill-Queen's native and northern series ; 72

FC3066.B43 2013   971.3'01   C2013-903962-7
C2013-903963-5

This book was designed and typeset by studio oneonone in Sabon 10/14

In memory of Cath Oberholtzer, 1940–2012

Contents

Figures

Sidebars

Acknowledgments

We gratefully acknowledge the generosity of the individual authors who contributed their time, expertise, and energy to this project, as well as of Laura Helmuth for her excellent advice. We also thank those who contributed images for the book, including the authors, James Conolly, Kate Dougherty, Laura Helmuth, Jean-Luc Pilon, and, above all, Archaeological Services Inc.

Publication of this book was made possible through financial contributions from TUARC (the Trent University Archaeological Research Centre), the Symons Trust Fund for Canadian Studies, Archaeological Services Inc., Timmins Martelle Heritage Consultants, Mima Kapches, Susan Jamieson, Andrew Stewart, and several anonymous donors.

Introduction
Seeing Ontario's Past Archaeologically

Neal Ferris

What do you see when you walk along a path, drive down a country road, or fly over Ontario? There is the physical landscape, certainly – the waterways, lakes, hills, and valleys, and perhaps the Niagara Escarpment. And of course you see the many signs of how we have altered that landscape, especially in the south: the roads, homes, and graded vistas that are the direct result of our collective, continuing efforts to shape, develop, and make the world around us serve our wants and needs. This is the landscape of the present: the spaces and places we all see and read into our sense of home, neighbourhood, community, and, ultimately, belonging. At the same time, this landscape is transitory, changing around us day to day as new roads, buildings, and neighbourhoods are built, others torn down, and others changed. We rarely keep track of these changes except to note that they happened, or occasionally to regret the loss of a woodlot or playground to a new highway or plaza.

Archaeologists – like me and the other authors of this volume – are perhaps more aware of that constant change. We tend to see the world as the accumulation of centuries and millennia of human history, reading the past into the present. We notice the appearance of a new retail complex on the site of a former main street, realize that the highways we drive first began as pioneer roadways opening up the region to European settlement, and see in the many knolls and ridges near creeks and rivers likely locations of ancient Aboriginal settlements.

Increasingly, archaeologists have played a role in the constant changing of today's landscapes, in that most of this development now requires documentation or protection of archaeological sites that may be present on the land before construction begins. So not only do archaeologists see ancient communities and landscapes when we drive through subdivisions or pass by gravel pits, we also see the woodlots, pasture, and farmland that we surveyed looking for archaeological sites, just prior to construction and change. In this way archaeologists serve as chroniclers, by action and by discovery, of the always changing past of this land, place, and society. In doing so, we link these many pasts to our present, revealing the story of the common heritage that has shaped this distinctive place that today we call Ontario. This book, written by archaeologists active in the province, is one way we seek to chronicle some of the many histories that are the legacy of the diverse peoples of this land.

Geography and Environment

This book covers the archaeology of what is now Ontario (figure 0.1). It focuses largely on the area along the north shore of the St Lawrence River and within the lower Great Lakes below the Canadian Shield (figure 0.2) (but see chapter 5). This area corresponds roughly with the southerly part of Ontario today, though this is a rather arbitrary space – as any archaeologist will tell you and as First Nations know, the current boundaries of the province of Ontario have only existed for a little more than 150 years. Even the national borders between Canada and the United States are only a few decades older. For the many thousands of years before Ontario, the area's inhabitants would have imagined this part of the world differently, and would have had very different understandings of boundaries and territory (see Oberholtzer, chapter 11).

Not only would this region have been thought of differently, southern Ontario itself was also, at various times in the past, a very different place (see Stewart, chapter 1, and Karrow and Warner 1990). The Great Lakes were vastly deeper and wider than today, leaving behind relic shorelines now visible as long ridges several kilometres inland from the current Great Lakes. The channels of rivers and streams have changed constantly, as both lakes and drainage patterns were altered over the millennia. And major climatic and environmental changes have occurred since humans first arrived in this part of the world after the retreat of glacial ice – from subarctic to boreal forest to, eventually, the temperate environment we know today in southern Ontario. All of these changes took place over thousands of years, meaning that many generations of people were born, lived, and died in a land that would be as foreign to those of us who live in this land today as today's landscapes would be to those ancient generations. Of course, all of these environmental changes affected human history. As Chris Ellis describes in chapter 2, archaeologists must take into account the relationships among humans and the environment they lived in and manipulated.

First Nations Archaeology

Much of the archaeological record – the materials, plant and animal remains, soils, and contexts recovered from the landscape – that we study in Ontario are the direct and ancient heritage of the various First Nations communities that live here and in

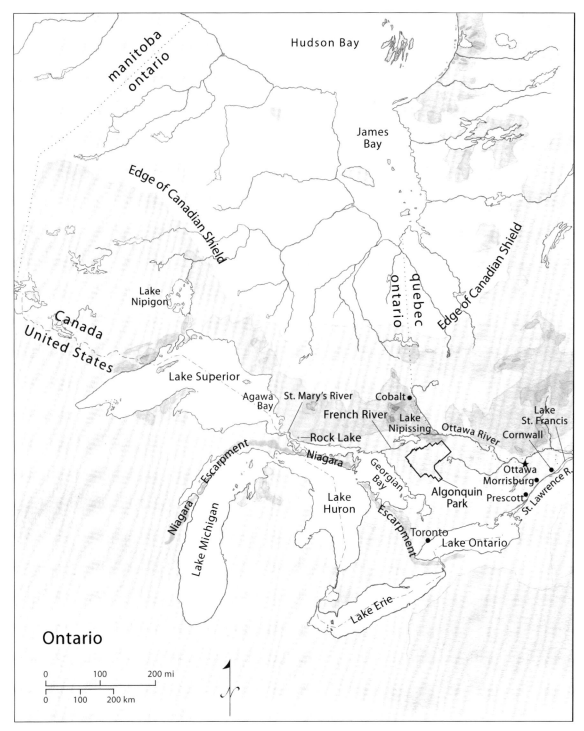

Figure 0.1
Map of Ontario (Map by Molly O'Halloran).

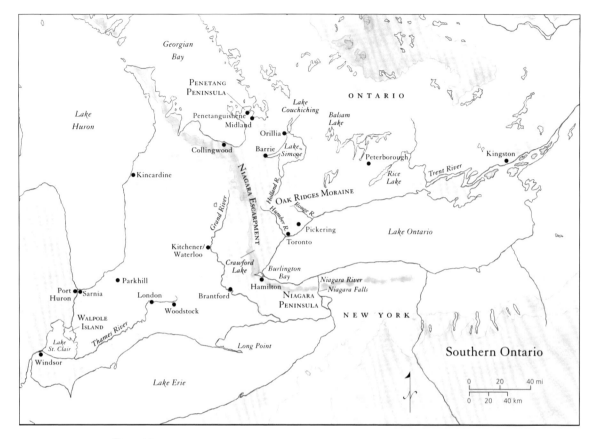

Figure 0.2
Map of southern Ontario (Map by Molly O'Halloran).

adjacent provinces and states today. Indeed, with the exception of the last 400–500 years, the archaeological record is the exclusive past of Aboriginal peoples. Over those thousands of years, people recorded the past through memory, myth, oral history, and retelling, while archaeology remains the sole nonverbal means of reaching back and reconstructing this ancient history of Ontario. This is the great value and privilege of the archaeologist, to see into the deep history that is so hard to access otherwise. But with that privilege comes a responsibility: to convey that material past and ensure that it is a vital part of our shared heritage today.

Who were these ancient Aboriginal people who lived and loved over the place we now know as Ontario? While it is easy enough to acknowledge that they were the ancestors of the descendant First Nations here in Ontario today, the particular challenge is in understanding the past beyond this basic fact. We know that there are many communities and Nations of Aboriginal peoples in Ontario today. These Nations generally divide along lines of culture and language, depending on whether they

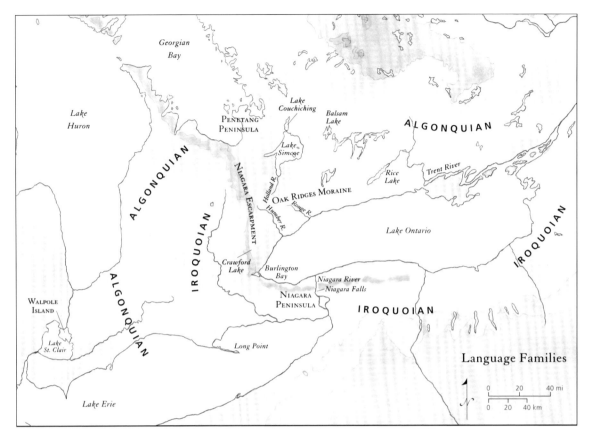

Figure 0.3
First Nations language families in southern Ontario, late 1500s to 1600s CE (Map by Molly O'Halloran).

identify themselves as descendants of particular Iroquoian- or Algonquian-speaking groups (Rogers and Smith 1994a).

The historic records of the Europeans who first met and interacted with the region's Aboriginal peoples in the late 1500s and early 1600s show that people variously identified themselves as belonging to specific nations. The members of these nations spoke particular languages from Iroquoian or Algonquian language groups (figure 0.3). Languages within each group were related but distinct, much as English, French, and Spanish are distinct but come from a common language group. However, I should hasten to add that a term like *nation* is probably an inadequate category to cover all the various political and social configurations of Aboriginal communities that existed even when Europeans first arrived in this part of the world. Indeed, a concept like nation, as it is understood today, is likely both too complex and too simple to capture the distinct group, village, and inter-village relationships that Aboriginal individuals and families defined for themselves (see Jamieson, chapter 12).

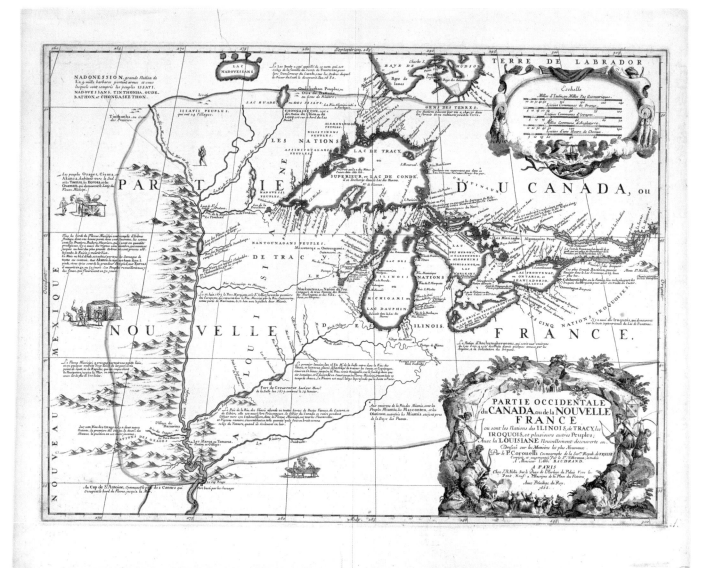

Figure 0.4A
Early European maps document explorers' attempts to make sense of North American geography, including the region that is now Ontario. This 1688 map of Western New France is based on the work of Vincenzo Maria Coronelli. The map focuses on the Great Lakes and major waterways, leaving inland areas mostly blank. (Courtesy of Library and Archives Canada, R3908-2-4-F.)

The Iroquoian groups in southern Ontario identified themselves to Europeans as belonging to one of the several Huron (Wendat), Petun (Tionontaté), and Neutral Nations (Trigger 1985). There were many Algonquian groups as well, whose descendants refer to themselves today as Anishnabeg peoples. We know that groups of these people often referred to themselves as both distinct and also belonging to broader nations. For example, in the 1600s in the area around the westernmost end of Lake Erie were people of the Fire Nation, including groups such as the Pottawatomi, Mesquakie, Mascouten, and Kickapoo.

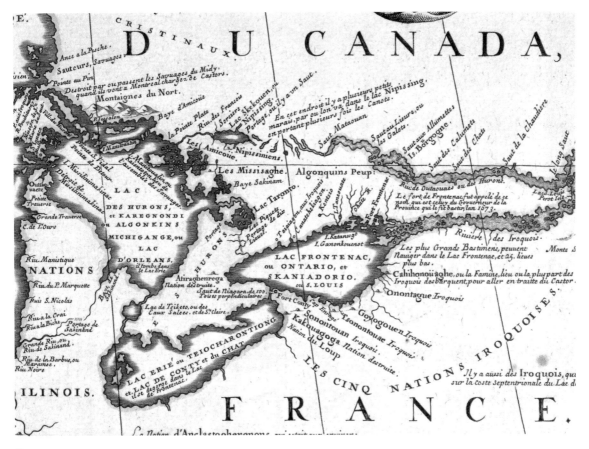

Figure 0.4B
Coronelli's map records considerable information about Ontario, from multiple names for each of the Great
Lakes to portages, rapids, and reported copper sources. Some of the place names identify Aboriginal villages
or nations in the approximate locations of historically-known groups; other names are more ambiguous and
difficult to link to specific groups. (Detail of Coronelli's map of Western New France, courtesy of Library and
Archives Canada, R3908-2-4-F.)

Archaeologists have augmented written accounts of Europeans with investigations
of the specific locales referred to in historic records, documenting the material record
of Aboriginal communities who encountered Europeans and then grappled with the
growing impact of European settlement and colonialism in southern Ontario (figure
0.4). As Gary Warrick discusses in chapter 4, this archaeological work was important
to understanding the material record in the Great Lakes, since archaeologists were
able to compare, for example, Huron villages from the 1600s with records from
French Jesuit missionaries living in those communities. This also allowed archaeologists to evaluate material evidence and patterns of settlement and subsistence with ancient evidence predating any written records, providing greater insight into daily life
from generations or even centuries earlier in time.

This method of working from the historic period back in time is one way that archaeologists have tried to understand the long-term social development of Aboriginal societies and communities, by tracing the historically known material of, for example, Iroquoian life – longhouses, villages surrounded by a palisade or stockade, distinctive pottery styles, farming of maize (corn), and so on – hundreds of years further back in time to when those material patterns first began to appear in the archaeological record.

But the deeper back in time we reach, the harder it is to link those patterns to historically identified peoples. We cannot assume that the ways people organized themselves in the recent past existed long ago. Archaeologists are certainly confident that the remains of several thousand years ago were left behind by the ancestors to modern First Nations. But did those ancient people think of themselves as Iroquoian or Anishnabeg, Huron or Odawa, or some other term now lost in time? Did they even speak the same form of language that they spoke in 1600? Learning what people ate is one thing, but it is an entirely different matter to discern exactly who ancient peoples thought they were, what nations or cultural groups they felt they were a part of, or how those ancient conceptions relate (or not) to modern nations and groups.

The reasons for this are several. Some have to do with the limitations of the archaeological record; others have to do with how we, as individuals and groups, think of our own identities. For example, archaeologists documenting the clay pottery of ancient Aboriginal peoples might study the shape and decoration of the pot and compare this to patterns seen at other times and from other sites of the same time period (see Kapches, chapter 10). In this process of comparison, archaeologists sometimes are tempted to assume people who had similar pottery all belonged to the same cultural group.

The problem is that shared patterns can reflect many different notions, and concepts like identity transcend material patterns – a pot is not a person's identity. Archaeologists of tomorrow, for example, may have a hard time defining an archaeological pattern that is distinctly Ontarian – or Canadian, for that matter. After all, we rely on exports from around the globe and share certain cultural values with the United States and Britain and, increasingly, with other countries as well. Even within a shared concept like nation or language group, people still hold many different identities – a Canadian might also be an Ontarian, a Torontonian, an Anglophone, a mother, a Maple Leafs fan, and an archaeologist. All of these identities shape an individual's sense of self, define their interactions with others, and affect their day-to-day lives in ways both profound and trivial.

Likewise, archaeologists studying villages or hunting camps from 1,000 or 10,000 years ago also need to account for the differing influences, or agency, of individual identities in the archaeological record. Women and men would have contributed differently to the material remains left on a site, as would children and the elderly. And, depending on the society represented at a particular archaeological site, some people who held special roles in communities, such as spiritual leaders or healers, may have contributed to distinct archaeological patterns through their life. Given all these complex realities of human life, it would not be surprising if people 3,000 years ago thought of themselves as something other than Iroquoian. After all, people 3,000 years ago on the British Isles did not think of themselves as English, Scottish, or even Briton or Pict – and yet there is no problem assuming that those people are the ancient ancestors of modern British peoples.

There are additional archaeological challenges to understanding identity and linking past to present. Over 13,000 years the way people lived changed greatly. Ancient hunters, travelling long distances in a subarctic environment 13,000 years ago (see Ellis, chapter 2), surely saw the land and their place in it in a manner quite different from the farmers of 800 years ago, who lived in villages, relatively permanent residences, and a temperate environment (see Williamson, chapter 3). Archaeologists seeking to understand the remains of the past must be acutely aware of these differences, which were so central to people's lives in different time periods.

Being aware of those differences can pose a challenge for the archaeologist, since the archaeology of the last millennium dominates the archaeological landscape of southern Ontario, marked by large villages that housed hundreds or thousands of people and left behind great quantities of archaeological remains covering many acres (see Warrick, chapter 4). The challenge is not to overlook the lives of people who followed alternatives to a village farming life (see Ferris, chapter 6), or the lives of more mobile hunter-fisher-gatherer peoples who lived thousands of years earlier – people who left far fewer material remains on the archaeological landscape.

These are just a few of the challenges that archaeologists face in our attempts to travel back in time through the broken, fragmentary material traces of human history in order to try and understand the lives of past peoples. So how do archaeologists get around these problems? How do we get beyond broken fragments and stains in the soil to bring meaning and understanding to Ontario's archaeological past?

Archaeologists at Work

Depending on where you are in the world, doing archaeology can look very different. In Ontario, almost all of the material remains of past human lives are found below the surface of the ground. For all but the last 400–500 years, these remains were left behind by Aboriginal people, who built their homes and earned their livelihoods from the soils, stones, waterways, and woodlands in which they lived (see Stewart, chapter 1). People used materials like wood, plant fibres, and animal bones, which, being organic, have typically decayed over the intervening years (see Needs-Howarth, chapter 7, and Monckton, chapter 8). They left relatively little in the way of monumental remains, although some built earthen mounds (see Spence, chapter 14). Even villages and longhouses are now visible only as dark stains in the soil where

SIDEBAR 0.1

Archaeological Cultures and Time Periods   Marit K. Munson

Archaeologists divide the past into distinct time periods that we believe were unified by common themes – a certain kind of projectile point, for example, or heavy reliance on maize. We also give names to archaeological cultures, assuming that people who left behind distinctively different materials might have seen themselves as separate from other groups.

Archaeological time periods are useful, but they can be a bit misleading – they neatly divide the past into specific periods and provide tidy labels, but just how realistic are they? There is nothing magical about 799 CE compared to 800 CE; the Middle Woodland inhabitants of Ontario did not wake up one morning and decide that they needed to make a different style of pottery in order to move into the Late Woodland. Some Late Woodland-type villages, like the Porteous Site, arose in the early 800s CE; in other parts of Ontario, Late Woodland traits are not obvious until almost three centuries later. Nailing down a specific beginning or ending date can be tricky.

In the same way, archaeologists have tended to assume that tracking historically known First Nations back into the Late Woodland period is straightforward. We know, of course, that the early historic period was a complicated time, with movement, conflict, and cooperation among Aboriginal groups (Jamieson 1992 and 1999); using terms from historic records, like Iroquoian and Algonquian, can be misleading.

Still, some of us continue to use these terms, including in this book. After all, talking about the Late Woodland period or Iroquoian-style pottery is a useful shorthand, like referring to the Renaissance period or Scandinavian design in Europe. The terms do give a general sense for what was happening at a broad time and place, but they're not very precise. (See opposite.)

the wooden support posts once stood (see Ferris, chapter 6). As such, when you look across the landscape of Ontario, it is not immediately obvious that the land is peppered with traces of the ancient past.

While those remains are difficult to see on the landscape, the traces left behind of that past are what archaeologists look for to find ancient places where people once lived. In order to find these traces, though, we need to know where to look. While people might have lived anywhere in the past, archaeologists know that there are some broad patterns to selecting a locale to hunt, fish, or build a village. The same features important to deciding where to build a house today (or, rather, where not to) are also shared with the ancient past. So we find that sites tend to be on dry, elevated, and relatively flat areas, near water, but without being on wet ground, and near places important for growing, hunting, or gathering food. Of course these priorities changed through time, with changing environments, and based on whether people were building temporary or permanent settlements. But taking these features into account helps us narrow down where to look for sites on the landscape.

Once archaeologists have an idea of where to look, we seek out evidence of sites on the land. This is a process called archaeological survey, meaning walking farm

General Periods	South ——————————————→ North					Calibrated Dates
European contact	Algonquian & Iroquoian			Algonquian		1800 CE
						1400 CE
Late Woodland	Western Basin Tradition	Ontario Iroquoian Tradition		Blackduck/ Selkirk	Sandy Lake	1000 CE
						600 CE
Middle Woodland	Couture	Saugeen	Point Peninsula	Laurel		200 CE
						1 CE
						200 BCE
Early Woodland	Meadowood					600 BCE
			Terminal Archaic			1000 BCE
Late Archaic						1500 BCE
		Old Copper Complex		Shield Archaic		2500 BCE
						3500 BCE
Middle Archaic	Archaic					4500 BCE
						5500 BCE
						6500 BCE
Early Archaic				Lakehead Complex		7500 BCE
		Plano-like				8500 BCE
Late Paleoindian						9500 BCE
Early Paleoindian	Clovis-like					10500 BCE
						>11500 BCE

fields, looking for artifacts pulled to the surface by the farmer's plough (figure 0.5). The plough mixes things up as it flips over the top layer of artifacts from a site. Still, it doesn't really drag those artifacts very far, so finding a concentration of artifacts in the field shows that the location is an archaeological site (see Warrick, chapter 4). Looking for sites in woodlots or pastures is a little more complicated, as plant cover makes it hard to see traces of ancient settlement. In these cases, archaeologists dig a series of small holes, or test pits, to look for artifacts present below the ground (figure 0.6).

The materials that archaeologists find on survey tend to be small and fragmentary, but they help determine the size of a site and identify roughly when it was occupied. Archaeologists hope to find artifacts that are "diagnostic," meaning that they have been previously identified as characteristic of a particular time or group in the past. Diagnostic artifacts are usually distinctive in shape or design, such as arrowheads or spear points (see Fox, chapter 9), or decorated pottery (see Kapches, chapter 10).

Figure 0.5

Brightly coloured pin flags mark places where archaeologists from a cultural heritage management company have noted artifacts in a ploughed field. These surface remains indicate the presence of a village from the 1200s CE, called the Gibson site, in Peterborough County. (Courtesy of Archaeological Services Inc.)

However, to be able to speak more specifically about the site and the lives lived at that place, archaeologists need to dig deeper, literally, by uncovering the remains sealed below the surface of a site.

Excavation, often thought of as the glamour work of archaeology, is a lot of hard work, physically and mentally. Excavation involves removing the soil over an archaeological site to expose the artifacts, deposits, and soil patterns of past settlement. Artifacts are often in soil that has to be removed, especially when a plough has churned up some of the soil on a site, so archaeological excavation usually requires hand removal of soil using shovels, trowels, or even brushes and sifting the soil through screens (see figure 0.6). In other contexts archaeologists may use heavy machinery, especially at the beginning of a dig, when skilled operators can carefully strip off the soil churned up by ploughs to expose the intact portion of the site remaining below that top layer (figure 0.7). What we find as we excavate is really the

Figure 0.6
Archaeologists screen material from small shovel test pits on Jacob's Island, north of Peterborough. They were examining an area, near a known Archaic period site, that is being considered for the location of a new building. (Courtesy of James Conolly.)

Figure 0.7
A Gradall strips off a thin top layer of disturbed soil, known as the plough zone, at a site in the City of Vaughan, near Toronto, that is slated for future development. Archaeologists located a Late Woodland village, called the Hope site. (Courtesy of Archaeological Services Inc.)

accumulated residue of material left behind after people stopped living on or using a locale. Depending on the nature and time period of the site being excavated, discoveries might consist only of scattered artifacts in the soil churned up by a plough, or we might find artifacts in discrete concentrations, reflecting their intentional or accidental disposal on floors, swept into the corners of a house, or into waste or storage pits (see Ferris, chapter 6).

The most time-consuming work begins after the excavation is complete, in the laboratory, when we clean, catalogue, examine, and analyse thousands or even hundreds of thousands of objects. Archaeologists may focus on dating artifacts or on chemical analyses of pottery, stone tools, and other objects. Other specialists focus on studying human bones (see Keenleyside, chapter 13), plant remains (see Monckton, chapter 8), or animal bones, scales, and shells (see Needs-Howarth, chapter 7). Indeed, it takes many people working together to fully draw out the stories that a particular site can add to our understanding of the past.

The goal of all of this work is to interpret the material from the site, moving from basic descriptions of what was present to interpreting findings. This means working from an assemblage of artifacts – the group of pots, stone tools, plant remains, animal bones, and other materials from an excavation – to reconstruct daily life and to un-

SIDEBAR O.2

Dating the Past Susan M. Jamieson

Archaeologists have many ways of dating the past. Some are more precise than others; some work only on specific materials. In Ontario, radiocarbon dating is one of the most important dating methods. Radiocarbon dating is based on the isotopes, or different varieties, of carbon that are present in all living things. Most of this carbon is stable (C12, or carbon 12), but a small fraction is radioactive (C14, or carbon 14). This radiocarbon decays into nitrogen at a steady rate. People, plants, and animals take in both forms of carbon throughout their lives, maintaining a constant ratio of C14 to C12. The clock starts ticking after death: the radiocarbon continues to change into stable nitrogen but no new C14 enters the no-longer-living tissues. Measuring the ratio of C14 to C12 in bone, wood, or another organic material makes it possible to calculate the amount of time that has passed since the organism's death – the less radioactive carbon, the older the remains.

Radiocarbon dating is a bit more complicated than this, though, for a radiocarbon "year" is not the same as a calendar year. To make a long story short, radiocarbon years can be longer or shorter than a calendar year. Fortunately, we have figured out how to count tree rings and layers of arctic ice in order to correct radiocarbon dates and convert them to calendar years. This correction, known as "calibrating" a date, works well for dates within the last 15,000 years or so.

A calibrated radiocarbon date is really a statement of probability about a date range. For example, a radiocarbon date on a deer bone might be reported as 700 years ago, plus or minus 20 years. Through a historic quirk, radiocarbon dates are given with 1950 as their base point, so this gives the basic date of the bone as 1950 minus 700, or 1250 CE. Then you have the "± 20 years" part, which is where the probability comes in. It means that there is a good chance that the deer died some time between 1230 and 1270 (1250−20 and 1250+20). To be really certain, you need to double the plus/minus, which puts the deer's death at between 1210 and 1290 CE.

derstand more complex processes, like where people lived, how they related to each other, and how they interacted with outsiders.

The reason for all this effort during and after excavations is because doing archaeology in the field is a kind of controlled destruction of the archaeological record. Once a site is excavated, it is gone. There is no longer any way to return to the location to check on the position of artifacts, the layout of a village, the appearance of the soil – all were obliterated in the act of uncovering, recording, and removing archaeological material and information from the site. The fact of this destruction creates a strong ethical obligation for all archaeologists to work carefully to fully document all possible information that might contribute to understanding the past as reflected at this one location.

Importantly, that obligation is not just to other archaeologists, nor is it an abstract notion of responsibility to the archaeological record. Rather, archaeologists' obligations extend to the descendants of those whose heritage we uncover, as well as to all citizens of Ontario, Canada, and the world. In fact, archaeologists have a kind of public trust to document and care for our collective heritage, reflected in specific laws that govern who can investigate a site, their responsibilities for documenting and reporting their findings, and the long-term public trust obligations that they accept for collections and records made in the act of removing the archaeological record from the ground.

In Ontario, the *Ontario Heritage Act* governs archaeological protection, fieldwork, and practitioners. A separate law, the *Cemeteries Act*, covers the discovery of ancient burials, because when human remains are involved, archaeological interests are entirely secondary to the concerns and wishes of the landowner and people representing the interests of the deceased – typically a contemporary First Nation in the case of ancient Aboriginal burials (see figure 13.1).

Under part VI of the *Ontario Heritage Act*, only individuals who hold an archaeological license from the Ontario Ministry of Tourism and Culture are allowed to conduct archaeological fieldwork. In other words, because archaeological sites are considered by the province of Ontario to be fragile, nonrenewable resources, and are recognized as a significant part of Ontario's heritage, the province regulates who can be considered qualified to conduct fieldwork and alter these locales. As such, all archaeological sites are protected from disturbances caused by people who are not licensed archaeologists.

Archaeologists must meet different criteria in order to hold a particular kind of license. An avocational license is available to anyone interested in walking fields and looking for sites on the surface of the ground, or documenting local collections. Avocational archaeologists often get hooked when they first look down at the ground and recognize a piece of stone as an arrowhead, a spear point, or some other artifact. They practice archaeology as a hobby and a personal passion, finding joy and excitement in finding sites and documenting collections. Although archaeology is not their profession, avocational archaeologists add a great deal to our knowledge of the archaeological record, helping to document the past in their own regions or counties.

To direct site excavations, an archaeologist must hold a professional license, which requires a graduate degree in archaeology and extensive previous experience in the field. An important part of licensing obligations for all categories of archaeologist is that they must document everything that they find in reports and forms they file with the province. The province, in turn, compiles all this work into a database, so that individual findings will combine to create a greater understanding of Ontario's archaeological past.

Managing Ontario's Archaeological Record

Over the last thirty years, archaeologists and lawmakers have worked together to ensure that the ancient heritage of Ontario is not bulldozed away (Ferris 2007). Provincial laws include provisions to make sure that development activities, from building homes and highways to extracting gravel or harvesting forests, do not accidentally destroy the archaeological record. Any archaeological sites that may be present on the development property must first be identified, and then either protected or documented and excavated before construction begins, so that the information in that site is not otherwise lost. All of this work is done by archaeologists who are hired by developers to address these requirements for specific development projects. These archaeologists, often referred to as consultant or commercial archaeologists, are trained and experienced in applied archaeology. Their day-to-day routine is not just finding and documenting the past but also directly managing the practice of archaeology as it impacts on landowners, developers, descendants, the public, and the government. This process is often referred to as cultural heritage management (CHM).

The motivations for archaeologically protecting and documenting this threatened part of the past were originally driven by the public's and archaeological community's concern for the ancient heritage of Ontario. But in many ways the success of these efforts has created a host of new challenges that we have only begun to grapple with. For example, documenting the archaeological record in advance of development means that hundreds of archaeological sites are identified and excavated every year. In a single field season, this work creates more collections and more raw information about the archaeological past than a single university professor would create in a lifetime. In short, archaeologists collect far more archaeological material out of the ground than they can possibly research and document in detail. And yet, every year, more material is taken out of the ground and added to these holdings. Concerns about housing and caring for these collections, and making them accessible for research in the future, have largely fallen by the wayside in the yearly rush to survey the next proposed subdivision and excavate the next site before the winter freeze. These challenges of modern practice are concerns voiced not only by archaeologists but by many in Ontario today who are concerned for the long-term care of the archaeological record we document.

Indeed, archaeology is no longer the exclusive domain and practice of archaeologists. The field is thoroughly entrenched in modern social realities, balancing the expectations of development proponents, the obligations of municipalities and provincial authorities, and the concerns of public citizens that our heritage be protected. All of these groups have a strong interest, and a heavy financial obligation, in the documentation of Ontario's archaeological past. Over the last few decades, archaeologists have slowly come to recognize that archaeology is no longer solely about archaeological practice. It is much more about all the various interests that are engaged with Ontario's archaeological heritage, demanding accountability in what archaeologists do every day.

Nowhere is this dynamic more evident than in the close and evolving relationship of archaeology and First Nations communities today (see Nahrgang, chapter 15). Over the last half-century, this relationship has been very rocky. It reached a nadir, really, in the late 1970s, when members of the Haudenosaunee Iroquois confederacy successfully laid criminal charges against an archaeologist from the Royal Ontario Museum for committing an indecency to a dead person – the archaeologist had been excavating a 1600s Aboriginal cemetery found during the early stages of a housing development in Grimsby, along the Niagara Escarpment.

It is fair to say that the relationship has changed considerably since then. Archaeologists and First Nations communities have worked hard to pursue common interests and to respect what each brings to the archaeological record in Ontario. Still, there are bound to be differences when multiple groups seek to interpret the past (see Nahrgang, chapter 15). Archaeologists and First Nations often see the world in different ways, with different kinds of understanding. Human burials may intrigue some individuals, archaeologists and First Nations alike (see Spence, chapter 14), but their investigation may also cause pain and dismay for others. The controlled destruction of a site through excavation is a necessary evil to many archaeologists, but it may be simply an evil to some First Nations people. First Nations know that they have been here since time immemorial; archaeologists prefer to think in terms of defining specific dates. All of these differences are sometimes the cause of conflict. At other times, they can be the basis for collaboration, with archaeologists and First Nations working together on community archaeology, with cooperative decision-making and good outcomes for all parties (see sidebar 15.1). What is certain is that both archaeologists and First Nations have important stories to tell about the past and both see that past everywhere across the landscape of this place we know today as Ontario.

Deep Pasts and Recent Histories

A vibrant, inclusive Ontario society is one that is aware of and celebrates the many pasts that make up the collective heritage of the province. The deep human history of the Aboriginal people of Ontario stretches back at least 13,000 years, accessible through oral histories and through the tangible material remains that archaeologists study. The more recent past of Euro-Canadian newcomers is a story of the last 400–500 years, documented in written records and in the material record of archaeological remains. These pasts intertwine, united into the collective, continuing material heritage of the many peoples, First Nations and newcomers alike, who together have shaped this province into the modern society that it is today. The province's heritage is the heritage of both. We hope that this book will bring alive the rich heritage and vibrant past of a time before Ontario.

Part I
A Land before Ontario

Marit K. Munson

Ontario is new land, geologically speaking. It began to emerge from melting glaciers about 15,000 years ago, at the end of the last ice age. On a human scale, though, the land has existed since time immemorial, providing a beloved home for hundreds of generations of Aboriginal peoples. The stories of this land and its people are preserved in oral history, in written documents, and in the material remains of ancient societies.

This book tells some of the many stories of the land that became Ontario, from the perspective of some of the province's leading archaeologists – researchers who have devoted themselves to exploring and better understanding the past. Some work in cultural heritage management (or CHM), locating and studying ancient villages and archaeological sites in advance of development; others are academics, training the next generation of archaeologists and carrying out their own research projects. Collectively, these archaeologists have a deep body of knowledge about Ontario's past. Too often, though, that information is buried in the archaeological literature or technical publications.

This book is intended to remedy that situation, bringing recent archaeological research to the broader public. To do so, Susan Jamieson and I gathered a group of archaeologists for a two-day workshop on the campus of Trent University (figure 1). The meeting was a rare opportunity for the experts to sit down and talk face-to-face about everything from the minute details of fish bones at a single village to the broad social implications of the move from hunting and gathering wild foods to farming maize (corn). In between hashing out the details of recent discoveries and mulling over new information, we used our time together to identify the key themes in Ontario archaeology and to decide how to cover the broad span of time and space.

Figure 1

The authors gather for a workshop on the campus of Trent University in 2008. Back row, left to right: Neal Ferris, Mima Kapches, Bill Fox, Kris Nahrgang (above), Susan Jamieson, Suzanne Needs-Howarth (front), Chris Ellis, Stephen Monckton (front), Gary Warrick, Ron Williamson (front). Front row, left to right: Michael Spence, Cath Oberholtzer, Marit Munson, Andrew Stewart. Not pictured: Scott Hamilton, Anne Keenleyside. (Photo by Laura Helmuth.)

The result is this book. We have tried to create a readable and entertaining volume that explains what we know about Ontario's past and provides a glimpse of the archaeologists behind the research. Part I provides an overview of the province's Aboriginal past, showing the practice and promise of archaeology as a means of understanding the past. Part II gives a closer look at what archaeologists do and, above all, asks how we know what we know about the past. Part III, the last word, tackles the relationships of archaeologists and First Nations, challenging the reader to consider the perils and the promise of archaeology in Canada.

The story of Ontario's past begins at the end of the last ice age, in an environment and landscape very unlike what we know today. In chapter 1, Andrew Stewart paints a picture of a land emerging from ice, with tundra plants the first to colonize the new land and forest following after. The people who moved into the newly ice-free landscape hunted game and gathered plants, ranging across great distances as they moved to areas where resources were available. Chris Ellis (chapter 2) explains that archaeologists call these earliest inhabitants Paleoindians and the later groups Archaic peoples. As the climate and environment continued to shift, the landscape settled into a pattern that is familiar today: the temperate forests and glacial soils of southern Ontario, framed with the boreal forest, lakes, and exposed rock of the Canadian Shield to the north.

Most Aboriginal people living in the north continued to hunt wild game, fish, and gather plant foods – a way of life exquisitely tuned to the northern environment, as Scott Hamilton describes in chapter 5. Some northern peoples began to plant and grow some maize and make pottery of their own, as they maintained ties with their neighbours to the south. In southern Ontario, Aboriginal people increasingly settled in larger villages, began to rely on farm fields of maize and other crops, and manufactured pottery. Ron Williamson (chapter 3) provides an overview of these innovations, which ushered in significant changes for Aboriginal people in the more temperate parts of the province and marked the beginning of a time period (and way of life) that archaeologists call the Woodland. When European explorers and missionaries arrived in Ontario in the late 1500s and early 1600s CE, they ushered in the historic period, that time when written records document Aboriginal ways of life – or, at least, French explorers' and missionaries' views of their lives. The newcomers also, tragically, brought with them epidemics that decimated Aboriginal populations and caused great upheaval and change, as Gary Warrick explains in chapter 4.

This is the big picture, an overview of the story as archaeologists see it. In writing it, we have tried to bridge the gap between the modern world and a past that can sometimes seem distant and unfamiliar. Most of all, we have tried to honour the lives of people from long ago, tracing the stories of the ancestors of modern First Nations, the people who lived here long before Ontario.

1
Water and Land

– · – · – · – · – · – · – · –

Andrew M. Stewart

… at length [he] stood wistfully on the brink of the clay cliff crumbling even then in huge clods beneath his weight … he studies the [raw] clay face of the escarpment for traces of the old grave fill or other evidences of the burial place … For an hour or more the Indians combed through the smashed shale, coarse gravel and huge clamshells that cover the wide beach.

Arthur Carty (quoted in Guy St Denis, *Tecumseh's Bones*, 95)

The people standing on the banks of the River Thames in southwestern Ontario in 1926, described in this newspaper article, were searching for a grave, the burial place of the Shawnee chief Tecumseh, killed at the Battle of the Thames in 1813. The searchers were members of the Nahdee family of Walpole Island, descendants of Aboriginal warriors from that battle who recalled their father's stories of Tecumseh's secret burial following his defeat in battle during the War of 1812. They hoped to find his grave, but their search ended in confusion. Though they remembered the country from their youth, little was familiar. Trees and entire forests were gone, the course of a river had shifted, its banks collapsed, and a slurry of 10,000-year-old sediment was now flowing to the Great Lakes. Memories and knowledge of events from a century before resonated uncertainly in the radically altered landscape that they now beheld.

The changes in the landscape of southern Ontario in the last two centuries are staggering. Forest clearance, cultivation, the introduction of exotic species, draining of wetlands, canalization of rivers, and urbanization – the scale and effect of human actions is astonishing. Nearly 70 percent of our rich mosaic of wetlands, for example, has been lost. But the changes are not limited to the past two centuries. Most of the landscape of southern Ontario consists of what geologists call "overburden" – rock pulverized by glaciers and left behind as the ice began to retreat 15,000 years ago. Ice and water laid down this mineral sediment, creating hills, plains, and valleys that have been subject ever since to weathering and reworking by forces of gravity, climate, plant growth, and human land-use.

For early Euro-Canadian settlers, the forest seemed primeval – an impenetrable and malignant presence to pioneers who had to kill and clear the trees to secure their land. Anna Jameson, an English writer and observant traveller in Upper Canada (Ontario), described the land in her 1838 book *Winter Studies and Summer Rambles in Canada* as "boundless wilderness … where foot of man hath never penetrated" (129). Just a few decades earlier, however, she might have glimpsed an Ojibwa family extracting sap from trees along the Sydenham and Thames rivers in late winter, or living with other families on the open meadows and plains around Lake St Clair, planting and harvesting maize. Farther east in Ontario, farmers had been growing corn in fields and on open river flats and floodplains for about 1,500 years. Even before that, Aboriginal people tended and harvested plants on floodplains like that of the Grand River. The people changed the landscape to suit their needs, opening up forest with fire, encouraging new growth, and preparing ground for cultivation.

Lakes, Forests, and Aboriginal Peoples

Before maize, before forests even, there was ice. Fifteen thousand years ago, Ontario began to emerge as an island from beneath the ice, surrounded by meltwater lakes. Within a few thousand years, the continental ice sheet had retreated northward, leaving southern Ontario an ice-free peninsula. People began to enter this emerging land (figure 1.1).

On the north side of the peninsula Lake Algonquin, which lapped the retreating ice to the north, filled the Huron-Georgian Bay basin (figure 1.1, A and B). To the east, it occupied much of today's Simcoe lowlands, with long embayments extending southward into the hills of the Oak Ridges moraine. (Today's Holland Marsh is a finger of this former lake.) The south side of the Ontario peninsula was bounded by diminutive early Lake Erie, about forty metres below present levels, and, until about 12,000 years ago, an enlarged Lake Ontario, which geologists call Lake Iroquois (figure 1.1A) (Barnett 1992; Chapman and Putnam 1984; Eyles 2002).

None of these lake stages was stable for long. Once freed from the weight of the ice, the land began to spring back, faster in the north than in the south. Water flowed from one lake basin to another, eroding through barriers of sand and rock. Catastrophic flows of water excavated gorges and channels through plains of gravel and mountains of sediment – the moraines, eskers, and other formations sculpted by glaciers that are the distinctive landmarks of our country. Levels in these lakes changed over the next 6,000 years or so as the land rebounded, at first rapidly and then more

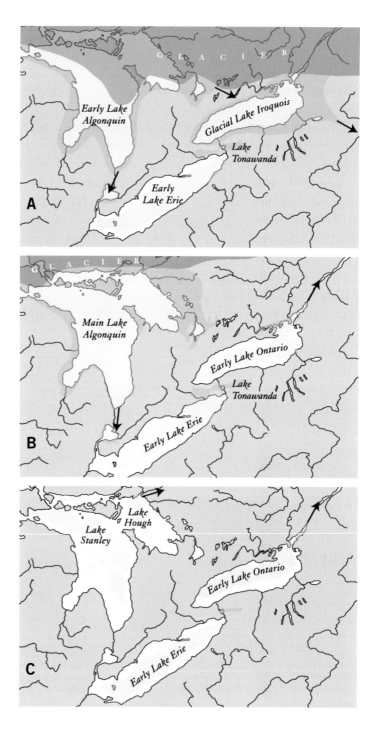

Figure 1.1
Generalized stages of lake formation in the lower three Great Lakes at the end of, and shortly following, the last ice age:

A (top) Early Lake Algonquin stage, showing outlets (arrows) for Early Lake Algonquin southward (through Sarnia-Port Huron) and eastward (through Fenelon Falls) between about 12,300 and 11,300 radiocarbon years ago;

B (middle) Main Lake Algonquin stage, showing the likely outlet southward through Sarnia-Port Huron, between about 11,300 and 10,400 radiocarbon years ago;

C (bottom) Early Holocene post-glacial low water stage, showing terminal lakes in the Huron-Georgian Bay basins at times between about 10,000 and 9000 radiocarbon years ago. (Maps by Molly O'Halloran.)

slowly (figure 1.1c). About 7,000 years ago, water levels began to change mainly in response to wetter and drier episodes.

The first people in Ontario probably came from the south at a time when lakes in the Erie and Ontario basins occupied only a fraction of their present area (figure 1.1, A and B). The land was full of ice-age animals, now extinct: mammoth, mastodon, stag-moose, giant beaver, peccary, and the California condor, among others. Hunters and their families set up their camps along the shores of Lake Algonquin, seeking caribou and other prey. Archaeologists find ancient hunting camps today by following the impression of the former lake's beachline, or strandline (figure 1.1B). The ancient beaches often take the form of slight terraces, wending their way through the fields and pastures of what is now open countryside. Standing at this elevation today, you overlook the smaller lakes that Lake Algonquin became – Lake Huron, Georgian Bay, and Lake Simcoe. When archaeologists search along these fossil beaches, they sometimes find distinctive tools that Paleoindians made from chert, a flint-like stone (see Ellis, chapter 2; Jackson and Hinshelwood 2004; and Storck 1997, 2004).

While water ebbed and flowed in the Great Lakes region, plant communities developed, eventually to become part of the great temperate deciduous forest that today covers southern Canada and the eastern third of the United States. Plant species spread into southern Ontario from their Ice Age refuges along the Atlantic seaboard and the southeastern United States, their spores and seeds borne by wind or carried by animals (Delcourt 2002).

Figure 1.2
This spruce parkland, where boreal forest meets tundra adjacent to the Clarke River, Northwest Territories, is similar to vegetation of southern Ontario at the end of the last ice age. (Photo by Andrew Stewart.)

Tundra and evergreen forest plants colonized the ground recently scoured by ice and water. Southern Ontario had the appearance of the tamarack and spruce parkland-forest that, today, is the meeting between boreal forest and tundra (figure 1.2). Lichen, sedges, and grasses flourished in open, sparsely treed areas. Over time, forests gained the upper hand, filling in open areas except where extensive marshes or dry sand, gravel, and limestone plains resisted the forest's spread. About 10,000 or 11,000 years ago, spruce was largely replaced by birch, red and jack pine, and then by eastern white pine. Beginning about 8,000 years ago, temperatures had warmed to near present values, allowing beech, hemlock, and other trees to become established. These mixed forests of needle and broad-leafed trees spread across upland areas (Karrow and Warner 1990; Yu 2000).

The evolving forests were to profoundly influence the way people came to live. For example, the rising fortunes of the McIntyre Site, a 4,000-year-old village on the north side of Rice Lake, were due to a complex ecological chain linking declining hemlocks and increasing mud to abundance. Beginning about 5,000 years ago, hemlocks disappeared from southern Ontario for a millennium, probably due to an epidemic of pests. When the hemlocks declined, the acidity of the soil decreased as well. The lower acidity allowed organic debris to build up on the forest floor. As the organic matter accumulated, some of it washed away, coming to rest on the bottom of Rice Lake. Muddy conditions in the shallows of the lake provided the ideal growing conditions for wild rice, an important food for local people. The replacement of hemlock by maple, birch, and beech trees probably also provided better habitat for white-tailed deer, whose population expanded. One small change – the disappearance of the hemlocks – may have set off a chain of events that doubly rewarded people in the village with a local abundance of both grain and game (McAndrews 1984).

Moving Shorelines and Shifting Ground

Aboriginal people have witnessed many episodes of rising and falling lake levels in the Great Lakes since the retreat of the ice began some 15,000 years ago. As lake levels changed, shorelines moved; the Ontario peninsula expanded and contracted, at times quite quickly in response to catastrophic flows.

For 2,500 years after the draining of Lake Algonquin through what are now the French and Ottawa Rivers, the levels of water fluctuated dramatically in the Huron basin and, to a lesser extent, in the Erie and Ontario basins. Episodes of flooding by glacial meltwater alternated with dry periods, when water bypassed the Great Lakes and flowed directly along the edge of the Laurentide ice sheet in northern Ontario toward the Ottawa River. The effect was amplified by the dry climate that prevailed during the early Holocene. During lowstands, water in Lake Huron and Georgian Bay pooled in basins, seventy metres below the present level (figure 1.1C). At times, these pools were disconnected, or hydrologically closed – on their way to becoming salt

SIDEBAR 1.1

Reconstructing Environments from Mud Andrew Stewart

A millennium of mud from Crawford Lake, near Milton, offers insight into changing environments in the area. The mud traps organic particles, including pollen, in layers of mud, known as varves, laid down annually on the lake bottom. The pollen of maize, weedy grasses, and purslane shows up in the mud from 1268 CE, disappearing in 1486 – clear evidence for two centuries of use of the area by Iroquoian villagers and their farm fields. Bird pellets loaded with pollen of maize, sunflower, and purslane also show up in the varves. Canada geese evidently invaded the corn fields, fouling the nearby lake just as they do today. Algal blooms depleted the bottom water of oxygen, which helped to preserve the varves.

Around this time, or slightly later, the pollen record shows that red oak and white pine succeeded beech and maple as the dominant tree species. These trees thrive in sunlight, growing in clearings like those created by abandoned fields and village sites. The clearings gave white pine and red oak good places to grow, but cooling climate might also have created an opportunity to gain a foothold. The newly dominant trees show up during a period known as the Little Ice Age, when climate around the world cooled during the centuries from the 1300s to the 1800s. The cooler conditions in southern Ontario probably favoured white pine and red oak, which began to thrive under the new climate regime (Campbell and McAndrews 1993; McAndrews and Turton 2007).

lakes. Today, remote-operated underwater vehicles and side-scan sonar from Lake Huron's surface are being used to explore this drowned landscape for archaeological sites. Eventually the levels rose and water resumed its old course along the French and Ottawa Rivers (Anderson and Lewis 2002; O'Shea and Meadows 2009).

As the land rebounded from the ice, the north end of the lake rose more quickly than the southern end. Water spilled southward, forcing people out of the Huron and Georgian Bay basins into higher areas of southwestern Ontario. By 6,000 years ago, the land was inundated along Lake Huron's southern shore, from Sarnia to roughly Kincardine, a high-water period in the lower Great Lakes that geologists refer to as the Nipissing stage. The rising water broke through a barrier of glacial sediment, or moraine, that had acted as a dam at Sarnia-Port Huron. The waters cascading through the breach enlarged the existing channel of the St Clair River, raising the water level in Lake Erie. The flow of water formed an enormous inland delta at Lake St Clair, which is the foundation for the rich marsh and prairie habitat of today's Walpole Island (Adams 1989; Karrow 1980).

Aboriginal people living along the southern Lake Huron shoreline found themselves stranded after the high Nipissing-stage water receded. They inherited a rich legacy of emerging wetlands, constantly changing in response to lake levels adjusting to climatic change. The ground was literally shifting under people's feet. Even the slight elevations of dunes along the shoreline or bars and beaches of former lakes offered suitable ground, at least for a few years, for year-round settlement. From these places, people had access to huge wetlands – vast storehouses like the Thedford embayment on Lake Huron south of Grand Bend, the Holland Marsh and Minesing Swamp in the Simcoe lowlands, and Cootes Paradise and the shallows of Burlington Bay at the west end of Lake Ontario. These watery environments provided resources such as shellfish, shallow-water species of fish, amphibians, reptiles, migratory waterfowl, and fur-bearing mammals, as well as plants such as wild rice (see Needs-Howarth, chapter 7, and Monckton, chapter 8).

The extensive lowlands in southwestern Ontario, with their moist soils, supported sycamore, walnut, chestnut, and basswood trees. Sandy levees bordered streams and sloughs, while prairie habitat was interspersed with marshes and channels teeming with aquatic resources. This rich environment probably provided enough food and materials that people could support themselves with a relatively unstructured pattern of movement, seasonally and year-to-year. The low relief and shifting balance between land and water in this distinctive environment is symbolically expressed in Mishipizhiw, the horned panther or serpent present in so much iconography of the Great Lakes (see Oberholtzer, chapter 11). Shallow lakes and broad areas of lakeshore marshland, with their opportunities and dangers, clearly resonated in the imaginations of generations of people living in this part of Ontario.

Rivers

Rivers and lakes formed important routes for travel and trade. Eastern Lake Ontario was connected to the upper Great Lakes for thousands of years through the Trent River system, including the Kawartha Lakes and Rice Lake, along with Lake Simcoe, Lake Couchiching, and the Severn River, which flows from its north end to Georgian Bay (Allen 2002). In fact, people paddled along established waterway routes carrying chert, a tool stone, for long-distance trade. As Bill Fox describes in chapter 9, Aboriginal peoples traded Onondaga chert from the northeast shores of Lake Erie and the Niagara River to sites all over southern Ontario. No boats have survived to the present day, but heavy specialized wood-working tools, like celts, from as long ago as 10,000 years suggest that Aboriginal people made and used watercraft.

Islands in the lower courses of rivers like the Ottawa, the Trent, and the Grand became fixed in the landscape and stable places for human settlement only after their channels entrenched their present courses. Formerly, many islands were shifting bars, subject to erosion (figure 1.3). Their bare surfaces yielded raw material for making stone tools, which people collected for flintknapping. As soil and vegetation developed, many bars became islands, or part of the riverbank, and the formerly exposed pebbles and cobbles disappeared from view.

Stable riverbeds also provided environments for seasonal concentrations of fish, giving people access to more productive fisheries (see Needs-Howarth, chapter 7). Hundreds of people gathered seasonally to harpoon fish at rapids on the St Mary's

River between Lake Superior and Lake Huron within the last 1,500 years and continuing into the twentieth century. The offshore fishery, established during the Middle Woodland period, was also famously rewarding, with gill nets set for whitefish and lake trout on reefs in autumn. The increasing importance of fisheries and elaboration of fishing technology through time show an expanding knowledge of lake environments through the Late Archaic and Woodland periods, particularly in the upper three Great Lakes (Cleland 1982; Rogers 1978).

Sites at the Couchiching Narrows, the St Clair River and the Niagara River also show how people gathered together on a seasonal basis to take advantage of fisheries at narrows and rivers. Large camps based on spring spawning runs of fish appear for the first time about 2,000–1,500 years ago. Sites along the middle and lower Trent River indicate a longer season of settlement, based on fish and shellfish during spring and summer and wild rice, nuts, and deer in autumn (Spence et al. 1990).

The St Lawrence River has been one of the most important waterways in southern Ontario since Paleoindian times. It has served as a route between the Atlantic Ocean and the continental interior since the ice age. The St Lawrence also has, at Lake St Francis, one of the most productive fisheries in Ontario, along the border with Quebec. Archaeological material from all cultural periods has accumulated on its shores. In contrast, the Ottawa River has been a much less stable and reliable location for settlement. During the Nipissing phase, before the opening of the Port Huron outlet, waters from Lake Huron poured through this channel, restricting human settlement to higher areas above its shores.

Rivers were also important as locations of cemeteries, which archaeologists often find beside major waterways and on islands. These cemeteries, which became fairly common about 3,000 years ago, seem to mark places of permanence in the landscape

Figure 1.3
Shifting bars of gravel in unstable rivers at the end of the last ice age provided good sources of tool stone for Ontario's early inhabitants. (Photo by Andrew Stewart.)

(see Spence, chapter 14). Some of the cemeteries may have been associated with large seasonal camps of people at spring spawning runs of fish. The forks of the Thames River (Blackfriars Bridge) is one such place. Further downstream, the Hind Site cemetery seems to mark a significant boundary in the natural landscape as Aboriginal people experienced it. The cemetery overlooks a major deviance in the southwestward direction of flow of the river. Just downstream from the site, the channel of the Thames River may have had a shifting, less stable course over time, in part because of its very low gradient and frequent blockage by ice during winter and spring.

Stable floodplains of rivers were critical to the first cultivation of native and introduced plants, such as maize (see Monckton, chapter 8). The lower Grand River, for example, has been stable over much of the past 1,500 years, neither eroding nor building up. This steadiness allowed topsoil to develop on the floodplain, creating a good place for harvesting and cultivating plants each year following the spring flood. The traditional Anishinaabe name for the Grand River seems to capture this knowledge: *Pesshinneguning*, "the one that washes the timber down and drives away the grass weeds" (Smith 1987, 20). This old topsoil now lies buried beneath silt and sand, washed into the river as a result of deforestation and agriculture across the drainage area between about 1820 and 1940. The buried topsoil represents the former surface where the grass weeds grew (figure 1.4), once used by generations of Aboriginal cultivators and farmers (Crawford et al. 1998).

Figure 1.4
This photo of a profile from the Davidson Site shows how excavations expose different layers of earth, much as slicing into a cake reveals its layers. The dark horizontal band across the middle of the photo is an ancient topsoil, rich in organic material. Once at ground level, it has long since been buried by sediments deposited during flooding of the Ausable River. (Courtesy of Christopher Ellis.)

The Enhanced Land

During the Late Woodland period (800–1650 CE), people began to intensify their use of existing land and to expand into new parts of the southern Ontario landscape. They continued to live on lakeshores and along lower river reaches, especially for spring fishing, but also made use of higher reaches of rivers that afforded greater protection and secrecy for the locations of villages. They built large, defended villages for the first time (see Ferris, chapter 6), often perched on bluff tops overlooking valleys. In some places, wetlands served as defensive ground. Where villages were more exposed, people sometimes modified the ground, building earthworks for added protection.

People also worked to shape the distinctive open woodland landscapes along the north shore of Lakes Erie and Ontario and south of Rice Lake. The sandy plains in these areas supported dry parklands – a distinctive open woodland landscape that was enhanced by fire (figure 1.5). Aboriginal people almost certainly used fire to maintain these landscapes, which were nearly ideal environments for settlement. With soil conditions favourable for growing maize, the sand plains also supported oak, pine, poplar, sassafras, and hickory trees. The nut-bearing trees attracted deer, providing good hunting.

Archaeological sites from these woodlands provide evidence that helps to understand the shift from hunting and gathering food to growing crops such as maize. Many people think of gathering food and producing food through farming as two completely different ways to make a living, but in fact many Aboriginal people combined both activities (see Monckton, chapter 8). For example, people living north of Lake Erie in the 1100s and 1200s spent part of their time in villages with farm fields

Figure 1.5
Sandy soils near Rice Lake supported open, park-like woodlands, similar to the current landscape at the Serpent Mounds. The long curve of the main mound is visible at the bottom of the photo, with Rice Lake peeking through the trees in the distance.
(Photo by James Conolly.)

surrounded by maple-beech forest, growing maize and other crops. In spring and autumn, they moved to smaller hamlets in areas of sandy soil and open oak woodland, where they hunted deer and collected nuts (Williamson 1990).

Fields, meadows, and prairie; sandy plains of oak and pine and poplar savannah; groves of nut-bearing trees and fruit-bearing shrubs along forest edges – all of these landscape features were part of the environment of southern Ontario and the lower Great Lakes at the time of European contact. All were deliberately encouraged or enhanced by Aboriginal people.

Yet the idea of deliberately managed landscapes is not without controversy among historical geographers and archaeologists. How prominent and widespread was this management, whether by fire and by other means? Many of these kinds of landscapes do not accord with our conventional notions of pristine forest inherited from the accounts of settlers in the 1800s. Anna Jameson described the forests of Upper Canada in 1837 as an unending wilderness. Nevertheless, on her journey between Woodstock and London she noted that a "forest of pines, rising tall and dark and monotonous on either side" gave way to "open flat country … covered with thickets and groups of oak, dispersed with a park-like and beautiful effect" (Jameson 1838, 139, 311).

To what extent were these openings in the forest the result of dry, cold conditions of the Little Ice Age in the 1300s–1800s CE? Could they be related to other episodes of climate change during the past 8,000 years, since hardwood and mixed forests became established? How much did this park landscape owe to the efforts of Aboriginal peoples who helped make the landscape part of a domestic environment (Crawford and Smith 2003)?

The 10,000-year history of the landscape tells of its evolution from the spruce parkland that early caribou hunters knew to the park landscape that Aboriginal peoples helped to shape through the early 1600s and after. During this long span of time, the forests of the Ontario peninsula were continually modified and opened up by agents of change and disturbance: fire, water, plant diseases, the introduction of new species. Separating the effects of human beings from other agents is impossible; people have been involved with and implicated in most aspects of the so-called natural world from the earliest times. Peoples' involvement with the world around them is what constitutes the archaeological record, which is not limited to stone tools and pottery fragments but is found everywhere, from soils to seeds, in the evidence of a changing environment.

2

Before Pottery: Paleoindian and Archaic Hunter-Gatherers

Christopher J. Ellis

The most ancient known peoples of southern Ontario lived in the region before pottery, before farming. They made a living by hunting, fishing, and collecting wild plants, a way of life that favoured a more or less mobile existence. People usually moved from season to season to make use of the natural resources available in different places at particular times of the year, a lifestyle that required detailed knowledge of the local environment and its variations. These early hunter-gatherers lived in Ontario from the retreat of the Ice Age glaciers that first exposed the land for human occupation through the invention of pottery about 3,000 years ago. Archaeologists use the term Paleoindian (literally "ancient Indians") for the earliest period of occupation in the New World, from about 13,500 to 12,000 years ago. The following period, from 12,000 until just 2,900 years ago, is known as the Archaic.

"Ancient Indians"

Archaeologists first discovered Paleoindian sites in the 1920s to early 1930s in the southwestern United States. The sites included distinctive stone artifacts, such as the points of hunting weapons, found together with extinct animals such as large, long-horned bison and elephant-like mammoths (see Wormington 1957). By the late 1930s, archaeologists began to realize that characteristic Paleoindian stone tools were widespread and occurred even in Ontario. Still, it was not until the 1970s that actual sites were reported in the southern part of the province. One reason for the delay is the fact that Paleoindian sites are extraordinarily rare. Also, most of these early sites are quite small. An average Paleoindian site in Ontario consists of thirty to forty stone tools, clustered in an area of less than 200–300 square metres, about half the size of a small lot in a modern subdivision. Discovering a Paleoindian site is like finding a needle in a haystack – locating even a single new site anywhere in North America generates a great deal of excitement among archaeologists. Researchers in Ontario have led the way in discovering these sites (Ellis and Deller 1990; Storck 2004). In the last thirty-five years, we have gone from no known Paleoindian sites in the province to more than one hundred.

Paleoindian sites are rare and small in large part because there were not very many Paleoindians. Plus, they moved their camps quite frequently throughout the year, so there was never much time for tools, animal bones, or other debris of daily life to build up. This way of life is not surprising, given the environment and resources of the time and the fact they were colonizing areas that were previously unoccupied. When Paleoindians came to the area, the environment was very different than it is today (see Stewart, chapter 1). Today, the most similar settings are the areas of the tree-line in Canada's north, where coniferous (needle-bearing) trees such as spruce and pine dominate. In these kinds of environments, resources are few and far between and plant foods are particularly rare. For these reasons, Paleoindian peoples undoubtedly focused on hunting, trapping, and fishing.

Evidence of what Paleoindian peoples ate can be hard to come by in Ontario, where acidic soils tend to eat away animal bones and other organic material. Paleoindian sites are so old that little remains other than stone tools and debris from their manufacture. Only one site in southern Ontario, near modern Lake Simcoe, has yielded burned food remains, including caribou, arctic fox, and either hare or rabbit (Storck and Spiess 1994). Other sites in adjacent areas of the United States also include caribou bones, suggesting that the species was central to the Paleoindian food quest, just as it is among Aboriginal peoples in similar environments in the modern north. Of course, Paleoindian peoples may also have hunted now-extinct animals, as they did in other parts of North America. So far, though, we have no direct evidence that Paleoindian peoples in Ontario hunted large mammoths and mastodons.

Archaeologists occasionally find larger Paleoindian sites, beyond the small short-term campsites that are most common. The larger sites may be more than 700–800 square metres in size, with multiple areas that were repeatedly occupied. Some of these sites were probably camps where small groups of Paleoindians congregated seasonally to intercept moving caribou herds. In fact, some of the better known sites that I have examined are located at narrow river crossings (Ellis and Deller 2000) – exactly the same settings favoured by modern caribou hunters in the north. The water crossing forced caribou to slow down, making them easier for hunters to kill.

Paleoindian peoples often camped along shorelines, probably drawn by the fish, waterfowl, and other animals in and around the water. As Andrew Stewart describes in chapter 1, water levels in lake basins like Huron and Erie were much above modern levels during Paleoindian times, flooding areas that are now dry land. Archaeologists looking for Paleoindian sites often target the abandoned and inland shorelines of these ancient lakes, realizing that the Paleoindian peoples once favoured lake shores for their camp sites. In fact, our understanding of Paleoindian preferences and of the geologic history of the region is one reason that archaeologists have been successful in locating these small and rare sites.

Learning from Stone

Paleoindian peoples surely used plants, animal skins and leather, and other perishable materials. (Just imagine trying to survive an Ontario winter without clothing.) The great age of their sites, though, means that stone artifacts are usually the only preserved items. As a result, archaeologists who study the earliest hunter-gatherers usually specialize in studying these tools, which can be remarkably informative about Paleoindian lives. For example, Paleoindian peoples used a range of stone raw materials for their tools, indicating that they were mobile, covering large areas over the course of the year in order to make use of the region's widespread resources. Archaeologists often find that the tools at a given site were almost completely made on stone from a source 175 kilometres or more away (Ellis and Deller 1990). I have had the privilege of investigating many sites in Ontario south of Lake Huron; most of the artifacts on these sites are made of stone that originates in the Collingwood area, near Georgian Bay to the northeast. Small amounts of more exotic stone materials from even farther afield show that Paleoindians had direct and indirect contact with other groups over vast areas encompassing thousands of square kilometres.

Wide-ranging social contacts were important beyond helping provide access to distant sources of stone. Indeed, such contacts were essential to people's survival, allowing individuals to maintain social ties and find mates of the right age and sex – often quite difficult among very dispersed, small populations. Moreover, they provided ties that could be drawn on for aid and assistance in times of trouble or poor hunting success, which probably occurred frequently in the rapidly changing, Late Ice Age environments. Anthropologists studying hunter-gatherers in many areas of the globe have found that people living in small, dispersed groups often give gifts of everyday items to one another in order to solidify their social ties. Perhaps the exotic stone materials from some Paleoindian sites represent similar exchanges.

Paleoindians produced toolkits made of fine-grained glassy stone, like cherts and flints, chipped or flaked into shape. They selected the finest flakeable grades of these raw materials, often choosing stone that is aesthetically pleasing. The result was a diverse and complex stone toolkit, which was certainly used to make other tools and equipment out of bone, antler, wood, leather, and other perishables.

Paleoindian stone tools were made with an outstanding degree of skill. Modern flintknappers, who practice the craft in order to gain insight into the production process (see Fox, chapter 9), have a difficult time replicating some of these ancient objects. The most characteristic Paleoindian tool is the most difficult to produce. The earliest forms of the exquisite lance-shaped spear or dart points have a grooved or fluted base (figure 2.1) that requires strength, finesse, and a thorough understanding of the stone's properties to create them successfully. These Paleoindian points were mounted on hand-thrown short spears or darts, launched with the aid of a throwing stick or spear thrower known as an atlatl (figure 2.2) (Bradley et al. 2010). (The bow and arrow would not be invented until later.) The remaining stone artifacts include a wide range of tools used for cutting, scraping, and engraving or incising, many of which would have been placed in long-decayed wood or bone handles (figure 2.3). Paleoindian peoples often recycled their tools, repeatedly sharpening and resharpening edges dulled by constant use. This reuse was undoubtedly due to the need for a practical, portable toolkit that could be easily carried long distances.

The rarest and most unusual Paleoindian artifacts are miniature stone tools. The best known are very tiny points of 25–30 millimetres in length (figure 2.3B) that mimic the form of regular-size fluted points. In fact, these are often made of the small chips or flakes that had been removed when making the flutes or grooves on full-size points. Some believe that these miniature items were children's toys, while others suggest a more spiritual use, such as an amulet or charm made to increase success in the hunt (Ellis 1994).

It is clear that Paleoindian peoples regarded many stone items as more than simply tools. They chose the highest grades of materials and made their tools with such consummate skill that the resulting objects are almost as much art as artifact. For Paleoindians, stone tools' importance went well beyond the ordinary. Two southern Ontario sites that I had the honour to study, the Crowfield and Caradoc sites, really indicate this special significance (Deller et al. 2009; Ellis 2009). In one case, more

Figure 2.1 *Opposite*
These early Paleoindian points, from the Thedford II Site in Ontario, date to around 11,000–10,500 BCE. The distinctive flute, or channel, of many Paleoindian points shows up clearly as the long scar down the centre of each tool. (Courtesy of Christopher Ellis.)

Figure 2.2 *Opposite*
Paleoindians used an atlatl, or spear-thrower, to increase the power and distance of their throws. Modern-day atlatl enthusiasts describe their delight when a properly thrown spear flexes with the force of the throw, whipping forward with a surprisingly snakelike movement that appears to help stablize the spear in flight. (Drawing by Molly O'Halloran.)

Figure 2.3 *Opposite*
A Paleoindian tool kit included many different stone artifacts. These tools, found at the Parkhill, Thedford II, and McLeod sites in Ontario, date to around 11,000–10,500 BCE. A: Fluted point. B: Miniature point. C-D: "Beaked" tools used for perforating, incising, and cutting grooves. E: End scraper, probably for processing hides. F-G: Needle-like "gravers" used for incising. C to E would have been placed in "sockets" in bone or wood handles. (Drawings by Janie Ravenhurst.)

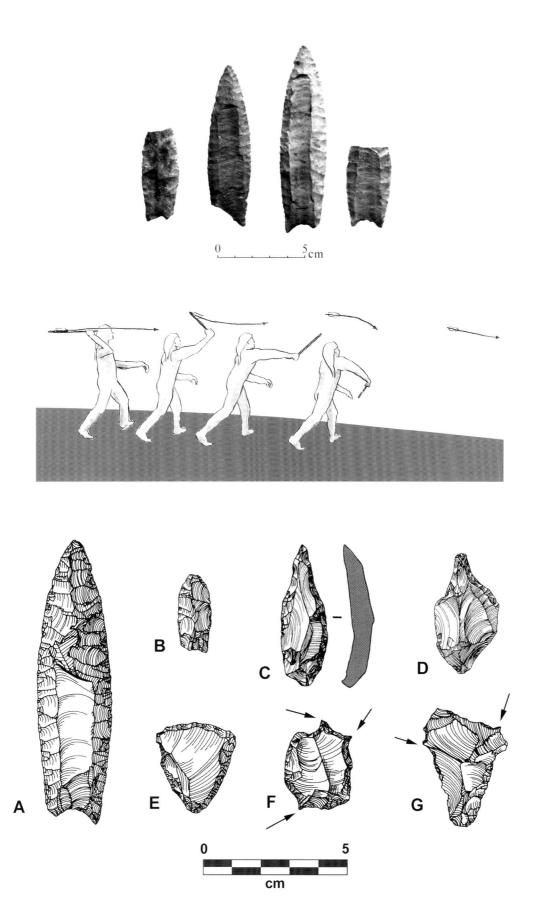

0   5 cm

0   5

cm

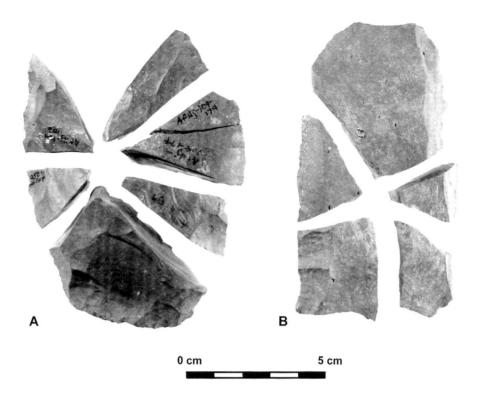

Figure 2.4
These Paleoindian stone tools were purposefully broken by striking them in the centre of one face, splitting them into multiple pie-shaped segments. All of the pieces were found at the Caradoc Site, a Paleoindian site near Strathroy that dates to around 9,500 BCE. (Courtesy of Christopher Ellis.)

than 60 useful and everyday artifacts had been smashed up by one or more blows (figure 2.4) and then left simply lying on the surface of the ground. This deliberate destruction suggests that the objects represent offerings or sacrifices to forces or beings who governed human existence. In the other case, more than 180 previously functional artifacts were destroyed by burning them in a shallow pit. The collection was apparently a single individual's personal stone toolkit. This could, like the previous example, represent simple sacrifices, but there are instances outside of Ontario of the deliberate burning of objects in the context of Paleoindian burial ritual. Whatever the details, Paleoindians' decisions to use stone tools and to destroy them in what must have been significant spiritual activities and events emphasize the tools' important role in Paleoindian views of the world. In Ontario, the use of stone artifacts in such activities would not be seen again until almost 8,000 years later, well into the subsequent Archaic period.

Archaic Lives

In the 1920s, archaeologists studying the oldest Aboriginal peoples in North America noticed that sites dating from around 12,000 years ago seemed somewhat different from the earlier Paleoindian sites. They began calling the sites and other finds from about 12,000 to 2,900 years ago "Archaic," using that term for the people who lived then as well (Ritchie 1932). Sites dating to the Archaic period have been found throughout eastern North America. Unlike the more uniform Paleoindians, there is much more regional variation in Archaic ways of life, particularly late in the period.

The Archaic peoples are the direct descendants of Paleoindian ancestors. Where one draws the line between the two is somewhat arbitrary, as the changes from Paleoindian to Archaic are gradual (Ellis et al. 2009). The first noticeable change was a shift from making the lance-shaped Paleoindian weapon tips to points with notches or stems at the base, which were used to attach them to a shaft (figure 2.5).

By around 11,000 years ago, Archaic peoples began to make tools made on coarser-grained rocks, like slate, granite, schist, and limestone, which are difficult or even impossible to flake. Toolmakers using these materials had to start by laboriously pecking the rock into the desired shape, then finish the tool by grinding and polishing. Most of these early ground stone tools were made for woodworking – items like axes, chisels, and adzes. Between about 9,000 to 7,000 years ago, Archaic toolmakers began to make elaborate stone knives, spear points, and weights for spear-throwers. The weights, known as bannerstones, were beautifully shaped into various tubular and winged shapes (figure 2.6).

Figure 2.5
These large stemmed (left and centre) and notched (right) spear points or knives date from the Late Archaic, around 2,500–1,500 BCE. (University of Western Ontario collections. Courtesy of Christopher Ellis.)

0cm   5cm

By the end of the Archaic, around 2,900 years ago, artisans began making exquisite ceremonial and decorative items, including small bird effigies, two-holed pendants known as gorgets, and tubular pipes (figure 2.7). Archaic peoples continued to make simpler tools on the coarser-grained rocks. Notched pebbles or cobbles helped weigh down fish nets, for example, while grinding stones were used to grind seeds and other plant foods. As in earlier times, Archaic peoples also used finer-grained materials like cherts to make flaked-stone tools. Unlike Paleoindians, though, Archaic flintknappers often used locally occurring stones. Other than points and the occasional drill or scraper, most flaked tools were just simple flakes or chips that were used briefly as cutting and scraping tools and then discarded. These items, while fully serviceable, were not made with as much skill or care as the earlier artifacts and lack the extensive use, resharpening, and recycling seen in Paleoindian times.

As on Paleoindian sites, preservation of organic materials is rare on Archaic sites – after all, most of these sites are older than the pyramids! Still, archaeologists have managed to document some bone and antler tools as far back as 6,500 years ago, including fishing tools like hooks, barbs, and harpoons. There are even the preserved remains of 5,000-year-old wooden fish weirs at Atherley Narrows, between Lake Couchiching and Lake Simcoe, where Archaic peoples took advantage of spawning runs to take large quantities of fish (see Needs-Howarth, chapter 7).

The Archaic peoples also seem to have been the first in southern Ontario to use the bow and arrow, just after 4,000 years ago – at least if the small size of weapon tips is any guide. They also began to use native copper, about 6,500 years ago. Native copper refers to relatively pure natural nuggets of copper, which chemical analyses indicate came mostly from sources in the western Lake Superior region (Chapdelaine and Clermont 2006). Heating the nuggets at low temperatures alters their chemical structure, making it possible to cold-hammer them, with a little care, into thin sheets.

Archaic peoples at first used these sheets of copper to make tools like spear- and harpoon-tips, fish hooks, knives, and axe heads. Decorative items like bracelets were quite rare, suggesting that trade networks were used mostly to exchange the goods needed for day-to-day existence. Over time, though, trade networks expanded to include many more decorative or exotic goods. By the end of the Archaic, copper was much rarer and apparently more precious. Most copper was used to make decorative items or ritual goods, which were often used for sacred purposes, like burial offerings.

Other trade goods used for decorative or ritual purposes came from far-flung locations. Archaic peoples traded marine shells from the Atlantic coast, which they used to make large pendants (figure 2.7B) and necklaces. They also traded for cubes of galena, a lead mineral, mainly from New York State sources although the exact uses to which they put that material is unknown. It may be that the unusual nature of this material, which feels surprisingly heavy, made it an attractive material for religious or spiritual purposes. As a whole all these goods indicate very widespread and regular trade networks of considerable antiquity.

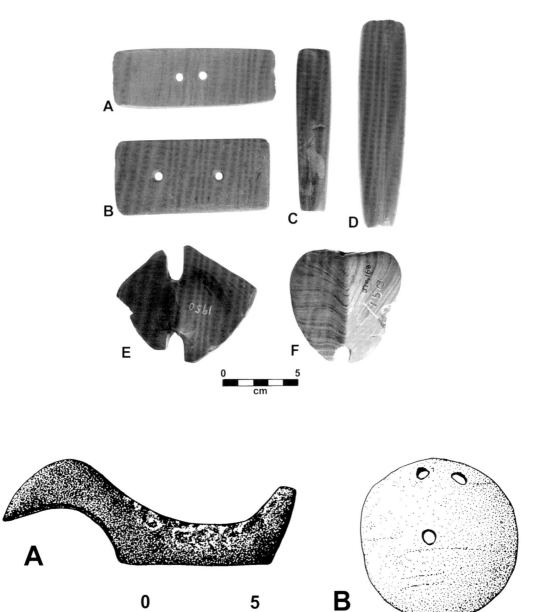

Figure 2.6 *Top*
Ground stone tools are typical of the Archaic period between about 8,000–1,000 BCE. These examples
include rectangular stone gorgets (A & B), tubular bannerstones (C & D), and winged bannerstones (E & F).
(Courtesy of Dr Robert Pearce and the Museum of Ontario Archaeology, London, Ontario.)

Figure 2.7 *Bottom*
Late Archaic artifacts from the Schweitzer Site (1,500–1000 BCE) include a bar-shaped birdstone
(A) and a circular gorget (B), or pendant, made out of shell traded long distances from the ocean.
(Drawings by Ian Kenyon.)

Changing Land, Changing Lives

The changes from Paleoindian to Archaic ways of life were probably triggered in part by widespread environmental changes, including rising water levels in the Great Lakes. Prior to about 6,000 years ago, water levels in lakes Huron, Erie, and Ontario were much lower than in modern times (see Stewart, chapter 1). Many favoured camp sites and hunting areas were surely flooded as water levels rose, leaving some of the record of the earliest Ontarians underwater today. The shift from the Paleoindian to the Archaic also coincides with the more widespread appearance of deciduous trees and more modern animals, particularly in southwestern Ontario. By about 8,500 years ago, resource-rich environments similar to today's were in place. Southwestern Ontario was covered by forests rich in plant foods and full of plentiful game.

The changing environment shaped the archaeological record as we see it today. Living sites became much more common over time, for example, suggesting that population density increased as well. Natural population growth, made possible by

Figure 2.8

Pins outline small excavation units at the ancient Davidson Archaic Site (2200–1000 BCE), Parkhill, Ontario, 2009. Each unit is only 50 cm² to ensure recovery of tiny and often delicate items, like fish remains and charred nutshell, and to maintain exact spatial control over find locations. Research at the site was supported by the Social Sciences and Humanities Research Council (SSHRC) of Canada, with the kind permission of landowners Rick and Marlene Davidson. (Courtesy of Christopher Ellis.)

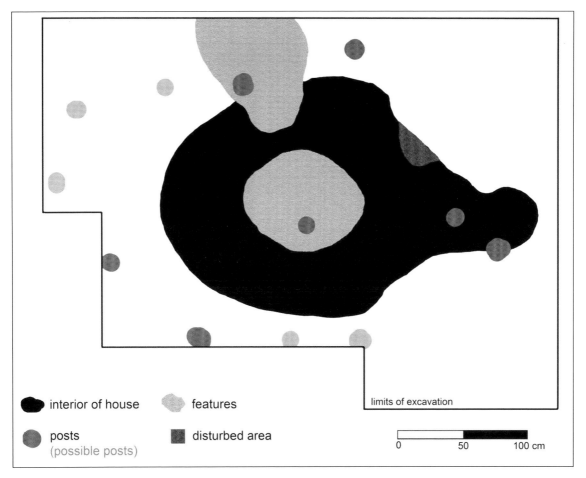

Figure 2.9

This house, from the Davidson Site, dates to 1000 BCE. The centre and narrow entrance of the house (to the right) were dug into the ground, typical of well-insulated houses occupied in winter. The house was ringed with posts that supported a sod-covered roof, including several (to the left) that indicate that the house extended beyond the central subterranean part of the building. One of the features, in the centre, is the same age as the house; the other, at the top, is a more recent pit that cut into the edge of the earlier house. The houses at this site are among the earliest known from Ontario. (Courtesy of Christopher Ellis.)

increasing resources, was probably one factor; at the same time, the rise in lake levels around 6,000 years ago also flooded large expanses of ground, forcing people into smaller areas. I also suspect that Archaic peoples began to spend more time settled in one place, a less mobile lifestyle made possible by locally abundant resources. Indeed, by the end of the Archaic, some living sites were quite large, covering hectares, with thick refuse deposits showing the accumulation of debris over time.

I am currently excavating at an Archaic site near Parkhill (figure 2.8), in southwestern Ontario, that has substantial houses, large food storage pits, and debris deposits that are almost a metre thick (Ellis et al. 2010; Ellis and Keron 2011). The houses include a circular, five-metre diameter house dug down a metre into the ground and two smaller pithouses (see figure 2.9), which were probably occupied throughout the winter months. This house, and the thick midden deposits that are true garbage dumps, are among the earliest ever reported from Ontario; they date to 1500–1000 BCE.

Garbage dumps might not sound very exciting, but archaeologists can learn a lot from them. Formal garbage dumps, or middens, suggest that people probably moved less often, staying in one location for long enough that they needed to set aside special areas for garbage disposal, something that was unnecessary at briefly occupied campsites. The substantial housing and the large storage pits also reinforce the idea that people were moving less often. Thick midden deposits also suggest that groups might have returned regularly to reuse certain locations, perhaps because the increasing populations made it hard to find good places that were not already claimed by others.

Burials provide additional hints that Archaic peoples began to settle down more. While early burials were rare and isolated, several sites from after about 5,500 years ago include burials of multiple individuals, suggesting that people moved less often and returned more regularly to the same locations. Burial practices themselves changed over time, suggesting that the nature of society changed as well. On the earliest sites with multiple burials, the deceased have few or no grave goods and were usually buried in occupied areas. They may even have been laid to rest in unmarked graves, as later burials sometimes cut down through and disturb earlier ones.

By about 3,500 years ago, though, Archaic peoples began to set aside specialized areas solely for burying the dead and carrying out appropriate rituals. These first true cemeteries were probably marked on the surface, serving as visible reminders of a group's history and rights to the area. The goods that people buried with their dead suggest that there may have been increasing differences in the status of different members of society. In contrast to the relatively equal status of earlier times, a few individuals in the late Archaic were buried with objects made from rare and valuable materials, like marine shell and copper. These honoured individuals, most often males, were given items that might have signalled their status, such as large pendants that would have been visible to all members of the group or pieces that must have had ritual and spiritual significance: stone smoking pipes, smoothly polished birdstones, and even masks made from bear skulls (Donaldson and Wortner 1995).

Understanding the Earliest Ontarians

The earliest Ontarians sometimes seem impossibly distant in time. Living in a time before farming and before pottery, the Paleoindian and Archaic peoples earned their living through hunting, fishing, and gathering plants, a way of life that is far removed from our modern age. It is not always easy to learn directly about these ancient peoples. So many of their sites are poorly preserved, relatively small, and with scarce artifacts – not to mention disturbed and churned up by modern developments. Archaeologists have only just begun to find and date the sites that reflect the presence of these early peoples throughout their 13,000–year history in Ontario. Yet every newly discovered site provides an opportunity to learn more, to study the artifacts that they left behind, to tease out new details of their lifestyles, and to consider their relationship with a changing environment. Understanding the lives of the most ancient Ontarians is both a challenge and a responsibility – one that will occupy archaeologists well into the future.

3

The Woodland Period, 900 BCE to 1700 CE

Ronald F. Williamson

Archaeologists call the era from 900 BCE to 1650 or 1700 CE the Woodland period. It was a time marked by the introduction of clay pots in the Early Woodland (900–400 BCE) and by ceremonial interaction among Great Lakes groups in both the Early Woodland and Middle Woodland (400 BCE–800 CE). Archaeologists define the Late Woodland period, from 800 through the mid-to late-1600s CE, based on the gradual adoption of farming.

Ceramics, Ceremony, and Regional Interaction (900 BCE–800 CE)

Ceramic vessels, used for cooking and water storage, were first introduced into Ontario about 2,400 years ago. Thereafter, fragments of broken pots are among the most common artifacts found on settlements, in addition to the small flakes created during flintknapping. Curiously enough, adopting this innovative technology did not profoundly change the hunter-gatherer lifestyle of Woodlands peoples. In fact, the people's seasonal routines changed little from Archaic times (see Ellis, chapter 2). On the other hand, archaeologists have found a few carved, basin-shaped vessels made of soapstone in southern Ontario. These vessels are linked with the intensive use and processing of the seeds of local plants such as goosefoot and knotweed (see Monckton, chapter 8). This suggests that the widespread adoption of ceramic containers and cooking vessels may indicate an intensification of plant use in people's diets.

The craftspeople who made ceramic vessels did not use a potter's wheel but skilfully coiled and pinched the clay to form the pots (see Kapches, chapter 10). The potters smoothed the pot's surface and added decoration to the interior and exterior surfaces of the upper rims. The first ceramic vessels were gritty and poorly fired, with thick, collarless rims and somewhat pointed bases. With time the potters developed new styles – still coiled and with pointed bases but featuring relatively short and thin, outflaring upper rims. The potters often stamped the rims with notched or bevelled tools that left scallop-shell or tooth-like impressions, using a rocking motion to make the decorations. Later potters made more globular pots, decorated with incised horizontal, oblique, opposed, and other impressions (see figures 10.1 and 10.2). The variation in motifs and decorative techniques helps date the sites on which they are found (Spence et al. 1990) and is probably related to the potters' identity. Exactly how these styles relate to historic ethnic affiliations is not always clear, though archaeologists often use the names of historic groups as a kind of shorthand for specific styles.

In autumn and winter, single families lived in small hunting camps, located in prime areas for harvesting nuts and the animals attracted to them. Individual families came together into larger settlements in spring and summer, usually near seasonal resources such as spawning fish. These seasonal movements probably took place within well-defined territories, with individual bands repeatedly returning to certain preferred sites.

The number and distribution of sites tells us that numerous small regional bands inhabited the southern Ontario landscape, collectively representing a population in the thousands. Archaeologists estimate that there were twenty to twenty-five regional bands in southern Ontario, each occupying a significant portion of a major drainage system. If so, then the population of southern Ontario may easily have reached 10,000 people by about 500 CE.

Although each band had their own territory, they kept in touch across southern Ontario and shared ideas with more distant groups (Jamieson 1999, 182). From 2,000 to 3,000 years ago, for example, people across the entire Great Lakes region typically sprinkled ground red ochre, or hematite, around the remains of their dead as well as on their grave offerings. The ochre was bright red in colour and likely symbolized blood, restoration, and rebirth (figure 3.1).

Some of the grave goods placed with loved ones were made from materials that were traded over long distances, such as exquisite chert bifaces made near the Onondaga chert sources around the east end of Lake Erie. Bifaces are an early to middle stage in the process of knapping pieces of stone into useable, fashioned tools, such as projectile points (see Fox, chapter 9). Between about 2,700 and 2,300 years ago, people who archaeologists call the Meadowood culture (a number of Early Woodland groups who lived in what is now New York State, southern Ontario, and Quebec) produced extraordinarily thin and finely made bifaces that are the hallmark of flint-knapping in northeastern North America (see figure 14.1) (Granger 1978a and b; Taché 2011a).

Other goods that were placed with the deceased include polished trapezoidal-shaped gorgets (suspended with a cord to rest on the upper chest) (see figure 14.2) and birdstones made of banded slate (figure 3.2) – some of the most beautiful carved stone

Figure 3.1
Red ochre, a mineral high in iron, stains the soil at the Bruce Boyd burial site, an Early Woodland site in Norfolk County near Long Point. (Photo by Ronald F. Williamson.)

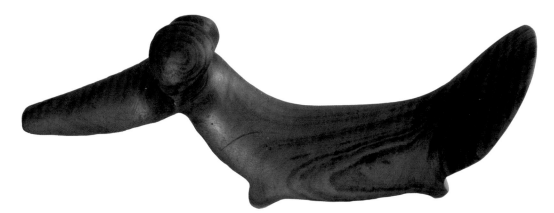

Figure 3.2
A birdstone, a weight or handle for a spear-throwing device, carefully shaped from a piece of fine-grained stone. (Robert Pearce, Museum of Ontario Archaeology – Wilfrid Jury Collection.)

art ever produced in northeastern North America. People also placed items of personal adornment in burials, including pieces made of native copper from the western end of Lake Superior or silver from northern Ontario and lead ore from the St Lawrence valley.

The contribution of these offerings, some of which represented a considerable investment of time and artistic skill, to the graves of fellow community members indicates that people were grieving, or at least marking the deaths of those other than their immediate family members (see Spence, chapter 14). Some archaeologists see these goods as the product of only a few individuals who, having manufactured and distributed such valuable items, sought and were afforded special status among their community members.

By 2,000 years ago, these increasingly sophisticated burial ceremonies sometimes involved the construction of burial mounds based on ceremonies originating in the Mississippi and Ohio valleys in the midwestern US. Earlier burials, around 3,500 years ago, were sometimes placed in prominent natural features such as knolls or sandbanks, but the deliberate construction of artificial mounds did not begin until about 2,500 years ago. The people built small oval or round mounds, which averaged ten metres in length and width and rarely exceeded two metres in height (figure 3.3). Most of these mounds were centred along the shores of Rice Lake, the lower Trent River system, and the adjacent waterways draining into the eastern end of Lake Ontario (see Oberholtzer, chapter 11). They have, however, also been documented in small numbers in most other parts of Ontario. The practice of burying community members in mounds ceased about 1,300 years ago.

Figure 3.3
An artist's rendition imagines how community members created mounds over the course of many years by bringing baskets of soil to add to the structure. (Painting by Shelley Huson, Archaeological Services Inc.)

While communities shared burial ceremonies across a large region, there were nevertheless differences between groups in the design of their ceramic vessels, stone tools, and other objects that they used in their day-to-day lives. In terms of ceramic vessels, archaeologists have been able to detect the presence of two or three social networks in southern Ontario in which individual bands participated. Archaeologists' interest in these ceramic trends has focused on the kinds of exchange and communication that existed among neighbouring and distant bands during the first millennium CE. Some archaeologists have argued, for example, that the broad similarities in the manufacture and decoration of ceramic vessels of this period reflect shared symbols exchanged among both neighbouring and distant communities (Jamieson 1999, 177; Williamson and Pihl 2002). People may have used similarities in design to reinforce their membership in an expanding social network. The most frequently expressed artifact styles may have signalled the most important affiliations of a group, making it easier for others to identify members by noticing readily apparent symbols (see Kapches, chapter 10).

In this way, small stone tools called blades found on sites in southern Ontario may signify that the people continued to identify with a larger Great Lakes ideological system called Hopewell, as they had earlier with Meadowood. Hopewell was a complex of related Middle Woodland communities centred in southern Ohio and Illinois. The Hopewell ideology was far-reaching, involving the construction of mounds and earthworks and the distribution of unique ceremonial items. The blades from the Ontario sites are made from Flint Ridge chalcedony, an exotic stone that outcrops in Ohio, suggesting that these communities exchanged goods with distant Middle Woodland people (see Fox, chapter 9). In short, the blades serve as markers of social identification with the Hopewell complex.

One fascinating development in Early and Middle Woodland times is that people began to cache certain stone tools with great frequency (Taché 2011a; Williamson 1996; Williamson and MacDonald 1998, 117–20). People have been caching stone tools for at least 10,000 years, yet almost 80 percent of the caches that have been documented in the archaeological record of the Great Lakes region date to between 2,000 and 3,000 years ago. About half of these caches are found with burials, while the other half are in contexts away from both burial and habitation sites. Also of special note is the number of these caches associated with wet sites; 30 percent of Meadowood caches were placed on lake shores or river banks, while almost a third of all later Early Woodland caches were recovered from the bottom of bogs or swamps. The latter are obviously caches of tools that were intended to remain forever inaccessible, a practice that is similar to some of the hoarding behaviour of early farmers in Europe. The caching of bifaces continues with some frequency into the subsequent Middle Woodland period but is not well known after that (figure 3.4).

Given the range and complexity of their cultural contexts, it is clear that cached bifaces represent more than simply burial goods or stored, surplus materials from

Figure 3.4
Archaeologists uncovered a cache of Middle Woodland bifaces on the Colborne Street site in Brantford.
Their tight grouping suggests that they were originally placed in a container that has long since disintegrated.
(Photo by Ronald F. Williamson, courtesy of Archaeological Services Inc.)

which a knapper might produce a variety of tools. The fact that caches contain very similar looking, well-made bifaces, suggests that a limited number of master knappers produced sets of tools beyond their individual needs or their local band members. If so, it is not surprising that few if any of the cache sites show any evidence of the thousands of small flakes that a knapper would discard during the production of the bifaces.

With time and the introduction of exotic flints and technologies, the shape of the bifaces became more variable, as did the skill with which they were made. Toward the end of the Meadowood period, for example, there was a proliferation in Ontario of ovate bifaces made of exotic flints from Ohio (Spence and Fox 1986). This would appear to mark the end of the period of Meadowood dominance and influence centred on Lake Ontario and the beginning of a period of substantial cultural influence originating in the west in the upper Mississippi valley – later strengthened with mound-building during Hopewell times.

The discovery and analyses of these caches have therefore helped us understand the direction of these evolving exchange systems and the changing nature of bifaces during Early and Middle Woodland times. Still, the fact that Early Woodland peoples placed caches in inaccessible places, combined with the lack of any evidence that they were intended for further shaping into tools, suggests that the exchange network may have been about more than economic transactions – it also played an important role in reinforcing religious beliefs shared across the region and in promoting individual and group status (Taché 2011a).

Caching may have marked important social occasions and events or contributed to maintaining community solidarity. Offerings of stone tools in burials, sometimes in large numbers, may have been part of the sacred realm accessible to everyone or perhaps only to the family of the deceased. On the other hand, isolated caches very well could have resulted from an entirely private act carried out at some distance, both spatially and socially, from the rest of the community.

Isolated caches may also have been votive offerings, in the sense that they were meant in gratitude for the stone itself. Among both Iroquoian- and Algonquian-speaking peoples, the origin of flint is linked with creation stories and the actual blood and bodies of important figures in those stories. It is conceivable that knappers or individual hunters who relied on stone for their weapons and hunting tools had a long-standing ceremonial tradition that at times required return of the stone that was so essential in their lives to the earth – a giving back of a cosmological figure's blood or body, or a refocusing of the object's value in the sacred realm, itself a reinforcement of the basic philosophical tenet of Aboriginal worldview (see Oberholtzer, chapter 11).

Caching is an activity that is only understandable in the context of historical tradition. In the Great Lakes region, the practice of caching bifaces appears to have come to an end at the same time as a far-reaching revolution began that involved the arrival and gradual adoption of domesticated plants from the south (see Monckton, chapter 8). Although hunting, fishing and gathering certainly continued, new rituals, reflecting an economy focused on the growing, harvesting, and consumption of cultivated plants, gradually supplanted older ones that revolved around naturally occurring resources and the tools necessary for their exploitation.

From Gathering to Growing Food (500–1300 CE)

The introduction of cultivated tropical plants such as maize and squash profoundly changed the lives of the people. Until then, tending plants for food, medicine, and other uses was incidental to hunting and other foraging activities that required seasonal movement. Berries and nuts supplemented the diet, but did not represent a substantial source of food around which to locate settlements. With the introduction of cultivated plants, people were able to grow enough food not only for immediate but for future use.

Maize was the focus of this subsistence revolution. By about 1300 CE, people were eating more than a pound of maize per day, comprising more than half of people's diet (see Keenleyside, chapter 13). Determining when exactly maize and other cultivated plants appeared in the Great Lakes region is still the subject of much archaeological research (see Monckton, chapter 8). Based on charred kernels and identifications of other plant parts, it appears that maize was widespread (though limited in use) by 1,500 years ago in New York and Ontario. People in the northeast were eating squash by around 3,000 years ago, yet its earliest evidence in Ontario also dates to about 1,500 years ago. By 700 years ago, all of the historic aboriginal cultigens – maize, beans, squash, sunflower, and tobacco – were in place.

As Stephen Monckton describes in chapter 8, the transition from hunting and gathering foods to growing crops was long and gradual and first involved growing crops on rich floodplain environments. The first communities to experiment with maize were not permanently settled and still relied considerably on hunted and gathered foods. Within centuries, however, communities had switched to establishing base settlements around which land was cleared for crops, while hunting, fishing, and gathering parties were sent out to satellite camps.

The first such communities in southern Ontario seem to have been established on the middle reaches of the Grand River in Brantford. The Holmedale Site, which is about 1,000 years old, is an excellent example of such a community (Pihl et al. 2008; Warrick 2000). It consisted of a small number of elliptical houses, most about six metres long and three metres wide, encircled by a flimsy fence or single-row palisade that likely served as a windbreak (figure 3.5). The discovery of large, deep pits, probably for storing crops, and the ubiquitous presence of maize on the site suggest that the crop contributed considerably to their diet.

With time, the adoption of a farming life resulted in changes to how people traced their descent. Eventually, a new "family tree" emerged, emphasizing the mother's rather than the father's side. This was a profound conceptual change. In pre-contact Aboriginal societies, the extended family was the basis for their entire social and political system (see Jamieson, chapter 12), and in early agricultural communities these systems came to be matrilineal, or linked to the woman's side of the family. The development of the Iroquoian longhouse, a communal residence during the subsequent period, was related to these earlier changes in social structure.

Some archaeologists argue that it was sometime during this period that Iroquoian-speaking peoples first entered the Great Lakes region, bringing with them maize, an influential lifestyle, and their new language (Snow 1995). Others believe that Iroquoian-speakers arrived prior to these developments, bringing ceramics or one of the new styles of spear points that so often swept the region (Ellis et al. 1990, 121–2). The exact timing of these changes is unknown, but it is clear that proto-Algonquian speakers and their ancestors had already lived in the region for thousands of years when Iroquoian-speaking peoples appeared in the lower Great Lakes region.

The people who came to reside along the central north shore of Lake Ontario were the ancestors of the Huron and Petun, while to their east along the St Lawrence Valley were Iroquoian groups that Jacques Cartier first encountered near modern-day Montreal (see figure 0.3). South of Lake Ontario, in what is now central New York State,

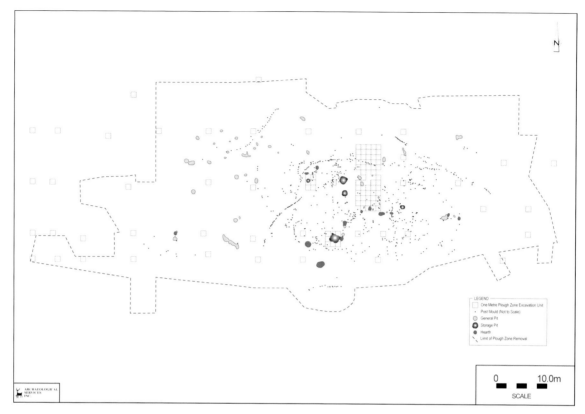

Figure 3.5

This map of the Holmedale Site, near Brantford, gives a good sense of what archaeologists face in figuring out the plan of an ancient village. The widely spaced outlined squares represent excavation units, one metre on a side, that helped archaeologists pinpoint the core of the site. Scraping with heavy equipment (in the area outlined with dotted lines) exposed post moulds, storage pits, and other features. The field crew excavated some of the features and mapped the entire site. The result appears rather chaotic, but an experienced eye can pick out the lines of posts that were originally walls of houses and a flimsy fence or palisade. (Courtesy of Archaeological Services Inc.)

ancestral Iroquoian-speakers became the Five Nations Iroquois (Seneca, Cayuga, Onondaga, Oneida, and Mohawk). The ancestors of the Neutral nation lived in southwestern Ontario, around the west end of Lake Ontario and throughout the Niagara Peninsula. While there were most certainly interactions among these Iroquoian-speaking groups, the Five Nations Iroquois did not actually inhabit southern Ontario until the mid-to-late 1600s.

The sites of these Iroquoian societies are often the focus of archaeological research in southern Ontario and New York State. Algonquian-speaking societies, however, continued to live throughout the rest of southern and northern Ontario, although their sites are often difficult to distinguish archaeologically because of the shared use of ceramic pots and other items. Many archaeologists believe that the boundaries between Iroquoian and Algonquian societies should be viewed as having been quite fluid and that Iroquoian villages may have been quite cosmopolitan in nature (Birch and Williamson 2013).

Northern Algonquian groups focused on hunting, fishing (especially sturgeon), and gathering wild rice, which they may have stored for use in winter. Recent research also indicates that maize, likely obtained through trade, was an important component of the diet of most northern groups by 1,000 years ago (Boyd and Surette 2010; see also Hamilton, chapter 5). In the warm season, people generally gathered at sites associated with good fishing locations at narrows, rapids, and sandy beaches. High ground moraines, drumlins, and eskers were also used in summer and would have provided good vantage points for observing caribou movements. Winter camps were smaller, typically consisting of one or two families through the fathers' line who moved into their winter hunting territories. These sites are often difficult to identify archaeologically.

Villages to Towns (1300–1700 CE)

By the beginning of the 1300s, during the Late Woodland period, the Iroquoian-speaking people of southern Ontario lived in much larger, fortified villages. In addition to a nearby source of freshwater, these settlements required hundreds of hectares of well-drained soil on which to grow crops and an ample supply of cedar trees for constructing longhouses. By the mid-1400s, feuding among neighbouring and more distant communities also necessitated an easily defensible location for good town sites.

Most of these villages were only occupied for a few decades. The fertility of the corn fields declined quickly as did supplies of firewood and nearby populations of fur-bearing animals. There was also the problem of managing considerable quantities of refuse. People began planning for their next communities years before abandoning the one in which they lived – clearing forests and preparing farm fields, planting and tending to the first year's crops, felling tens of thousands of saplings, cutting hundreds of sheets of elm and cedar bark to build dozens of houses and a palisade. All the while, the current community had to be maintained in good repair.

While the villagers relied on many plant and animal species to meet their needs, maize became the major part of their diet. Archaeologists find charred maize cobs and individual kernels in pits throughout their houses and in refuse areas. There is also direct evidence of the contribution of maize to people's diets in their skeletal remains. In 1997, for example, an ancestral Huron village and its associated ossuary (Williamson and Pfeiffer 2003), dating to the late 1200s to early 1300s, was discovered within Toronto. At the instruction of Aboriginal elders, the ossuary was completely excavated and the remains re-interred in another location. The ossuary, situated on the periphery of the village, was a circular pit about two metres in diameter that contained the mixed remains of eighty-seven people who had died during the village's occupation.

They had been buried together as part of a ceremony when the villagers prepared to relocate.

Archaeologists studying the remains were able to analyse the chemistry of the people's bones to see what they had eaten (see Keenleyside, chapter 13). The studies suggested that older adults, who died after age fifty, had a diet of 54 percent maize during their growing years. For those aged twenty to twenty-nine years when they died, the proportion of maize reached an astonishing 70 percent of their diet! These figures suggest that the need to produce more maize may have become more pressing in some communities of the late 1200s and early 1300s, even within as short a period as one generation, perhaps due to greater numbers of people living together in one place. Tooth decay and gum disease also attest to the people's increasing reliance on maize, which they probably prepared as a sticky gruel.

In addition to cultivated and wild plants, animal protein was a crucial part of the diet. Hunting and fishing provided most meat (see Needs-Howarth, chapter 7), while dogs, which were the only animals to be domesticated by the Aboriginal peoples of southern Ontario, served both as companions and as ceremonial food. Animal hides and pelts provided material for clothing and bones made useful tools. Most game and fish were likely taken during autumn, when people probably mounted large expeditions to hunt white-tailed deer and to catch spawning fish.

The length of people's longhouses varied with the size of the family, each housing a mother and her daughters, or a group of sisters, along with their husbands and children. The houses could be lengthened or shortened to accommodate changes in the number of people living in the house. Two families shared each of the hearths, located along the central corridor of the structure, and sleeping benches lined the interior walls (see Ferris, chapter 6). The house ends were often partitioned to create storage areas for firewood or dried corn. In the 1400s, some households became consistently larger and more variable in membership compared to others in the same community (see Warrick, chapter 4). The trend peaked with some longhouses being repeatedly enlarged to reach lengths of over 120 metres – longer than a football field!

In theory, holes in the roof allowed smoke from the hearth fires to escape, although Iroquoians' health suffered as a result of spending too much time in smoke-filled longhouses. Not only were respiratory infections common but the severe winter climate of southern Ontario ensured that people spent substantial periods of every year indoors, where smoky air irritated their sinuses. Some also contracted tuberculosis. Living in close proximity to organic refuse along with rodents, dogs, and considerable numbers of people would have heightened susceptibility to disease, as would the harmful effects of smoke (see Keenleyside, chapter 13).

Toward the end of the 1400s, smaller villages coalesced into large ones, reaching a size of more than four hectares (figure 3.6) (Birch 2012; Birch and Williamson 2013). The variation between houses, which may have signalled dominant lineages within villages, began to decrease, perhaps reflecting the increasing importance of

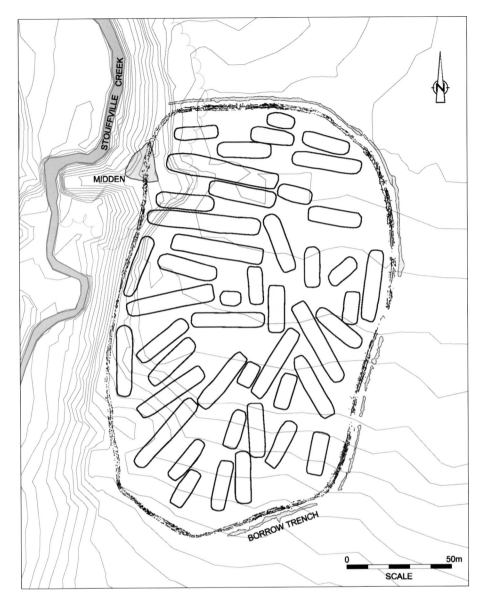

Figure 3.6
A map of the early sixteenth-century Mantle Site, near Stouffville, shows dozens of longhouses, all visible during excavation as simple lines of post moulds. The trench on the outside of the palisade was filled with refuse, indicating the site inhabitants streamed their waste from the inside to the outside of the village. (Courtesy of Archaeological Services Inc.)

clans over lineages. Clan membership, defined by those who claimed a common female ancestor, cut across related communities, so this aspect of kinship was an important means of integrating villages, where chiefs were elected from the principal clans (see Jamieson, chapter 12).

Regional clusters of Iroquoian villages in the archaeological record may represent two or more contemporary communities that shared a hunting territory or other common resources. In this way, several communities may have belonged to a large social network, with people moving back and forth between them. Social ties were likely stronger with neighbouring communities than with more distant groups. On the other hand, exchange with more distant groups would have afforded Iroquoians exotic goods and ideas, whereas local networks probably resulted in spousal exchanges, military alliances and trading relationships, all of which may have prepared people for community amalgamations. Moreover, social ties established by the exchange of marriage partners among the formerly autonomous communities would have helped address the social and political tensions inherent in the new larger residential populations.

Villages housing hundreds if not thousands of people required new social and political structures to regulate village affairs and relations between villages. Village councils, more formalized community planning, social groups such as curing societies, and group rituals like feasting and community burial all emerged during this time period. Curing societies are first visible in many of the longhouses in the form of semi-subterranean sweatlodges – a special type of feature that makes its appearance in the late 1200s (figure 3.7). These large, deep, rectangular structures with ramped entrances at the end were likely used for religious and medicinal purposes (figure 3.8), as the practice of sweating is thought to have been a means by which to communicate with the spirit world (see Ferris, chapter 6). They may also have served as venues to cement the newly emerging social and political ties among the various members of the village (MacDonald and Williamson 2001).

The end of the 1500s and first half of the 1600s saw major population movements. The effects of European-introduced diseases, warfare, and trade through the mid- to late seventeenth century contributed to further population reductions along with continued migrations, fission, and amalgamations of formerly independent groups (see Warrick, chapter 4). Most if not all the ancestral Huron-Petun populations inhabiting the north shore area of Lake Ontario had moved from the lake northward by about 1600, joining with other groups in present-day Simcoe County, between Lake Simcoe and Georgian Bay. Similarly, the Neutral Nation formed and inhabited the Niagara Peninsula and the area around the west end of Lake Ontario between Hamilton and Brantford.

While this movement of communities likely took place over several generations, the final impetus was conflict with the Five Nations Iroquois of neighbouring New York State. Intertribal warfare with the Five Nations during the first half of the 1600s, exacerbated by the intrusion of Europeans, ultimately resulted in the collapse and dispersal of the three southern Ontario Iroquoian confederacies – the Huron, the Petun, and the Neutral.

As a consequence, in the 1660s, the Five Nations Iroquois establish for the first time a series of settlements in southern Ontario at strategic locations along the trade routes inland from the north shore of Lake Ontario. Their settlements were on the canoe-and-portage routes that linked Lake Ontario to Georgian Bay and the upper Great Lakes, through Lake Simcoe. By the 1690s, these settlements were abandoned by the Iroquois. The Mississauga had moved into the territory; they were the Nation

Figure 3.7
An excavated sweatlodge, with the ramped entrance to the right. The white straws mark the location of posts around its perimeter. (Courtesy of Archaeological Services Inc.)

Figure 3.8
The bear skull in the centre of this photograph was found on the living floor of a sweatlodge at the Late Woodland Wiacek Site in Barrie. Animal skulls found occasionally on the floor of a lodge might symbolize clan identity. (Courtesy of Archaeological Services Inc.)

with whom the British eventually reached land agreements. The earliest Europeans were attracted to the area because of its strategic importance for accessing and controlling long-established regional economic networks. In many places, the first European settlement of Ontario was simply a continuation of patterns that had been in place for thousands of years.

4

The Aboriginal Population of Ontario in Late Prehistory

Gary Warrick

Four hundred years ago, Ontario was home to about 75,000 Aboriginal people, divided in two major language and cultural groups – Algonquians (15,000) and Iroquoians (60,000). Algonquians lived primarily in the vast expanse of northern Ontario. They hunted, gathered, and fished, moving seasonally through the forest and across the countless rivers and lakes of the Canadian Shield. During spring and summer, Algonquians lived in small bark-covered cabins, in villages of over 100 people at preferred fishing spots. In late autumn and winter, the villages broke apart into small camps of ten to thirty people.

The Iroquoians occupied southern Ontario, sharing hunting territories with some Algonquian groups, and lived in villages surrounded by fields of maize, beans, and squash so vast that you could get lost in them. The largest villages were encircled by fences of tall wooden poles, or palisades. They covered as many as five hectares, or the equivalent of eight soccer fields, and contained several dozen multi-family longhouses, home to more than 2,000 people. When French explorers, traders, and missionaries, such as Samuel de Champlain, Gabriel Sagard, and Jean de Brébeuf, visited such villages in the early 1600s, they recorded details of how the original peoples of Ontario lived – and how they died. Epidemics of European infectious diseases – measles, pneumonia, and smallpox – spread throughout Ontario in the 1630s, killing young and old indiscriminately. In the space of a few years, these diseases reduced the population from 75,000 to a mere 30,000 (Warrick 2003 and 2008, 81–6).

Disease changed the political landscape, prompting the Haudenosaunee (originally the Five Nations Iroquois – today the Six Nations) of New York State to launch a series of devastating raids against the various Aboriginal groups of Ontario. By 1652, southern Ontario was emptied of its original inhabitants, opening it up for resettlement by the Haudenosaunee and the Algonquian-speaking Ojibwa and Mississaugas from northern Ontario. In the 1780s, Six Nations peoples settled in the Grand River area, adding to the historical and archaeological landscape.

A Census of the Past

Aboriginal Ontario of the early 1600s is well documented historically, but the pre-European story can only be told through oral tradition and archaeology. With the deaths from disease of many elders and chroniclers of community history in the 1630s, much of the oral history in Ontario was lost. Archaeology offers an alternative means of revealing the pre-European history of Aboriginal Ontario, by helping to write the history of regions and peoples for which we have either no or few written or oral records. Even when historic records exist, archaeology provides additional valuable information about the distribution and number of people in a region and about the ways that those people were influenced by and interacted with the environment, their neighbours, and disease. The challenge for an archaeologist who desires to write a population history is how to identify and count past peoples.

Archaeologists who are interested in population are essentially census-takers of the past. In southern Ontario, archaeologists find material evidence of several groups of Aboriginal peoples from 1400–1650 CE. Some were the ancestors of Iroquoian speakers, such as the Attiwandaron (Neutral), Wendat-Tionontaté (Huron-Petun), and St Lawrence Iroquoians. Others were the relatives of Algonquian speakers, like the Assistaeronon (Fire Nation or Western Basin Tradition), Odawa (Ottawa), and Nipissirini (Nipissing). Most of these groups lived in specific territories until the late 1500s and 1600s, when disease, the fur trade, and shifting political alliances led several groups to abandon old homelands and coalesce into new and sometimes multi-ethnic communities.

Aboriginal farmers of pre-European Ontario are fairly easy to identify and count. Iroquoian-speaking and Algonquian-speaking farming peoples (like the Assistaeronon) lived in longhouse villages, covering tens of thousands of square metres, sometimes for more than forty years. Thick refuse piles, called middens, built up next to houses and palisades. A large village midden can contain more than 100,000 potsherds, stone tools, and food bones – sufficient to keep a labful of archaeologists cleaning, counting, and identifying for months.

The remains of these village sites show up clearly in a ploughed field, where the surface is littered with broken artifacts and darkly stained patches of soil. Archaeologists trace the size of a village using a technique called surface collection – walking over the entire site, marking artifact locations with wire flags, recording their location, and collecting and bagging them individually (figure 4.1A & B).

I will never forget surface collecting on the Cleary site, a Wendat village inhabited in the late 1400s, located just south of Barrie (Warrick 2008). The site was discovered in the 1890s, but its location had been forgotten over time. Working from

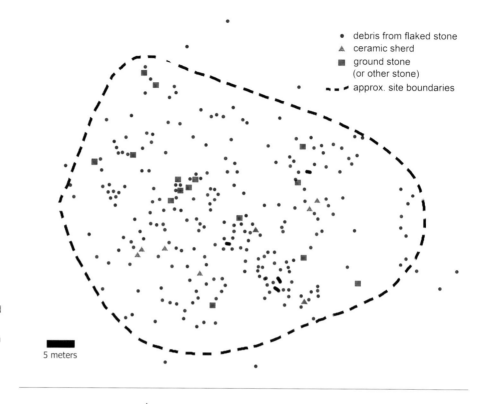

Figure 4.1A
This map shows the position of artifacts that archaeologists found on the surface of a ploughed field near Burlington, Ontario. Although it was clear that these artifacts constituted a major site, the full details only became visible after excavation (see figure 4.1B). (Courtesy of Museum of Ontario Archaeology.)

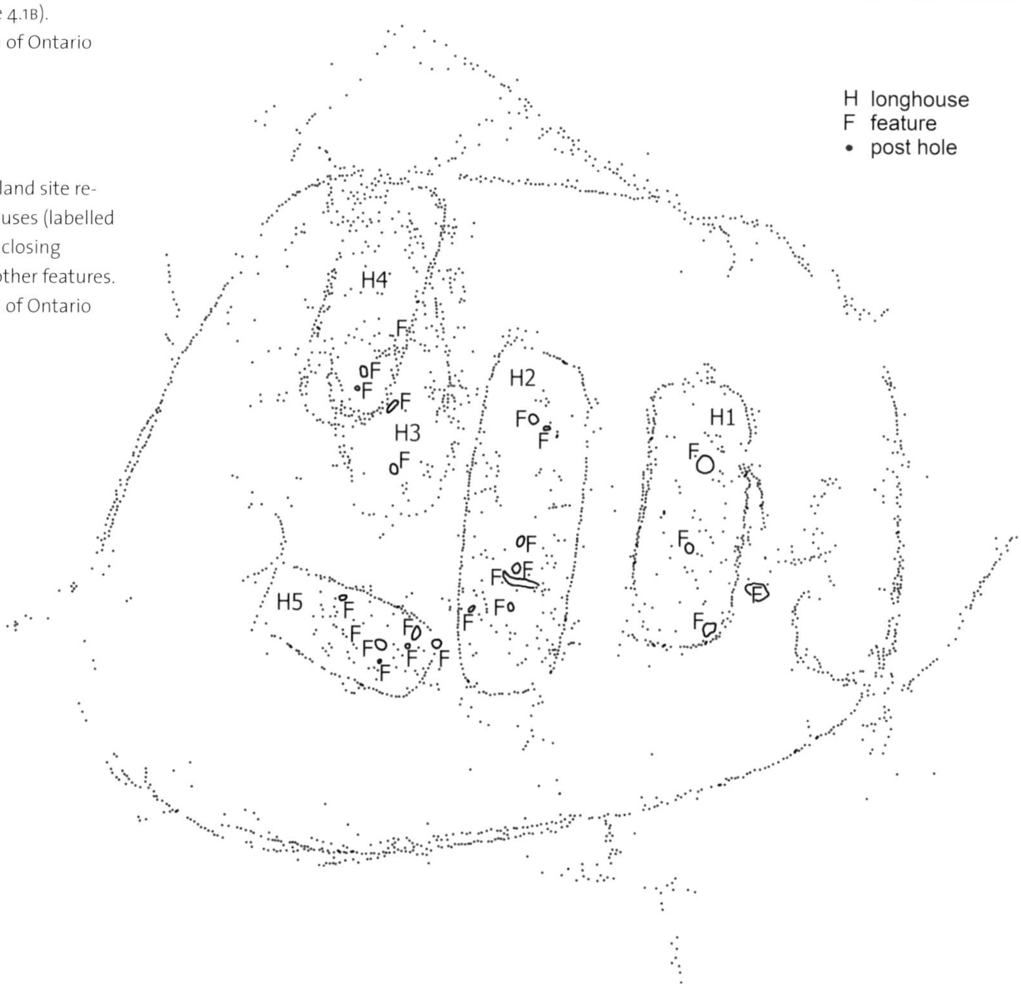

Figure 4.1B
Excavations of the Ireland site revealed several longhouses (labelled H1, H2, etc.) and an enclosing palisade, along with other features. (Courtesy of Museum of Ontario Archaeology.)

archival notes in the Royal Ontario Museum, we pinpointed a likely location and drove there, finding a bare, ploughed field awaiting exploration. Three crew members and I immediately noticed artifacts on the field surface just metres from the road. After walking over the site for a couple of hours and marking hundreds of artifact finds with fluorescent red flags, I realized that the field was covered in black patches almost as far as I could see. I sent one of the crew members marching across the field to investigate a black patch that was barely visible in the shimmering air of a hot May day. He walked more than two hundred metres across the field, bent over for a minute, stood up, and waved excitedly – he had found more artifacts. The site turned out to be one of the largest Wendat villages in the region, covering 4.8 hectares – an area equal to eight soccer fields. It took us three days to collect artifacts and map the entire site.

We can estimate the population of a village like the Cleary site based on its size. Ontario archaeologists have excavated portions of over 100 village sites and 1,000 longhouses since 1950, one of the largest number of houses and villages excavated anywhere in the world for early farming peoples. These excavations show that long-houses were remarkably consistent from 1000–1650 CE in the spacing of house wall posts and central fireplaces or hearths, as well as the number of longhouses relative to the area of a village. We use the average of number of hearths per hectare of village area (fifty) to help estimate the size of unexcavated sites. For example, the Cleary Site, at 4.8 hectares, would have about 240 hearths.

We can translate from hearths to people by using historical documents that refer to two families sharing a central hearth. In fact, according to historical linguist John Steckley (2007, 161), the Wendat word for hearth (*te onatsanhiaj*) makes reference to being divided in half. Burial remains and French historical accounts suggest that Wendat family size in 1600 was relatively small – two adults and three children, some-times with an unmarried relative or a grandparent. Thus, to calculate the population of a Wendat village site, you simply multiply the fifty hearths per hectare by ten people (two families of five). If the Cleary Site had 240 hearths, then we can estimate its population at 2,400 people.

My PhD research focused on just this kind of population count (Warrick 2008). I found that the Wendat-Tionontaté population grew rapidly between 1300–1430 from 8,000 to 24,000 people, stabilized at 30,000 people from 1430–1630, and then plum-meted catastrophically in the 1630s as a result of European disease, leaving only 12,000 survivors (figure 4.2). Archaeology and history reveals a similar story of growth, stabilization, and then a decline in the 1630s for the Neutral. The St Lawrence Iro-quoians in eastern Ontario waned in the late 1500s and then disappeared completely by 1600, probably the result of a combination of warfare and disease.

The estimation of the pre-European population of Algonquian speakers, who earned their living by hunting, gathering, and fishing rather than by farming, is a problem for archaeology. First of all, Algonquians lived so lightly on the land that

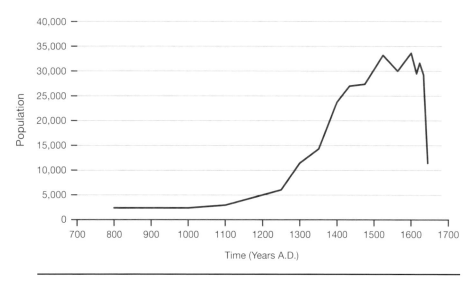

Figure 4.2
This graph depicts the growth and sudden decline of the Wendat-Tionontaté population.
(Courtesy of Gary Warrick.)

Figure 4.3
Archaeologists excavate at the Molson Site in 1985. Molson was a Wendat village from the late 1500s that included both longhouses and smaller cabins, perhaps built to accommodate visitors. The coloured straws mark the location of post moulds. (Courtesy of Gary Warrick.)

they left behind few physical traces. Archaeologically, they are sometimes invisible. Secondly, they obtained pottery and sometimes arrowheads from their Iroquoian neighbours, which adds great confusion to the archaeological record. Do the Wendat-style pots found in a campsite in Algonquin Park mean that Algonquians camped there, or Wendats? Were the small cabins at the Molson Site (figure 4.3), a Wendat village from the late 1500s in Barrie, occupied by Algonquians or Iroquoian visitors (Fox and Garrad 2006; Lennox 2000)?

Even if you can be certain that you have an Algonquian site, how do you determine who they were, how many people lived there, and for how long? According to historical accounts, Algonquian hunter-gatherer-fishers moved across the land in a seasonal cycle, living in at least three or four different places over the course of a year. Archaeologically, Algonquian peoples are difficult to identify and even more difficult to count – a census-taker's nightmare!

The archaeological invisibility of Algonquians is even more challenging after European contact, especially when pottery and stone and bone tools were replaced by metal kettles, knives, awls, and guns. At the early 1800s Davisville settlement, more than seventy Mississauga hunter-gatherers lived along the Grand River, just west of downtown Brantford in the mid-1820s. Except for concentrations of burned food bones, virtually no archaeological remnants of their two-year occupation could be found. They had vanished without a trace.

The best way to estimate the number of Algonquians in Ontario just before the arrival of Europeans is to use historical accounts and maps from the seventeenth, eighteenth, and nineteenth centuries. The writings and maps of European explorers, missionaries, and fur traders indicate sparse Algonquian settlement in northern Ontario. In the early 1600s, the Cree of northwestern Ontario likely numbered no more than 3,000 and the Ojibwa and other Algonquian groups of north-central and northeastern Ontario had a combined population of 6,000. The Odawa, Nipissing, and Ottawa Valley Algonquians totalled 4,000 people. Algonquians clustered in groups or bands of 100–300 in the warm season at fishing stations. In the cold season, each band dissolved into single families to hunt and trap in the forest. Archaeologically, Algonquians are most visible at the fishing stations, locations on lakeshores at the mouths of major rivers or near rapids. Some fishing stations, such as Michipicoten on the northeast shore of Lake Superior, were used for centuries and contain deep deposits containing stone tools, some for cleaning fish, and cooking pots (Wright 1968).

The Growth of Nations

Prior to European contact, the Aboriginal people of Ontario continually rearranged their households, villages, and regional relationships. Before 1300, Iroquoian peoples across Ontario lived in small longhouses of 20–30 people and tiny villages of just

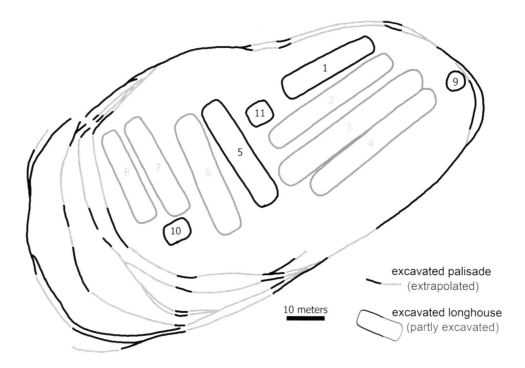

Figure 4.4
The Uren site, a village with eight longhouses and several smaller structures, is one of many settlements that grew rapidly in the early 1300s. This map shows changes over time in the area enclosed by the palisade around the village. (Drawing by Marit Munson, adapted from Wright 1986.)

100–150 people. In the early 1300s, longhouses suddenly doubled in size and village populations tripled (figure 4.4). Population increase from births alone cannot account for this growth in houses and villages.

The only explanation is that two or three smaller villages came together, and households likely merged as well. Perhaps this reflects the formation of political alliances and the beginnings of tribes or nations, bringing together two or more groups of distantly related households or clans, associated with an ancestral animal or bird totem and related by descent along maternal lines (see Jamieson, chapter 12). The villages of the 1300s have obvious defensive palisades and occasional victims of violence in middens, suggesting heightened levels of warfare between villages. Wendat and Haudenosaunee oral traditions tell of times in their past when warfare between nations was common.

Beginning around 1330, Iroquoian population in Ontario began to increase rapidly. For the Wendat-Tionontaté, population more than doubled between 1300 and 1400, from 10,000 to 22,000 people. The reasons for this boom are not clear, but skeletons from the Fairty ossuary (Katzenberg 1992), located east of Toronto and dated to the mid-1300s, indicate that women had more children than in previous

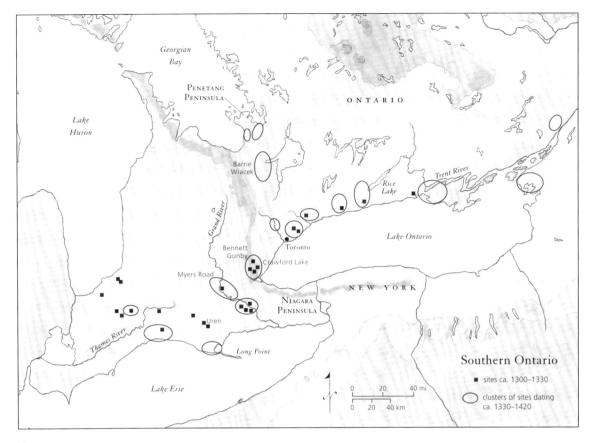

Figure 4.5

Iroquoian speakers expanded into new territories in the 1300s CE, a movement visible in clusters of village sites in specific areas of southern Ontario. (Map by Molly O'Halloran, based on Warrick 2000: fig. 8.)

centuries and more of those children survived into adulthood. Health indicators on the bones of the dead show that they had a protein-rich diet, based on a combination of beans, maize, and fish (see Keenleyside, chapter 13). Episodes of rapid population growth in human history occur whenever childhood death rates drop but birth rates do not. For example, in Britain, in the late 1700s and early 1800s, childhood deaths plummeted but families continued to have many children for a couple of generations, resulting in a massive population explosion and the migration of British people to the four corners of the world.

Population growth in Ontario during the 1300s resulted in the colonization of previously unoccupied lands. The Neutral expanded into the Kitchener-Waterloo and Crawford Lake regions. The Wendat-Tionontaté moved into the Lake Simcoe-Georgian Bay and Balsam Lake areas, while the St Lawrence Iroquoian settled in Prescott-Cornwall (figure 4.5). In the new "colonies" and in the original homeland, Iroquoians began to build neighbouring villages within a few kilometres of one another on the same drainage or height of land overlooking a lake or major river. These villages absorbed more and more people throughout the 1300s, with many more houses leading to larger and larger villages. In fact, village size doubled between 1300 and 1400.

In the mid-1400s, village size and the size of the longhouses themselves grew bigger still. Longhouses averaged 50 metres in length, and one third were remodelled to add family compartments, sheltering 100 residents. The largest longhouses are found in Neutral sites of the 1400s and are longer than a football field – a single house at the Moyer site was 93 metres long, and another house, at the Coleman site, in Kitchener-Waterloo, was 124 metres in length (MacDonald 1986; Wagner et al. 1973).

Villagers from several smaller sites joined together to form these large villages (Warrick 2008, 134–8). By the late 1400s, major villages, such as the Cleary Site south of Barrie and the Lalonde Site in Simcoe County, covered 4–5 hectares and would have contained over 2,000 inhabitants each. The Draper Site, in Pickering, was occupied for forty years. Its overlapping palisades, middens, and longhouses show that the village grew over time as five smaller communities joined the original core village (figure 4.6).

Archaeologists interpret concentrations of village sites and the appearance of very large villages across southern Ontario in the early 1400s as evidence of the origins of tribes or nations. An Iroquoian nation was either a single large village or a cluster of village communities whose residents spoke a distinct dialect and cultivated trade and political alliances with neighbouring and distant Iroquoian and Algonquian nations. Oral history supports this. The Wendat told the Jesuits in 1639 that the Attignawantan and Attigneenongnahac were the founding nations of the Wendat confederacy and that they had coexisted in Simcoe County since the early 1400s.

Archaeologists have identified seven clusters of Wendat-Tionontaté in south-central Ontario in the 1400s (Warrick 2000, 447), including two groups in Simcoe County precisely where the Attignawantan and Attigneenongnahac were living in the 1600s. Other village concentrations in the 1400s include two clusters of St Lawrence Iroquoians in eastern Ontario and seven groups of Neutral sites in southwestern Ontario (figure 4.7). The St Lawrence Iroquoian clusters persisted into the 1500s, but the other groups joined together into large villages. The Wendat-Tionontaté, for example, concentrated in six clusters, with only one large village remaining in the Toronto region, on the Humber River. The Neutral largely abandoned the London area, settling in three main clusters, mostly east of the Grand River. By 1615, the St Lawrence Iroquoians had disappeared, the Wendat-Tionontaté had concentrated in the Collingwood-Midland-Orillia region, and the Neutral occupied the region of Brantford-Flamborough-Hamilton-St Catharines, having abandoned all lands west of the Grand River.

The origin of Algonquian nations is more difficult to identify using archaeology. In Late Woodland times, there are two styles of pottery found in sites across northern Ontario: Blackduck and Selkirk (Wright 2004, 1500–17). Both pottery styles were made between 500 and 1700 CE. While it is tempting to claim that Selkirk pottery users were ancestral Cree and Blackduck users were Ojibwa, the two pottery styles are found in sites of the same age in the same region (see Hamilton, chapter 5). Even

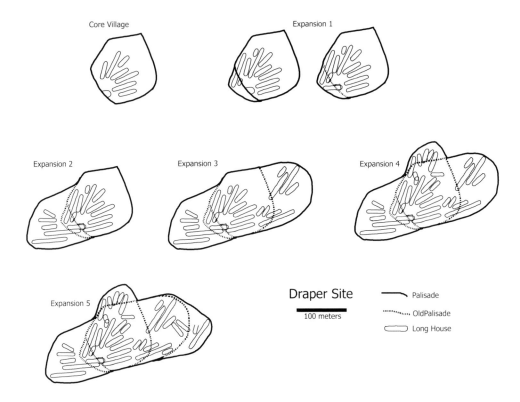

Figure 4.6
The Draper site, in Pickering, grew dramatically in the thirty-five to forty years that it was occupied, from about seven longhouses to three dozen. (Courtesy of Gary Warrick and the Museum of Ontario Archaeology.)

if pottery could distinguish one group from another, membership in historical Algonquian groups was fluid and groups joined together and broke apart frequently, mixing artifact styles and changing territorial boundaries.

Uniting in Confederacies

Beginning in the late 1500s, neighbouring Iroquoian nations stopped fighting with one another and began to join together to form larger political groups called confederacies. In Ontario, confederacy formation is reflected in the abandonment of long-term site clusters and their re-establishment in closer proximity to other site clusters, such as the Neutral concentration east of the Grand River and the Wendat concentration in Simcoe County. Patterns of cross-nation trade and warfare in New York State suggest, to me, that the Five Nations Iroquois confederacy also formed around 1600.

The Wendat, Tionontaté, and Neutral of the 1600s consolidated into distinct political confederacies – alliances of several nations. The Wendat confederacy united four or perhaps five nations, the Tionontaté two, and the Neutral six, or possibly eight, member nations. The five nations of the St Lawrence Iroquoians, on the other hand, never came together politically into a confederacy; they disappeared because of warfare among themselves and with the Wendat, Abenaki, and Five Nations confederacies, and also because of European diseases.

It can be quite difficult for archaeologists to identify differences between confederacies like the Wendat and the Neutral, much less among individual nations within a single Iroquoian confederacy. Most researchers rely on differences in the styles and decoration of clay smoking pipes and cooking pots among certain Iroquoian groups (see Kapches, chapter 10). The St Lawrence Iroquoians, for instance, made and decorated their clay pots with distinctive styles. Just identifying St Lawrence Iroquoian style pottery is not enough, though. The pots show up in villages from the 1500s occupied by the Mohawk, Delaware, and Arendarhonon ("the Rock" – the easternmost Wendat nation). In fact, the number of St Lawrence style pots increased through time, even as the St Lawrence Iroquoians themselves began to decline. Most archaeologists believe that St Lawrence Iroquoian-style pots in Wendat, Delaware, and Mohawk sites were made by refugee or captive St Lawrence Iroquoian women (Kuhn 2004; Ramsden 1990; Warrick 2008, 201–3). After all, oral history recorded in the early 1600s describes "cruel wars" between St Lawrence Iroquoians and their enemies.

Warfare among Iroquoian confederacies was probably caused by the need to protect deer hunting territories and prime fishing grounds and to ensure access to trade routes and scarce resources. The Wendat concentrated their villages in Simcoe County for safety and security against raids from Five Nations Iroquois and for easy access to Algonquian traders and the furs, fish, and hides of the Canadian Shield (see Hamilton, chapter 5). For the Wendat and Tionontaté, their land also led to preferred trade status with the French, who established their main trade route in the 1600s along the Ottawa River, across Lake Nipissing, and along the eastern shore of Georgian Bay. Access to French traders increased Wendat and Tionontaté political stature among other Aboriginal nations of the Northeast. The trade advantage also raised jealousy and rivalry among the Five Nations and the Neutral, leading to raiding for furs and trade goods.

European diseases also had a major impact on Iroquoian confederacies (see Keenleyside, chapter 13). In the 1630s, smallpox, measles, pneumonia, and other diseases swept across Ontario and New York State, killing two thirds of all Aboriginal people in a period of just six years (Warrick 2003 and 2008, 81–6). In an effort to replenish their numbers, the Five Nations Iroquois attempted to convince the Wendat-Tionontaté and Neutral to join them. When this failed, the Five Nations conducted massive raids with hundreds of warriors in the 1640s and early 1650s into the heart of Wendat, Tionontaté, and Neutral territory, killing the men, burning villages, and taking hundreds of women and children captive. Many of the Wendat and Tionontaté sought refuge with other groups and most of the Neutral were adopted into Seneca villages in New York State.

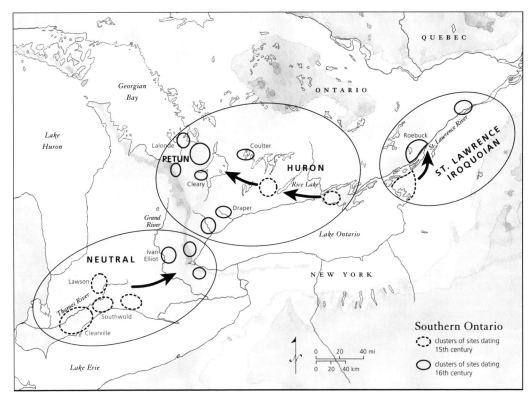

Figure 4.7

Archaeologists have combined historic accounts and archaeological information to map clusters of sites that may correspond to the Wendat-Tionontaté and other historic First Nations. (Map by Molly O'Halloran, based on Warrick 2000: fig. 10.)

The archaeological evidence of the epidemic years is meagre. The spread of European disease among northern Algonquians in the early 1600s is not well documented historically and would be impossible to determine from current archaeological information. At the very least, European diseases did infect Ottawa Valley Algonquians, Odawa, and Nipissing in the 1620s and 1630s. Many Wendat and Neutral survivors stayed in their villages after the epidemics, living in fewer houses in emptier villages; these small groups left little archaeological trace of their demise.

On the other hand, the horror of the Wendat confederacy's destruction by the Five Nations Iroquois is clearly visible in the archaeological record. In 1991, a team of archaeologists investigated the Charity site, a Wendat refugee camp on Christian Island in Georgian Bay (Jackson et al. 1992). Their work revealed hurriedly constructed houses, a lack of food remains, and cannibalized human bone. Over the winter of 1649–50, more than 3,000 Wendat perished in this camp from starvation and disease, leaving only 600 survivors. The last 200 Wendat left Christian Island in 1651 and journeyed to Quebec City.

The abandonment of southern Ontario by the Wendat and Neutral in 1652 and the retreat of Algonquian groups further north and west created a gap in the permanent Aboriginal occupation of southern Ontario. In 1667, the Seneca, Cayuga, and Oneida briefly filled that gap, establishing seven villages along the north shore of Lake Ontario. The short-lived villages were abandoned within a dozen years, after attacks by French-allied Ojibwa, Mississauga, and Wendat warriors. After 1690, the Mississaugas, about 1,000 strong and originally from north of Georgian Bay, moved south into Ontario and settled along the major rivers flowing into Lake Ontario and Lake Erie. Iroquoians did not return permanently to southern Ontario until 1784–85, when about 1,800 Six Nations Iroquois (Haudenosaunee) settled along the lower Grand River, where their descendants live today.

Continuity with the Past

Archaeologists know little about the Algonquian-speaking hunter-gatherers, such as the Ojibwa, Mississauga, and Delaware, in southern Ontario during the 1700s and early 1800s. Written census records from about 1800 suggest that as many as 1,500 hunter-gatherers were in southern Ontario, but they lived so lightly on the land that they left only meagre archaeological traces. Excavations at a few houses and camps near Chatham, Brantford, and Hamilton (Ferris 2009, 32–9) reveal remains of small bark-pole houses or tents with dirt floors, burned animal and fish bones, and broken and lost European items, such as glass embroidery beads, trade silver jewellery, flintlock gun parts and lead shot and balls, iron knives, and fish hooks. According to missionary accounts, Algonquians of historic Ontario moved their camps seasonally to take advantage of available resources, a pattern known as a seasonal round. They hunted and went fishing in spring, summer, and autumn, trapped and hunted through winter, and maple-sugared in early spring.

In contrast, Six Nations Iroquoians and allied Aboriginal peoples established long-term settlements on the lower Grand River in 1784–85, after they were pushed out of their homelands in New York State as a result of their loyalty to the British in the American Revolutionary War. A group of roughly 1,800–2,200 Six Nations, Delaware, and other Aboriginal peoples ultimately settled in eight to ten villages on the Grand River, living there until 1841. The Six Nations people built most of these villages right on top of 1,000–1,500-year-old Iroquoian villages, suggesting amazing continuity in Iroquoian knowledge about living in a river landscape.

The villages themselves consisted of several log cabins oriented to the river, with fields of maize, beans, squash, and potatoes planted on the rich floodplains and islands. Archaeologists have added to our knowledge of Six Nations life in the early 1800s by excavating cabins at Mohawk Village and Davisville (Warrick 2006), located in present-day Brantford. They found that Six Nations log cabins were modelled after those built by colonial Americans but kept some features of the ancient longhouses. Cabins were small, with a floor plan covering 25 square metres and two doors, one opening out to the river and the other to the forest. The cabins were far from basic, for each

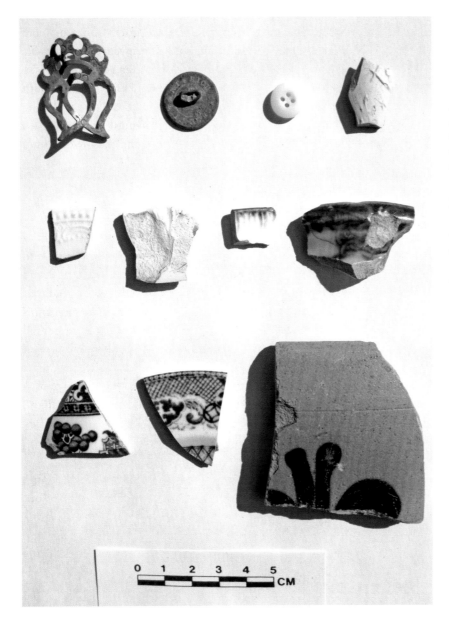

Figure 4.8
Archaeologists surface collecting at the Eagles Nest Site, an 1840s Cayuga village, found many different trade goods, including a silver Luckenbooth brooch (top left), buttons made of brass and glass (top centre), and a piece of the bowl of an imported ball clay pipe (top right) and ceramics. The ceramics in this image range from fine china-like blue transfer ware (bottom left and middle) to heavier hand-painted crockery (bottom right).
(Courtesy of Gary Warrick.)

might have a covered porch, a fireplace with a brick hearth and stone chimney, a root cellar for storing provisions, sleeping benches, and windows with glass panes.

Like their Algonquian neighbours, Six Nations did a lot of hunting and fishing; 90 percent of the food bones at the cabins are of wild game and fish. They also raised livestock such as pigs, cows, and chickens for food. Maize fields cleared on the opposite bank of the river from the cabin provided additional food. Six Nations traded furs and wild game to settlers in exchange for general store goods like china dishes and cloth and also received goods as gifts from the British government. Archaeologists routinely find these trade items in and around the cabins, including silver jewellery and glass beads, gunflints, gun parts, lead balls, iron knives, thimbles and scissors, and buttons (figure 4.8). Coins with holes punched in them were probably used as earrings, pendants, or clothing decoration.

Overall, the archaeology of Aboriginal Ontario in historic times describes a life of continuity with the pre-European past in terms of location of settlement, house layout, contribution of hunting and fishing to the diet, farming practices, and relationship to the land. By 1850, Aboriginal peoples of southern Ontario were concentrated on small parcels of land reserved for their exclusive use and their vast former hunting, trapping, fishing, and farm fields became part of the Ontario landscape seen today.

5

A World Apart? Ontario's Canadian Shield

Scott Hamilton

For most Ontarians, the north is an afterthought – a vast and empty wilderness of lakes, muskeg, and forest, populated only by moose and mosquitoes. It is not popularly thought to be a place to live or even, beyond a camping weekend or a fishing trip, to visit. In fact, many Ontarians use "north" as a kind of shorthand for isolated and remote country.

As with all stereotypes, this image is part fact and part imagination. The north is indeed vast, making up most of Ontario's landmass. The region is dominated by the boreal forest that lies over the Canadian Shield, an arc of some of the oldest rock on Earth that extends across much of northern Canada. Even farther north, the terrain shifts to the boggy muskeg of the Hudson Bay Lowlands and, along the coast, a narrow strip of tundra. The rugged land makes travel difficult. The "near north," or the southern part of the Canadian Shield (figure 5.1), consists of scattered multi-ethnic communities connected by a sparse network of all-weather roads and railways. "Far northern" Ontario, sometimes called the "forgotten north," is located beyond the all-weather road system. Its predominately Cree and Ojibwa population live in widely scattered villages, accessed mostly by air or over short-lived winter roads.

The north may be remote and rugged, but that is a far cry from empty. Aboriginal people know that the north has been a beloved home for millennia, from the end of the last ice age through treaty signings in the mid-nineteenth and early twentieth centuries and up to the present day. Archaeologists, working with First Nations, are documenting the complex, longstanding relationship between the people and the land.

As we piece together a more complete picture of northern Ontario's ancient past, we are beginning to recognize the shared trends that united the north and the south. As in more southerly latitudes, Paleoindian peoples moved into newly available land after the retreat of the glaciers. Along the edge of the Canadian Shield, land became

Modern Life in the North Scott Hamilton

After the mid 1800s, Ontario's southern Canadian Shield rapidly changed as the railroad and Great Lakes steamboats encouraged non-Aboriginal settlement. This increasingly marginalized Aboriginal people within the "near north," contributing to treaty signings intended to protect harvest rights and to secure reserves, annuities, and other modest benefits. Today, most First Nations reserves in Ontario's "near north" are small enclaves surrounded by a non-Aboriginal majority engaged in the industrial natural resource economy. Elements of traditional life persist, but under considerable acculturative and regulatory pressure.

In far northern Ontario the situation is different, with First Nations residents forming the vast majority and remaining (until recently) comparatively autonomous. Early twentieth-century life in the far north revolved around summer residence in widely scattered hamlets and winter dispersal to trapline camps. People harvested most of their food locally, earning cash from fur trapping and commercial fishing. After the Second World War, provincial and federal authorities encouraged people to move permanently to villages with services like nursing stations, day schools, trade stores, and air transport. As individual families moved to one or another centralized community, extended families became dispersed and summer hamlets were abandoned. People continued to use distant traplines, replacing dog sleds with snow machines, but climbing fuel costs and plummeting fur prices have made them less frequently harvested. Nonetheless, community members retain resource harvest rights and historic family roots over large territories.

The extent of these territories is not always fully recognized, due in part to the effects of a 1947 provincial trapline registry requiring that trappers purchase licenses for exclusive harvest rights to specific territories. These traplines are now often treated as forming part of the "traditional territory" of the First Nation to which the licensee is a member. However, other people in the same extended family (with inherited interests in the same land) might be members of other First Nations. While shared territorial interests might be informally recognized between related First Nations, outsiders might incorrectly assume that the trapline registry uniformly serves to identify the exclusive territorial interests of each First Nation.

Over the past thirty years northern First Nations communities have grown rapidly, forcing greater reliance on nonlocal food and fuel, and other imported supplies, and straining already limited housing and infrastructure capacity. Increasingly fewer young people regularly engage in harvesting

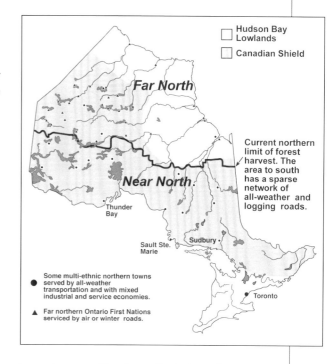

Hudson Bay Lowlands

Canadian Shield

Far North

Current northern limit of forest harvest. The area to south has a sparse network of all-weather and logging roads.

Near North

Thunder Bay

Sault Ste. Marie

Sudbury

Toronto

● Some multi-ethnic northern towns served by all-weather transportation and with mixed industrial and service economies.

▲ Far northern Ontario First Nations serviced by air or winter roads.

beyond seasonal hunts, particularly as they are assimilated into mainstream North American culture. For many communities, retaining and strengthening intergenerational economic and spiritual connections with the land are viewed as essential for cultural survival. Cultural heritage documentation and education, including archaeology, are often seen as an important part of that process.

available about 9,500 years ago; farther north in the Hudson Bay Lowlands, persistent ice and flooding may have prevented people from settling until 6,000 or 7,000 years ago. From the time of the earliest human presence in the north through to recent periods, artifacts found in the northlands show signs of influence from traditions better known in the more temperate south, like the Plano, Archaic, and Woodland. At the same time, northern hunter-gatherers apparently did not take part in many of the trends typical of the south, like increased population, heavy reliance on farming, relatively settled villages, and more complex social and political organization.

Life in the north underwent rapid change in the late 1500s and 1600s, when First Nations began to trade furs with Europeans. Some of Ontario's oldest European colonial settlements are found in the north, including coastal Hudson's Bay Company depots and inland French trading posts. Through Middlemen and other power brokers, new technology and economic pursuits spread throughout the interior long before Europeans ventured there (Ray 1974), and, in general, northern Ontario's resident population retained relative political and social autonomy. By the mid-1800s, though, a growing flood of Euro-Canadians encroached upon the more accessible southern parts of the Canadian Shield, drawn by natural resource abundance. As mining and lumber camps, railroad towns, farming hamlets, and commercial centres sprang up along the new transcontinental railroad, Aboriginal people came under increased pressure to negotiate treaties. Many of the people in northern Ontario today descend from the signatories of five different treaties signed between 1850 and 1929 (figure 5.2). These treaties, and their evolving legal meaning, profoundly affect contemporary northern life – including the practice of archaeology.

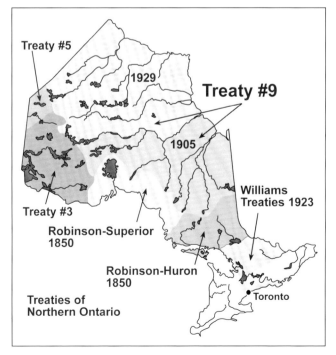

Figure 5.1 *Opposite*
Ontario's "near north" and "far north" differ in topography, environment – and degree of isolation. (Map by Scott Hamilton.)

Figure 5.2
Treaties signed between 1850 and the 1920s have had a profound effect on life in the north and on the practice of archaeology in the region. (Map by Scott Hamilton.)

Working in the North

Fieldwork in the Boreal Forest is challenging. The combination of rugged topography, wetlands, and dense forest cover make access difficult and expensive, requiring boats or aircraft and complicated logistics. Field seasons are short, shaped by weather and by the logistics of moving food, fuel, and people to remote areas. Northern field archaeologists need to master a wide range of bush skills that are seldom part of urban experience and academic training. In effect, northern archaeologists need an extended "apprenticeship" period to ensure that they are able to work safely and efficiently.

The difficult logistics and the vast area of northern Ontario have together resulted in a virtual void of cultural heritage information in many parts of the north. Our understanding of the region's past is relatively immature, and in some places we have only limited knowledge of even the basic physical geography – the topography, sediments, hydrology, ecology, and geomorphology that affect our research. As a result, most archaeological research in the north focuses on reconnaissance, trying to locate sites and collect basic information about them.

Survey methods in the north tend to be expedient, relying on the archaeologist's judgment and examining areas that provide a glimpse of what is underground – cutbanks, eroded beaches, game trails, the roots of toppled trees, animal burrows, and surfaces exposed by recent forest fires. The only other alternative involves laboriously excavated shovel test pits to search for what lies buried underground.

The challenges of locating sites are compounded by environmental conditions. The acidic soils of the north consume most organic materials and permafrost can prevent excavation even in mid-summer. Sediments accumulate very slowly and are chronically disturbed, mixed by the roots of falling trees, distorted by permafrost, and churned by cycles of freezing and thawing (Hamilton 2000; Reid 1988b). As a result, most Boreal Forest sites are sparse, with poor organic preservation and few (or none!) of the stratigraphic layers that archaeologists rely on to tease out the sequence of events over time. Short-term camps might be represented by limited and rather ephemeral artifact scatters. More heavily used locations, like prime spots along shorelines, usually yield more artifacts. Even then, the thin soils and many disturbances mean that archaeologists are often left puzzling out overlapping deposits of mixed debris. Imagine trying to make sense of dozens or even hundreds of different camp events spanning several millennia – all mixed together in pockets of soil just ten or fifteen centimetres deep.

The challenges of working in the north have prompted serious debates about how best to discover, test, and interpret these archaeological sites. If we want to find sparse and localized artifact scatters, how many test pits should we dig, and how big should each pit be? If we assume that most habitation sites were located near water, do we focus upon modern shorelines that might be only a few thousand years old? Maybe we should also search the abandoned shores of post-glacial lakes and streams where older sites might be expected. But do we know where those ancient shorelines are located? Are they accessible, or is it inefficient – or just plain impossible – to try to survey them? These and many other unresolved questions confound Boreal Forest archaeologists as they consider a region larger than most European countries.

Adding to the challenge, relatively few archaeologists work in this vast region. Archaeologists with academic appointments seldom work in the north, in part because of the difficulties associated with winning academic grants to fund the most basic work in presently unexplored regions. Consequently, few undergraduate and graduate students get formal training and "bush time" in Boreal Forest archaeology. Most northern Ontario archaeological fieldwork is conducted as CHM, undertaken as part of environmental impact assessment of some natural resource harvest or infrastructure development projects (see Ferris, introduction). Only a few professional consulting archaeologists are resident in northern Ontario. Few large archaeological consulting firms maintain a direct presence in the region, generally "parachuting in" to conduct projects when they win contracts. Although these large companies do significantly improve research capacity, such contracts can be problematic when archaeologists without local northern experience or established relationships with local First Nations undertake investigations that are more complex (and costly) than they first imagined. As in other parts of Ontario, most of the information from CHM work languishes in obscure publications or unpublished reports, with minimal contribution to the updating of the archaeological synthesis (Reid 1988a).

The relative lack of publication on northern archaeology means that, to a certain extent, knowledge of northern culture history has lagged behind that of other areas. In fact, entire generations of archaeologists have been trained with the stereotype of the north as remote wilderness. Pioneering researchers James V. Wright (1981) and K.C.A. Dawson (1983) saw the vast Canadian Shield as a uniform landscape that dominated the lives of past peoples. For Wright in particular, the landscape was a useful metaphor for the apparent uniformity of human adaptation and culture history across enormous areas and over thousands of years. The result? Three decades of northern research has been dominated by the image of timeless hunter-gatherers engaged in an unrelenting search for food in a harsh and demanding wilderness (see also Holly Jr 2002). In one widely used textbook, for example, archaeologist Brian Fagan (2005, 401–2) described northern people as "profoundly conservative" and living in "almost complete isolation from the more temperate world to the south." This was, Fagan continued, due to "[t]he sheer vastness and isolation of their harsh, forested wilderness [that] shut off most possibilities of cultural transmission from more sophisticated societies to the south." (Although Fagan was writing about a specific time period, the Shield Archaic, he clearly implied that that there was little or no change in economy, land use, and social organization from thousands of years ago through to the historic period.)

These ideas dominated my perspective in the early 1980s, when I began fieldwork in northwestern Ontario. Over time, my original image changed as I learned more about the dynamic relationships of people and environment in the Boreal Forest (Winterhalder 1983a and b) and read through the rich anthropological record of Subarctic ways of life (e.g., Feit 1973 and 1986; Helm 1981; Rogers 1969 and 1988; Rogers and Smith 1994b; Tanner 1979).

Most importantly, I learned from Cree and Ojibwa knowledge holders, gaining a growing appreciation of the complexity, dynamism, and surprises yet to be discovered in this huge and underexplored region. With time, the scope and frequency of archaeological investigation in northern Ontario is improving, in large measure because of regulatory changes in the environmental impact assessment process. Demands by First Nations also play a major role, as they insist that cultural heritage issues be more comprehensively addressed (see Nahrgang, chapter 15).

Ways of Understanding Life on the Canadian Shield

Anthropologists working in the north tend to think of traditional life in the region as fundamentally shaped by ecology. Bruce Winterhalder (1983b), for example, pictured hunting, gathering, and foraging in the Boreal Forest as a balancing act between groups of people and seasonally available resources. Winterhalder recognized that the Boreal Forest is an environment with patchy habitat, meaning that different resources become available (and sometimes abundant) in different places during specific seasons. Spring- and autumn-spawning fish, for example, provide a major reliable food supply, blueberries ripen in recently burned forest clearings in mid-summer, and migratory waterfowl also provide brief seasonal bounty. The key problem for foragers, Winterhalder proposed, is predicting when and where these resources will be available, then making sure that a suitable group of people is in the right place at the right time for the harvest.

Models of foraging suggest that bands gather together in places and times of food plenty (usually the warm season) in order to collect food, hold feasts, seek marriage partners, trade goods, build alliances, and share information. Such gatherings help otherwise scattered bands define and maintain a larger network of kin, neighbours, and associates. With the passing of seasonal plenty, and as winter approaches, individual family groups once again disperse widely in search of more diffuse and less predictable food prey. Winterhalder's ecological model demonstrates how a seasonally mobile lifestyle, coupled with a deep understanding of plant and animal communities and habitats, make it possible to sustain a foraging lifestyle in a sometimes difficult environment.

Ethnographic studies show that wide-ranging mobility is an essential part of making a living by foraging in the north. People travelled by canoe to optimal harvest places, using water routes to avoid difficult terrain, dense forest, and muskegs. In the cold season, people foraged more broadly for dispersed and unpredictable resources. Fortunately, winter weather offered more transportation options, with snowshoes and dogsleds (and now snowmobiles) enabling rapid movement across frozen wetlands as well as dry ground.

Regardless of season, successful foraging requires expert decision-making based upon a detailed understanding of the landscape, its travel routes, and its resource potential. Individuals must manage a complex mental inventory, predict seasonal resource productivity, and monitor environmental recovery from fire, wind damage, and previous foraging. Foragers draw on technical, physical, and intellectual abilities, coupled with supernatural assistance, to move freely and make a living within a familiar landscape.

Social bonds and cultural values are also critical to northern life. In cultures that rely on hunting, gathering, and foraged foods, the family is the basic social and economic unit, including parents, their adult children and spouses, and their grandchildren. At the same time, membership in forager groups tends to be fluid, varying from year to year. Reciprocity and hospitality are core cultural values, ensuring mutual support when illness, injury, and other misfortunes strike. Far from being isolated or insular, Subarctic peoples have traditionally moved widely and were connected through social networks between hunting groups, ensuring the spread of ideas, information, and technology. Such lifestyles are a matter of living memory with many contemporary elders, but dramatic change has occurred since the 1950s (see sidebar 5.1). Many people live relatively settled lives in First Nations communities, with shorter-term trips to harvest resources from extensive hinterlands.

Despite the changes of modern life, individual families retain an intimate understanding of the homelands used by their grandparents. Their foraging territories are familiar places, bisected with travel routes and dotted with named places. In recent years, researchers have begun to recognize the importance of this Aboriginal relationship with the land, drawing on the concept of a "cultural landscape" imbued with the spiritual interconnectedness of people, the land, and other-than-human beings with whom they share it (see Oberholtzer, chapter 11). Far from being the trackless, harsh, and austere wilderness of Euro-Canadian imagination, the north is a familiar and much-loved homeland where Aboriginal people have lived, sustainably harvested the land, raised their families, and buried their dead for at least 300 generations.

Paleoindian

Northern Ontario human history began shortly after the late Pleistocene glaciers had melted enough to support life along the ice front (see Stewart, chapter 1). In southern Ontario, this began as early as 13,000 years ago (see Ellis, chapter 2), but occupation of the Canadian Shield and Hudson Bay Lowlands was delayed by persistent ice and then by the time required for plants to establish themselves on the newly exposed land (figure 5.3). Vegetation typical of the tundra-taiga pioneered the newly ice-free land, likely attracting grazing animals northward as more southerly lands became forested.

Archaeologists assume that early human populations migrated northward in pursuit of favoured prey, though only a single study has tried to test this idea. Researchers Margaret Newman and Patrick Julig (1989) examined blood residues on thirty-six Paleoindian stone tools from the Cummins Site, near Thunder Bay. They tested the residues for specific antigens, which differ depending on the animal that was the source of the blood. A quarter of the tools showed blood residues, with antigens deriving from four different families of animals. Some of the blood was from the presumably desirable large game, including bovids (such as bison or musk ox) and cervids, which include deer, caribou, moose, and wapiti (elk). Other samples showed traces of rodents (like porcupine, muskrat, and beaver) and of humans. Although these results remain controversial, they are a good reminder that, even if Paleoindians sought large game, they surely ate smaller animals as well.

The best-known Paleoindian sites in northern Ontario are located on the ancient beaches of former glacial lakes, now overlooking both Lakes Superior and Huron, near bedrock exposures that were used for toolmaking (Julig 1994 and 2002). In the Thunder Bay area, it seems that Paleoindians strongly preferred silica-rich stone deriving from the Gunflint Formation, returning over the centuries to the now-abandoned shores of Glacial Lake Minong, located far inland from the current Lake Superior (see figure 5.3). Water-worn flakes from the Cummins Site suggest that the now-stranded beaches were still lakefront property when Paleoindians lived there (Fox 1980). Archaeologists have dated cremated human remains from the Cummins site to around 9,500 years ago (Julig et al. 1990). The density of artifacts found at the Cummins Site suggests that Paleoindians returned to this single location numerous times. Workshop sites in the area also yield more recent Shield Archaic tools (Hinshelwood 2004), suggesting that people continued to use some of the same locations long after the decline of Glacial Lake Minong.

Paleoindians probably lived in shoreline sites like Cummins during the warm season, taking advantage of the lake's resources and the opportunity to collect stone for tools. Other probable Paleoindian sites are found in former sheltered coves, on knolls within former wetlands of ancient river deltas, along inland river terraces and floodplains, on escarpment edges that provided good views over the surrounding land, and on well-drained knolls in the interior uplands (Hamilton 1996).

Archaeologists have called these early northern sites the Lakehead Complex (Fox 1980) or the Interlakes Composite (Ross 1997), names chosen to reflect the importance of former lakeshore locations and to link sites yielding similar artifacts found throughout the peninsula between Glacial Lakes Agassiz and Minong (see figure 5.3). These sites are recognized in part by diagnostic tools, including a variety of unfluted lanceolate (lance-shaped) projectile points (figure 5.4). These points seem to have

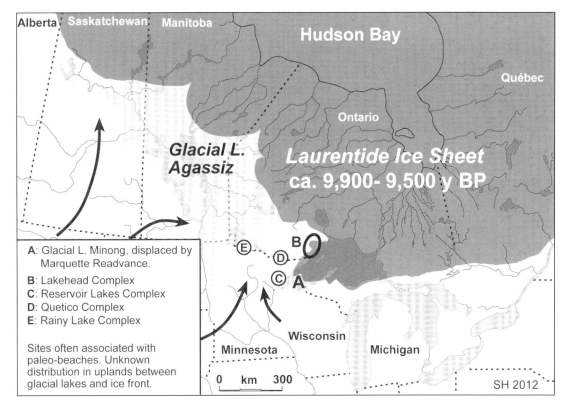

Figure 5.3

Ten thousand years ago, much of northern Ontario was still covered by the Laurentide ice sheet and, along with much of Manitoba, with Glacial Lake Agassiz. (Map by Scott Hamilton.)

considerable stylistic diversity, though they are so few in number that it is difficult to identify meaningful patterns in their form. In general, the artifacts fit well within the Plano Tradition (Ross 1997), a late Paleoindian tradition that was widespread across much of western North America.

Information about such ancient northern sites is unfortunately rare, with few solid dates, poor organic preservation, and minimal archaeological exploration. New CHM research by Western Heritage at the Mackenzie Site (near Thunder Bay) is yielding an uncommonly large tool assemblage. Archaeologists hope that these tools, paired with new geophysical and absolute dating methods, may help clarify some of the unknowns.

The Shield Archaic

As the glaciers melted and retreated northeastward, people expanded rapidly into the emerging landscape of the newly exposed Canadian Shield (figure 5.5). The evidence for these Shield Archaic peoples' move north within Ontario is sparse but growing. For example, Mike McLeod (McLeod 2004) recovered a projectile point from Rowdy Lake, north of Kenora. The tool is undated, but it appears to be related to the late Paleoindian Plano tradition, suggesting that people moved north earlier than archaeologists thought.

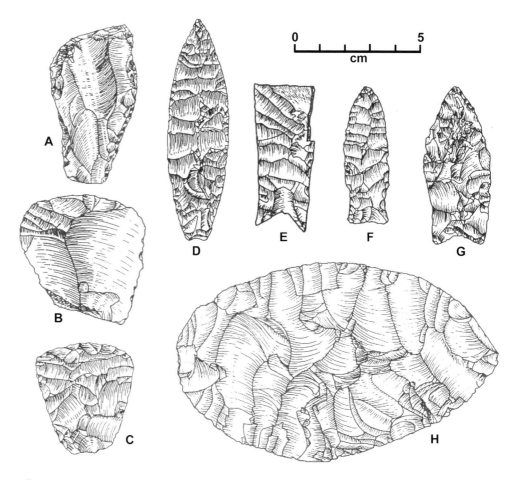

Figure 5.4
Paleoindian tools from the Cummins Site, near Thunder Bay. A–C are scrapers worked on just a single face; D–G are lance-shaped projectile points; and H is a large biface. (Courtesy Scott Hamilton, based on Julig 1994, 140, 141, 176, 177, 179.)

Human remains found near Big Trout Lake in Ontario's far north provide more evidence of unexpectedly early northward expansion. The remains, recovered at the Wapekeka First Nation airstrip, are radiocarbon-dated to about 7,600 years ago (Hamilton 2004, 355).

A collaborative project with Kitchenuhmaykoosib Inninuwug First Nation recovered two separate human burials near Big Trout Lake, dating to about 5,300 years ago (Hamilton et al. 2011 and 2006). The Allen site, near Lac Seul, appears to be even older; archaeologists found debris from flaking stone tools within buried soils that date to around 9,200 years ago (Pilon and Dalla Bona 2004, 331).

The relatively early dates at the Allen and Wapekeka sites may challenge long-held ideas about the origins of the Shield Archaic culture. James V. Wright (1972b), a pioneering Ontario archaeologist, defined the Shield Archaic culture in the early 1970s

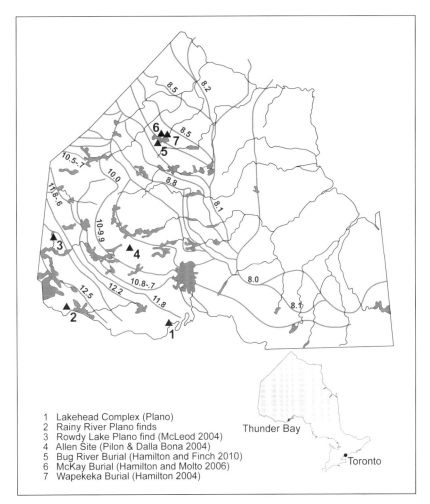

Figure 5.5
The retreating ice exposed new
land, rapidly occupied by Archaic
peoples moving to the northeast.
(Map by Scott Hamilton.)

1 Lakehead Complex (Plano)
2 Rainy River Plano finds
3 Rowdy Lake Plano find (McLeod 2004)
4 Allen Site (Pilon & Dalla Bona 2004)
5 Bug River Burial (Hamilton and Finch 2010)
6 McKay Burial (Hamilton and Molto 2006)
7 Wapekeka Burial (Hamilton 2004)

Thunder Bay

Toronto

based upon lance-shaped projectile points with side-notches for hafting, along with a range of other chipped- and some ground-stone tools (figure 5.6). Wright proposed that the Shield Archaic arose from Northern Plano origins in southwestern Nunavut, gradually expanding southeast around Hudson and James Bays to colonize the developing Boreal Forest of the Canadian Shield (Wright 1972a and 1995a). The Allen and Wapekeka dates suggest that the earliest pioneers of Ontario's Canadian Shield may actually have originated in the south. In fact, this scenario seems more plausible, given that the glacial ice melted earlier in the south than the north and that the shifting boundaries of Glacial Lake Agassiz would have affected peoples' movement. In either case, it is clear that the Shield Archaic culture was profoundly influenced by the environmental transformation that took place in the wake of the melting glaciers. Vegetation shifted with changing climate, entire lakes of meltwater were created and then drained, and the Tyrell Sea formed over an area that extended beyond present Hudson and James Bays. The land, freed from the great weight of the ice, began to rebound in a process known as isostatic uplift, causing widespread transformation of the entire hydrologic system.

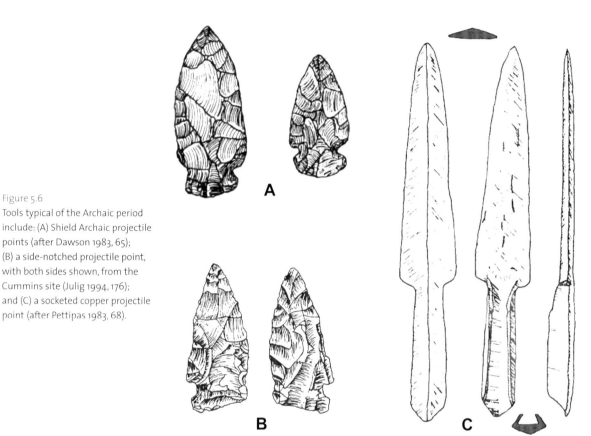

Figure 5.6
Tools typical of the Archaic period include: (A) Shield Archaic projectile points (after Dawson 1983, 65); (B) a side-notched projectile point, with both sides shown, from the Cummins site (Julig 1994, 176); and (C) a socketed copper projectile point (after Pettipas 1983, 68).

The western Lake Superior basin was also home to the Archaic-age "Old Copper Culture," or Complex, known for quarrying native copper from bedrock and glacial deposits (figure 5.7). They demonstrated an astonishing metal-working ability (see Wright 1972a) by heating, hammering, annealing, and grinding copper to produce a variety of projectile points, cutting tools, gaffs, chisels, and other objects (see figure 5.6C). These copper items are widely distributed throughout the upper Midwest of the United States and across the Canadian Shield of Ontario and Manitoba, with some items found beyond this range. Unfortunately, few such tools have been found with good stratigraphic context or associated with datable organic materials, due to the generally acidic soil in the region. Archaeologists assumed that the copper tools dated relatively late in the Archaic Period. In rare cases, copper salts helped to preserve wood, charcoal, or other organic materials, thereby enabling a precise kind of radiocarbon dating called accelerator mass spectometry, or AMS. AMS dates suggest that copper technology dates at least as early as 5,760 to 6,120 years ago (Buekens et al. 1992), making the Old Copper people among the world's first metal workers (see Fox, chapter 9).

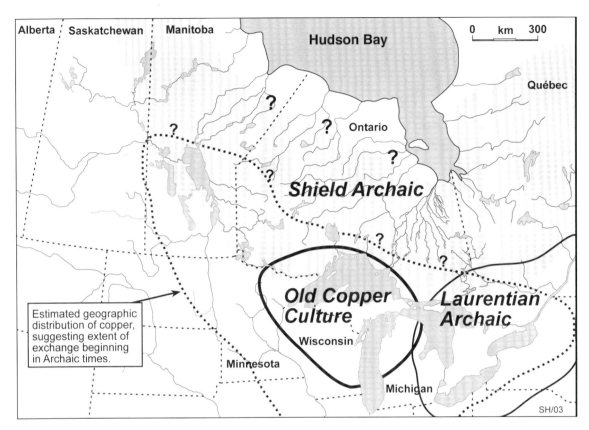

Figure 5.7
Archaeological cultures of the Archaic period in northern Ontario, about 8,000 to 2,000 years ago.
These cultures were quite long-lived, with wide geographic distribution. They are also weakly documented,
with poor dating and little organic preservation. (Map by Scott Hamilton.)

The Woodland in the North

The Woodland tradition was the next great social and technological trend to affect eastern North America, beginning as early as 3,500 years ago in the southeastern United States. As Williamson describes in chapter 3, archaeologists define the Woodland tradition in large part by the introduction of pottery, along with intensification of earlier Archaic themes: population growth, intensive foraging paired with farming of domesticated crops, construction of earthworks, burial mound ceremonialism, and broad trade networks for raw materials and finished goods that were often used as burial offerings. Some of these trends also occurred in parts of northern Ontario.

In the Boreal Forest, for example, people began using a style of pottery known as Laurel (figure 5.8) about 2,200 years ago, during the Middle Woodland period. Laurel pottery is typically cone-shaped, with plain body surfaces and complex stamp impressions upon the upper shoulder and rim. This style probably first appeared in

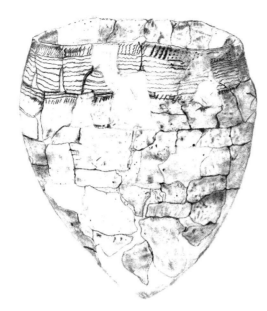

Figure 5.8
Artist's sketch of a reconstructed Laurel pot, recovered from the McGillivray site, Whitefish Lake. (Courtesy Department of Anthropology, Lakehead University.)

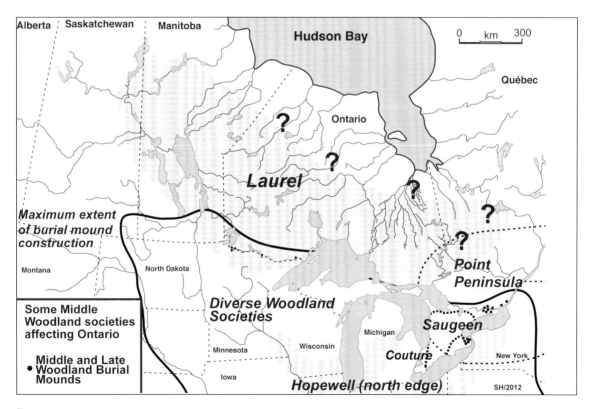

Figure 5.9
Archaeological cultures related to the Middle Woodland period in Ontario. The northern and eastern extent of Laurel pottery is not well known. (Map by Scott Hamilton.)

northern Minnesota, then spread widely across the Canadian Shield from east-central Saskatchewan to western Quebec. Unfortunately, the limited research in northern Ontario means that archaeologists are still uncertain about the northern extent of Laurel pottery (figure 5.9) (Dawson 1983; Meyer and Hamilton 1994). Few Laurel sites have been securely dated, but archaeologists believe that the style persisted until about 1,000 years ago.

SIDEBAR 5.2

Technology at Killarney Bay Susan M. Jamieson

Archaeologists' understanding of the past changes continually with new information and improved methods. A case in point is the Killarney Bay 1 Site, located on the northeast shore of Georgian Bay. The site includes a number of Middle Woodland burials, initially investigated by archaeologists in the late nineteenth century and again in the 1930s and 1940s. The site contained a variety of lithic, copper, organic, and shell artifacts, some from distant locales (Buchanan 1992; Fox 2010; Greenman 1966; Julig et al. 2008).

The artifact assemblage is similar to those found in burial mounds – but were there mounds at the Killarney Bay 1 Site? An archaeologist and a geologist who collaborated on an early study of the site (Greenman and Stanley 1941) believed that it included mounds deliberately built by Middle Woodland people. Decades later, the eminent Canadian archaeologist James Wright visited the site and declared that the mounds – by then excavated and largely destroyed – were natural features in which people had been buried (Wright 1967, 110).

Recent investigations may have solved the puzzle. Archaeologist Patrick Julig and a team of researchers from Laurentian University in Sudbury revisited the Killarney Bay 1 site, using methods drawn from geology to try to determine if sediments accumulated naturally over time or were built up by people. Based on a combination of coring and grain size analysis, they believe that the site was in fact created by deliberate human activity – in short, mound-building (Julig and Brose 2008).

If these researchers are correct, their results will require archaeologists to reconsider what we know about the past. The presence of mounds at the Killarney Bay 1 Site would mean that Middle Woodland burial mound ceremonialism occurs farther northeast than previously believed. This would reinforce previous interpretations that Laurel may have been part of the Hopewell Interaction Sphere, with ideas or influence spreading from south to north by water transportation routes. However, our understanding of the likely routes for water travel would probably need to include a Georgian Bay/Lake Huron route into the eastern part of northern Ontario. This expanded interpretation of interaction in the region is also supported another likely Middle Woodland mound burial, at Honey Harbour, on southeastern Georgian Bay (Fox 2010; Thor 2006).

The new information about these mound sites may encourage archaeologists to look for additional mounds. Given the logistical difficulties associated with doing archaeology in the north, it is possible that there may be other Middle Woodland mound sites yet to be discovered in this vast area.

Sites from the boundary waters between Minnesota and Ontario suggest that Laurel people may have been part of the Middle Woodland tradition of burial mound ceremonialism (Kenyon 1986). This ceremonial activity sometimes included burial offerings of nonlocal goods, suggesting that the Laurel traded for raw materials or finished items with people living to the south. In fact, the boundary waters may have been the northernmost extent of the Hopewell Interaction Sphere (Mason 1970 and 1981), a widespread exchange network centred in Ohio that encompassed many eastern North American societies at this time. It is easy to imagine that the biological productivity of the boundary waters was necessary to support the northern people who built burial mounds; it is curious, though, that equally rich boreal forest locations yield no evidence of these mounds. Perhaps the spread of Hopewell ideas or influence was more strongly linked to water transportation routes. After all, the headwaters of the Mississippi River fall only a short distance to the south of the Rainy River valley, an important east/west transportation corridor (Hamilton 1988). Groups that controlled the intersection of such important transportation routes may have been more frequently and profoundly influenced by cultural developments in the south.

Northern population levels seem to have increased during the Middle Woodland period, as archaeologists note an increase in the density and visibility of sites. Large sites with Laurel pottery are typically found along resource-rich lakes or at good fishing locations, indicating large seasonal gatherings and intensified harvesting of available foods. Archaeologists have conducted large-scale digs at several of these large Middle Woodland sites (Hamilton 1981; Reid and Rajnovich 1991), opening up contiguous excavation units that provide an unusually complete view of house structures and other features. Despite the usual constraints of poor organic preservation and shallow disturbed deposits, researchers were able to reconstruct pottery and to analyse the use of space within each site. The results suggest that the sites hosted the kind of large seasonal gatherings described in ethnographic studies of Subarctic peoples.

Both Buchner (1979) and Rajnovich (1980) have suggested that the large sites (and the implied larger populations) of the Laurel people were made possible by gathering wild rice to supplement more general hunting and gathering. In fact, charred food residues on Laurel pottery show that the people did, indeed, consume wild rice – but sometimes the same residues also show that Middle Woodland people ate domesticated plant foods, such as maize (Boyd et al. 2006; 2008; and 2010). This pattern of domestic plant consumption is even more obvious in the residue from Late Woodland pottery.

The source of the maize is not yet clear; northern people may have traded food with farmers living farther to the south, or perhaps they grew a few of their own plants in suitable northern micro-habitats. In any case, the presence of maize in the Boreal Forest reinforces the point that northerners were hardly isolated from the developments affecting temperate North America.

After about 1,200 years ago, new technological innovations appear in the northern Ontario archaeological record, indicating that Late Woodland cultural influences spread widely throughout the Boreal Forest and even beyond into the northeastern plains (Meyer and Hamilton 1994). Archaeologists define the Late Woodland period by the use of the bow and arrow and by a variety of new pottery wares that differ markedly from the earlier Laurel style.

The most archaeologically prominent of such pottery in northwestern Ontario includes Blackduck, Selkirk, and Sandy Lake wares, each with its distinct form and decoration (figure 5.10). These wares also differ slightly in timespans and overlap geographically (figure 5.11) (Meyer and Hamilton 1994; Pettipas 1983). Recent research in western Quebec indicates the eastern limit of Blackduck pottery (Coté and Inksetter 2001), but it looks as if pottery in general is less evident in northeastern Ontario. Although the picture is far from clear, the current evidence suggests considerable overlap and cultural interchange between diverse Boreal Forest populations, each presumably making different styles of pottery.

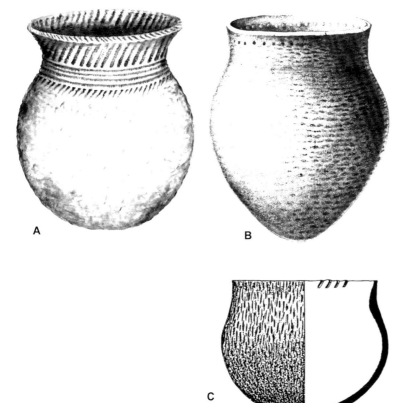

A

B

C

Figure 5.10
Late Woodland pottery from northwestern Ontario includes: (A) Blackduck (after Pettipas 1983, 129); (B) Selkirk or Clearwater Lake Punctate (after Pettipas 1983, 163); and (C) Sandy Lake Ware (after Taylor-Hollings 1999, 33). (Courtesy of Scott Hamilton.)

Archaeologists are often tempted to equate pots with specific ethnic groups or speakers of a common language (see sidebar 10.1), and researchers in the north are no exception. Archaeologist Kenneth Dawson (1983), for example, strongly asserted that Late Woodland peoples were Algonquian-speaking ancestors of the Aboriginal residents of northern Ontario who traded with French and English fur traders in the 1600s (see also Meyer and Hamilton 1994). However, the ethno-historic record and some archaeological data indicate a more complicated situation, with Sandy Lake Wares possibly reflecting the presence of Siouan speakers (Lake Superior Basin Workshop participants 1987; Taylor-Hollings 1999).

Archaeologists tie the end of the Late Woodland period to the time of Aboriginal contact with European fur traders, at some point in the late 1500s and early 1600s. The fur trade in northern Ontario began first with the French and, after 1670, also with the Hudson's Bay Company. While Aboriginal people continued to dominate northern Ontario, the fur trade introduced new technology and economic relationships into the forager lifestyle. Bartering surplus food and fur for European manufactured goods, Aboriginal people replaced some traditional technologies with imported European commodities. Although fur-trade era archaeological assemblages look quite different from those of earlier times, it seems likely that Aboriginal people simply incorporated the new tools into their traditional forager lifestyles.

Aboriginal people were central to fur-trade production and initially retained relative political and socioeconomic autonomy in these relationships. However, the fur trade introduced a new dynamic: increased resource harvest to supply an insatiable European demand for furs. By the 1760s, many Aboriginal groups began to be hard hit by the significant ecological damage associated with over-harvesting and also by the spread of European communicable diseases (see Helm 1981; Lytwyn 1986 and 2002; Rogers and Smith 1994a). Throughout much of the nineteenth and twentieth centuries there has been a steady erosion of economic and social autonomy as Aboriginal people became integrated into modern Canada. Archaeologists have not yet devoted much attention to post-contact Aboriginal sites to document the details of this transformation.

The Complexity of the North

The basic archaeological framework of Ontario's past is in place, but little of northern Ontario has been archaeologically explored to fill in the details. Current insight relies mostly on a limited number of archaeological surveys and test excavations, with even fewer projects being well published. For more than twenty-five years archaeologists have called for methods and theories better suited to the Subarctic (Reid 1988b), rather than adopting those deriving from eastern North America. Despite these efforts, we have made relatively little progress in overcoming the methodological and sampling problems that come with working on northern sites; at this point,

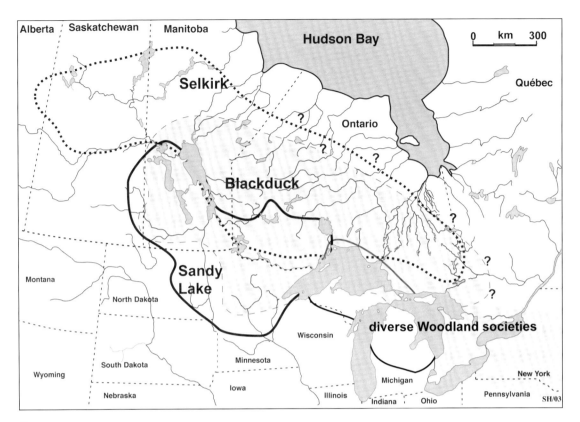

Figure 5.11
Distribution of major Late Woodland ceramic wares in northern Ontario. (Map by Scott Hamilton.)

we still remain focused on describing artifacts and documenting the basic sequence of events.

Despite the challenges of northern archaeology, one thing is abundantly clear: the Subarctic past is much more complex than we realized. Early Holocene human burials in the northern Canadian Shield show that the far north was occupied much earlier than previously thought (Hamilton 2004). Copper working in the Upper Great Lakes is an early and important innovation, contradicting the outdated notion that northern peoples were conservative. And the relatively rapid spread of pottery technology across vast expanses of the Canadian Shield defies the stereotype of remote and inhospitable landscape occupied by isolated people. Most surprisingly of all is the emerging evidence that Late Woodland people ate domesticated plants like maize much farther north than ever imagined. We have learned all of this from just a handful of boreal archaeologists and a limited number of projects. So much of the region's archaeology remains unexplored. With natural resource development poised to expand in Ontario's far north, new archaeological work will become more and more important to document, interpret, and conserve this largely untapped record. The challenge will be to ensure that this new information gets distributed beyond the conventional CHM reporting process so that new discoveries can become part of the bigger picture of archaeology in Ontario's north.

Part II
Telling Archaeological Stories

Marit K. Munson

Any archaeologist can tell a good tale – just ask about field accidents or near-misses, mosquitoes or poison ivy and get ready for an earful. Interpreting the past is also akin to creating a story, spinning out the long narrative of prehistory like that presented in part I of this book.

The difference between these kinds of stories, though, is that the field stories are told for entertainment and prone to exaggeration, while stories of the archaeological past are constructed through painstaking documentation, description, and analysis of material remains. Those remains – the evidence that archaeologists use – can range from a grain of pollen to a deer bone, a dark stain in the earth to a whole pot. But how do we move from stained earth to the layout of an entire palisaded village? How do we know what it might have been like to live in a smoky longhouse during a cold Ontario winter, to move through a landscape populated with human and other-than-human persons, or to celebrate the Feast of the Dead?

In part II of this book, the authors explain their archaeological specialties and describe how specific kinds of evidence create a more detailed story about the lives of Woodland peoples. In chapter 6, Neal Ferris describes the houses and other structures that make up villages, using information from excavations, historic records, and modern experiments to shed light on ancient architecture. Lithic analyst William Fox (chapter 9) and ceramic analyst Mima Kapches (chapter 10) turn their attention to the tools of stone, metal, and clay that were used for everything from daily activities to feasts and other special occasions. Evidence of hunting, cooking, and feasting also comes from the remains of plants and animals themselves. Paleobotanist Stephen Monckton and faunal analyst Suzanne Needs-Howarth discuss Aboriginal use of plants (chapter 8) and animals (chapter 7), including the changes that occurred when people in southern Ontario increasingly began to rely on domesticated plants, such as maize.

As anthropologists, archaeologists are also concerned with the less tangible aspects of peoples' lives, like beliefs and social organization. As Cath Oberholtzer and Susan Jamieson explain (chapters 11 and 12), we can understand, or at least consider, these themes by drawing on information from historic and current societies, locally and around the world. Oberholtzer describes what we know about Aboriginal relationships to the land and the beings that inhabit it, while Jamieson tackles the question of personal and political relationships based on reciprocity and obligation.

Finally, bioarchaeologists consider how all of these aspects of life in the past affected individuals directly, by studying human remains and burial practices. Anne Keenleyside (chapter 13) discusses what she and other bioarchaeologists have been able to learn about the diets and health of past peoples, while Michael Spence (chapter 14) describes how the living cared for and mourned their relatives in death.

Studying human remains is not without controversy. Archaeologists have, at times, treated remains without the respect due to every human being, and contemporary First Nations are quite rightly concerned the treatment of their ancestors' bodies (see Nahrgang, chapter 15). As Keenleyside and Spence address, however, archaeologists' attitudes have changed considerably in the last few decades; most bioarchaeologists now try to maintain good relationships with First Nations, hoping that they will be able to work together to tell the stories of individuals who are long gone but not forgotten.

6

Place, Space, and Dwelling in the Late Woodland

Neal Ferris

That the past is a foreign place becomes clear from the space and comforts of the twenty-first century, when we try to think beyond our own time to imagine ways of living in and through the ancient landscapes of southern Ontario. How do we understand lives lived in a world so different than the one we know, when notions of home, community, place, outside, inside, territory, and landscape had very different connotations?

Take a moment to notice your surroundings as you read this chapter. Perhaps you are in a chair inside your heated home during a cold winter's day, the sun shining through a window, warming your hands as you hold this book. Perhaps you need to caulk that window because it is letting in a draft – but meanwhile you know you can turn up the thermostat to warm yourself and your family.

Now imagine yourself on a similar sunny and cold day, inside a pole and bark-covered longhouse around 1500 CE (figure 6.1), part of a village whose descendants would come to be known as Iroquoian people, at a place that later was known as the Lawson Site, in London, Ontario, on the grounds of the Museum of Ontario Archaeology (Anderson 2009). As you stand in the longhouse, you feel the cold leaking in and around you every time someone enters or leaves the building, and you feel it rising up from the ground along the sides of the walls. The inside is a dim place, though there is a brief flash of blinding light some thirty metres down at the other end of the longhouse as someone moves the flap back to go through the other entrance. You see sunbeams shine in through vents in the rounded roof, slicing through the dried plants hanging in the rafters and outlining the bundled forms of the ancestors who lie wrapped and resting in the upper platforms of the long bunkbed-like benches that run down either side of the house. The sunbeams also highlight the smoke that hovers

Figure 6.1
This artist's reconstruction gives an idea of what Late Woodland long-houses may have looked like. The interior of the house was divided into separate compartments, each probably inhabited by a family on either side of the central hearth. The lower platforms along both sides served as beds, while the upper level provided convenient storage. Note the dried corn hanging from the rafters in the upper right and the large log bins (bottom left), also used for storing food. (Courtesy of Archaeological Services Inc.)

near the ceiling, rising from the glowing and flickering hearths spaced every few metres down the centre of the longhouse.

Members of your family squat or sit around the hearth in front of you, talking, cooking, or entertaining a child. You can smell food cooking, the earthiness of the soil floor, the mustiness of the plants hanging from the ceiling, and, always, the smell of wood smoke, tanned hides, and people living together in their home. Your ears are filled with the chatter of family and friends, the crackling of fires, and the wind howling outside. You feel the heat of the hearth on your face, the cold from the outside on the backs of your legs, the drip of water from snow melting on the roof falling on your head, and the slickness of the ground underfoot. This is the place where you sleep, eat, play, and share hopes and fears. You have lived in places like this all of your life, except in warmer weather when you sleep outside or in smaller huts at places away from here. You have known better and worse longhouses, and you like some features of this one and dislike others. It is the way things are ... or were then.

This picture is speculative, drawn from descriptions I have read of Europeans who visited and dwelled with the descendants of the Lawson Site and other Iroquoian speaking peoples a century later. It is also drawn from my experiences excavating and interpreting the floors of longhouses at Iroquoian villages like the one described, and from helping to build a longhouse, and even from sitting, eating, and listening to stories and songs inside a longhouse built in the present. More than any other thought that crosses my mind when I am in a longhouse, I often try to imagine living in that longhouse during a cold winter's day, similar to the many that I have experienced over the years also living in this same region of Ontario – but always inside a brick home with central heating.

Living Indoors

Understanding what life was like in the past requires a kind of time travel of the mind, which begins when archaeologists read the archaeological traces of the structures and living spaces left behind in the ground. In southern Ontario, these traces are usually just discolorations in the soil, visible after stripping away the top layers of dirt on an archaeological site. These discolorations or stains, which archaeologists often call cultural features, are all that remain of holes the site's inhabitants dug into the ground for any number of reasons. Over time, the holes filled in, intentionally or not, with soil, organic waste, artifacts, or other materials, so that the former holes end up holding a darker, richer soil than the surrounding light-coloured subsoil (figure 6.2).

When people built the wall of a house, for example, they dug holes to hold wooden poles, or pushed the pointed end of a post into the ground. If the post was pulled out later, wood and darker topsoil would have fallen into the hole. Or the pole might have been left where it stood, eventually rotting into a richer, darker soil. Either way, when an archaeologist, centuries later, shovels away the grass and topsoil over a site, those filled-in holes where poles stood appear as small, roughly circular stains – a

Figure 6.2
Kris Nahrgang excavates at the Bark Site, a village site west of Peterborough that dates to the mid-1400s. The dark circle next to his foot (under the pair of gloves) is the stain from a pit, which shows up clearly against the lighter dirt around it. Some stains are easier to see than others; the inset photo shows four post moulds, each marked with a straw stuck in the ground. (Courtesy of Susan Jamieson.)

feature archaeologists call post moulds. Rows of these post moulds outline house walls, a stockade or palisade surrounding a village, and other structures that ancient peoples used day-to-day.

The most common type of structure found by archaeologists working on sites from the Late Woodland period are longhouses (e.g., Dodd 1984; Kapches 1990 and 1994; Warrick 1996). Longhouses are typical of villages that archaeologists tend to assume are ancestral to Iroquoian-speakers, although other peoples used longhouses too. Most longhouses had an elliptical or cigar-shaped outline, with straight sides and rounded or slightly squared-off ends outlined by rows of posts (figure 6.3).

The space inside these walls is often distinct from space outside, due to visible concentrations of post moulds, features, and other soil discolorations that mark interior walls, support posts, hearth areas, and even buildup of waste and dirt. One or two lines of post moulds often run along either side of a central corridor through the middle of the house – probably bunk lines that supported benches or raised sleeping platforms. A number of hearths are usually visible along the central corridor, made up of reddish soil baked by wood fires maintained in those spots. House floors contain other features, too, such as holes or pits that were used to hold garbage or ash from hearths, or to cache food or supplies, or as burial places (see Spence, chapter 14). At either end of the house, where the straight side walls begin to taper, open spaces may have served as storage areas for food or firewood. Entrances usually appear as simple gaps in the row of wall posts, at one or both ends of the longhouse or slightly to one side. Occasionally, a house had an entranceway or tunnel sticking out from the entrance, probably serving as a windbreak or heat sink.

From a strictly archaeological perspective, we cannot tell exactly what a longhouse looked like above ground (Wright 1995b), as walls and roofs did not survive. Sometimes, the angle and direction of post moulds in the ground can hint at the orientation of poles to the structure's roof. In general, though, archaeologists turn to historic accounts written by Europeans in the 1600s and 1700s who visited or lived in longhouses and to oral histories and craft traditions in communities today. Experimenting with replicas of these buildings also provides some insights. Based on these sources, we think that longhouse walls were covered with bark or hide over wall poles that were bent over and tied off to create a closed, curved ceiling. Vents or flaps in the ceiling probably allowed smoke from hearths to escape and air to circulate. Depending on the season, entrances may have been covered with a hide flap or barrier.

From historic sources we know that it was common for two families to share each hearth found along the central corridor of the longhouse (see Warrick, chapter 4). These families would have lived on opposite sides of the fire with personal space around, under, and on the benches adjacent to the hearth. Historic descriptions and census records suggest that a longhouse could have been home to many families, with anywhere from a dozen to nearly one hundred people living in a single longhouse. The people in a single longhouse were likely all connected to each other by extended

Figure 6.3
Archaeologists map a longhouse from the Alexandra Site, a mid- to late-fourteenth-century village in Toronto. The straws marking the post moulds highlight the building's oval shape and its two remodelling episodes, visible in the three curving lines marking the end of the house. The first expansion added six metres to the longhouse; the second provided another four metres. (Courtesy of Archaeological Services Inc.)

family ties or lineage. And since we know that Iroquoian societies historically traced family connections through the mother's family, it was probably the women in the longhouse who shaped and defined who belonged in that particular house. So while a longhouse would have been a crowded, noisy, and lively place to reside, all that noise was the sound of a family living together.

Archaeologists know that longhouse shape and style – and probably function and the rules of residence – changed over time. At the beginning of the Late Woodland period, longhouses were relatively small in size – generally less than twenty metres long, and sometimes with only a single hearth. By about 800 years ago, longhouses usually shared a common shape and similar layout of interior space, even if individual longhouse length varied. This change happened at a time when community size and village populations grew. While some longhouses from this period were fairly small, many more range from twenty to fifty metres long. There are even examples of individual longhouses extending more than one hundred metres in length!

Archaeologists often point to more "complex" settlement patterns (which usually means bigger sites, more structures, evidence of rebuilding, and so on) that appeared during this time as evidence that the rules of household living and social relations evolved along with the places people lived in. This includes the appearance of distinctive features found in or connected to longhouses as evidence of new social practices adopted to address the stresses of living in bigger longhouses and larger communities (MacDonald and Williamson 2001). These features appear as large holes, two to three metres wide and a metre deep, dug either inside the longhouse or immediately next to it, but with the only entrance through the longhouse itself. The pits are encircled by their own row of post moulds, suggesting that they were enclosed. They often contain layers of ash and fired soil, along with artifacts like distinctive smoking pipes that may suggest ceremony or sacred importance (see Kapches, chapter 10). Archaeologists interpret these features as being semi-subterranean sweatlodges or saunas (figure 6.4). Longhouse inhabitants might have used ritual or healing sweats to address (or redress?) some of the social tensions that came from the reorganized social structure and rules of residence inside the longhouse.

Toward the end of the Late Woodland period, longhouses became even more standardized and on average somewhat shorter in length, perhaps reflecting more established social conventions around rules of residence and family or lineage membership.

Figure 6.4
This large Late Woodland longhouse includes an astonishing nine sweatlodges, shown in light grey on this map. Five of them were inside the walls of the house, while four (#12, 96, 98, and 147) had ramped entrances inside the house leading to exterior sweatlodges. This is the largest house at the Hubbert Site, a mid- to late-1400s village in Simcoe County. (Courtesy of Archaeological Services Inc.; modified from MacDonald and Williamson 2001, figure 5.)

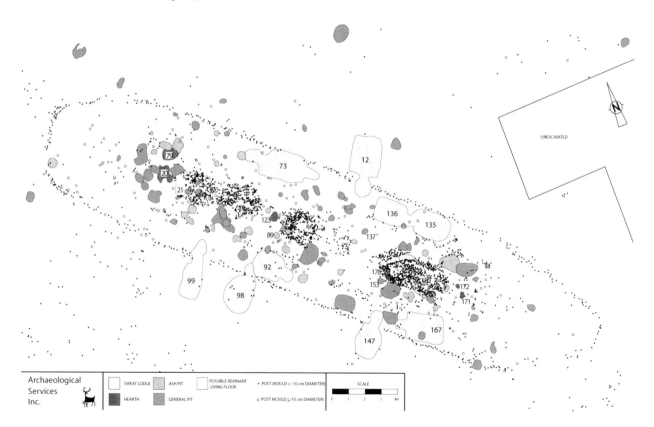

By the end of the 1500s, smaller longhouses of just one or two families were present in villages of otherwise larger longhouses, a pattern that increased and became more popular over the next 200 years (Jordan 2004).

By the 1800s, few longhouses were still in use as residential dwellings. Instead, many Iroquoian-speaking peoples lived in log cabins with earthen floors and a central hearth, reminiscent of the hearth and side bench spatial arrangement in longhouses (Ferris 2009). Longer longhouses remain important as communal buildings in the 1700s and 1800s, serving as community council houses. Into contemporary times, council longhouses took the form of elongated log cabins, with interior layouts in the style of traditional longhouses: rows of benches along either side of the house; council fires along the centre or end of the structure (facilitated by the use of cast iron stoves by the mid-1800s); traditional meals served by clan mothers; even places to host white dog ceremonies and communal burial locations when the longhouse was moved (Kenyon and Kenyon 1986).

Inside the Village

Of course, daily life in the Late Woodland was not restricted to the inside of dwellings alone. So we can now step out of the longhouse and into the space inside the village. If we return to the Lawson Site at the time of occupation we would see in front and around us many other longhouses with open areas in between and garbage dumps to one side. Encircling all this would have been a large palisade or wall of poles, made of larger poles either pressed tightly together or, more commonly, spaced a little ways apart with branches or bark interwoven between the poles. If it were warmer weather we would see many people around us, some talking or playing, others working or cooking at outdoor fires. We would also see wooden pole structures scattered around the village, holding stretched deer hides or drying meat or fish.

Even in cold weather, people would be moving about, perhaps coming back from a hunting trip, following paths in the snow leading from the main entrance in the palisade to longhouse entrances. Signs of cooking and other outside activity would be less, but we'd see smoke and steam rising from the roofs of longhouses, reflecting people working and living inside on a cold day.

Archaeologists define village limits by the concentration of settlement patterns and artifact debris in a fixed area, usually including several longhouses, sometimes surrounded by one or more rows of palisade (Warrick 2008). Palisades, though not used at every village, helped to define boundaries, marking the line between inside and outside, and helping to provide shelter from wind and wandering predators (Ramsden 1991). In the earlier Late Woodland, palisades were typically a single row of posts. By 800 to 500 years ago some village palisades become more elaborate, with multiple rows of wall and raised earthen embankments along the base. These earthworks, as they are referred to by archaeologists, remain long after a village is abandoned and, in locations where farming has not eradicated them, are visible as linear mounds by archaeologists who investigated the sites. Archaeologically earthworks are typically evident from linear, filled-in ditches visible in the settlement patterns for a site (Keron 2010; Lee 1958).

Some palisades, such as at the Lawson Site (Anderson 2009; Wintemberg 1939) even created mazelike paths to get into the village itself. These elaborate palisades suggest to archaeologists that villagers felt an increased need for defense, as do villages built on points of land surrounded by steep slopes.

From the early part of the Late Woodland, the space inside the palisade reflected the needs of the community. Some longhouses were carefully aligned, with open spaces between the buildings serving as outdoor work spaces or places for social activities. Communal garbage dumps or middens were set aside in one area of the village. Evidence of smaller structures, either smaller longhouses or rounded structures, may have been single family homes or visitor residences, storage spaces, or even areas for rituals or medicinal practices (Bursey 2006; Kapches 1984).

In the first half of the Late Woodland in particular there is plenty of evidence of reuse and remodelling of village space as villagers' needs changed, with plenty of signs of repairing, lengthening, or replacing houses – multiple lines of wall posts, extended longhouse ends, and overlapping structures (e.g., Williamson 1998). Some villages also show evidence of major rebuilding episodes, with older longhouses razed and entirely new longhouses built over the top, sometimes with entirely different orientations. Villagers might build additional longhouses to fill previously open space between houses or perhaps expand the palisade to increase interior village space. This speaks to the importance of the village location for the community, as well as to the continual revisions needed to accommodate the always-changing makeup of a community.

Even after a village was abandoned, people continued to use the location for more seasonal uses, such as hunting camps (Timmins 1997). Former village locations, cleared of trees and overgrown with grasses and weeds, remained visible on the landscape long after their inhabitants and their children had moved elsewhere, serving as memory markers on the landscape that speak to a community's sense of space, place, heritage, and belonging. Later on in the Late Woodland villages became bigger, and the space within the palisade was more formally laid out, with communal open spaces that might have served as central village plazas and with large communal middens in designated spaces both inside and outside the village proper. It even looks as if some groups of longhouses were clustered together and separated from others across the village (Birch 2010; Wright 1986). Archaeologists also see walls connecting individual houses in these clustered groups, which would have helped reinforce the distinct space around these longhouse groupings. Even the placement and orientation of longhouses within these clusters and relative to the village palisade helped to create more private spaces behind or between longhouses that were inaccessible to people except through those longhouses. The more exclusive spaces and even middens within villages speak to the logistics of managing the living space of one or two thousand individuals in one concentrated village. But they also reflect the result of several centuries of social change and experimentation through the Late Woodland, as these Neolithic-like village farmers worked out sophisticated and complex rules governing village and longhouse residence (Ferris 1999). Village architecture and settlement patterns hint at elaborate structures of marriage and family, as well as lineage, village, and nation membership. Individuals maintained reciprocal social obligations of debt and exchange. Archaeologists studying the settlement patterns and architecture found inside villages quickly learn just how nuanced and complex these societies were before, during and after the centuries and decades in which Europeans also came to reside in this part of the world.

Beyond the Palisade

If you were to walk around the outside of the palisade at the Lawson site at about 1500, you would have seen an open area, cleared of trees, and perhaps some scattered fields of maize or other plants. But you would also have noticed paths heading off in many directions – into the distant woods, through fields, and down to the creek valley. Some of the paths would lead to nearby places to get water, to gather plants, or perhaps to find clay for making pottery. Some might even lead to a place where the ancestors were buried or would be buried later. Still other paths would lead off to more distant locales. After all, people travelled widely in order to harvest or trade for cultivated crops, meat, fish, wild plants, and the raw materials needed to make things. The world beyond the palisade was connected to the world inside by radiating pathways that made distant spaces into familiar places.

Such domestic places included small sites of just one or two longhouses, which have been documented throughout the Late Woodland period. Such areas were probably used by members of one family/longhouse, spending part of a season at a location well-suited for hunting, fishing, tending to fields of maize, or similar purposes (Pearce 1996; Williamson 1983 and 1990). These smaller communities probably fended for themselves, creating surpluses to bring back to the larger village community. Even smaller camp sites, with roughly circular or oval huts, probably served as temporary houses for a single individual or a few people for a short time.

Later in the Late Woodland, some people began to live in hamlets – small communities consisting of a few longhouses, often without palisades. Most archaeologists assume that these were satellite settlements connected to a larger village community. Despite their small size, though, these sites may have trash middens and other substantial features, suggesting that people lived there on a relatively long term – either year-round or for a full season – or revisited them on a regular basis (Lennox 1984 and 1995).

Archaeologists also find the occasional single, isolated longhouse and midden, beyond the geographic limits of community territories (Lennox and Fitzgerald 1990). These may represent a segment of a village community moving beyond the territory and establishing new settlement areas, perhaps in response to increasing populations or the constraining rules and social stresses of life in the old village. This pattern is seen, for example, in southwestern Ontario at about 700–600 years ago, presaging the expansion of ancestral Iroquoian village settlements west into the region between western Lake Erie and southern Lake Huron that was previously either shared territory, or the land of peoples not connected to ancestral Iroquoian traditions.

Other Houses, Another Story

I want to make sure I am not leaving the impression that the settlement archaeology of southern Ontario is solely related to the ancestors of the Iroquoian peoples who Europeans encountered in the 1600s. While longhouses and palisaded villages are a significant part of southern Ontario's Late Woodland past, the record is more than just that and also reflects the material past of peoples who may have been the ancestors of the Algonquian-speaking Anishnabeg peoples who live in Ontario today.

In the region west and south of London, for example, archaeologists study a different Late Woodland tradition, referred to as the Western Basin. Western Basin archaeology suggests that people lived in seasonal settlements during the early part of the Late Woodland, moving frequently across their territories over the course of a year (Murphy and Ferris 1990). Many of the known archaeological sites consist of large clusters of deep storage pits (figure 6.5); we seldom are able to find dwellings, likely because people used temporary structures that were not substantial enough to leave clear post mould patterns that would survive over a century of modern farming activity. The large pits on these sites can be up to a metre wide and a metre deep, but seldom have much in the way of artifacts (although a few include the occasional complete pot or sealed waste deposits). These pits were probably used mostly as storage or cache pits – little cold cellars, in effect, to store surplus harvests from fishing, hunting, nut-harvesting, or farming maize. The group might leave the supplies after they moved on from the camp, to recover the stored goods when they next passed through the area, perhaps at a different time of year.

The most common house documented from the early part of the Late Woodland was probably similar to wigwam-like oval huts, with a single entrance and perhaps a single hearth (figure 6.6). These small buildings were probably home to one or two extended families. Elsewhere, some sites only appear to have a single walled row of posts, either partially or totally enclosing a living space (Ferris 1989). Archaeologists have found these enclosure walls on sites with extensive storage pits, as well as at locations that seem to be short-term harvest locales. In one instance, a large enclosure of about twenty-five metres in diameter was associated with a single-family burial pit.

These settlement patterns are quite distinct from the archaeological record documented to the east and reflect a different relationship of people to the landscape. In the west, people moved across the landscape over the course of a year, staying for a

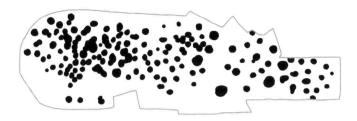

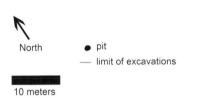

Figure 6.5
The Robson Road Site, in the Western Basin, consists of two clusters of hundreds of large pits, shown in black, but no buildings at all. (Drawing by Marit Munson, based on Murphy and Ferris 1990, figure 7.26.)

North

● pit
— limit of excavations

10 meters

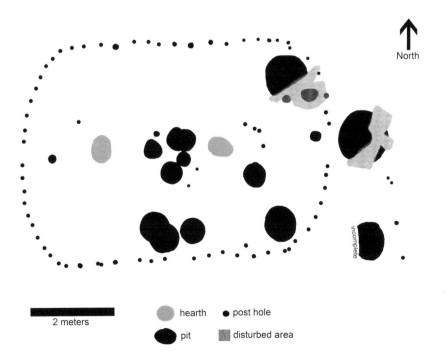

North

Figure 6.6
This small house from the Sherman Site is a good example of a winter cabin or wigwam from the Western Basin tradition. Features inside the house include two hearths (7 and 10) and several small pits. The doorway is at the east end. The Sherman Site, near Thamesville, dates to the Late Woodland period. (Drawing by Marit Munson, based on Murphy and Ferris 1990, figure 7.35.)

incomplete

2 meters

hearth   ● post hole

pit   disturbed area

Figura Site

· post mould
● pit or other feature
h hearth
b burial

5 meters

House 4

House 3

House2

House 1

midden

midden

Figure 6.7
Archaeological sites in the Western
Basin are quite different from those to
the east. The Figura Site, for example,
includes numerous storage pits (shown
in black) but only a few small oval
structures. (Drawing by Marit Munson,
based on map from Neal Ferris.)

season or for a shorter time at a locale; at the same time, they returned to use some
of these same locales over and over again, sometimes for centuries, especially at sites
used to harvest seasonally abundant foods. Yet despite the differences in their way of
life, recent scientific studies show that Western Basin people from this period ate as
much maize as peoples living to the east (Dewar et al. 2010).

As well, recent work in what is thought of as a borderland between this Western
Basin Tradition and the Ontario Iroquoian Tradition to the east revealed a diverse
array of settlement patterns including a palisaded village with both wigwams and longhouse-like structures and "villages" of wigwams surrounded by a palisade (figure 6.7).
These patterns suggest a community fully engaged and aware of the differences to the
west and east, experimenting with multiple ways of living and organizing their community. The overall pattern for this period from southwestern Ontario suggests that
these Late Woodland people farmed and ate similar foods to people further east but
organized their lives and defined themselves in ways distinct from those seen further
east.

After this period Western Basin communities across southwestern Ontario more commonly use longhouse-like buildings as residences (Kenyon 1988). These "longhouses," though, were less substantial than those seen to the east, as well as different in their use of space and internal structure. The size of some settlements also increased during this period, with evidence of multiple longhouses and enclosures around groups of large storage pits (Lennox and Dodd 1991). It appears that people located their settlements near diverse environments, perhaps as part of a community's effort to use many different food sources without having to travel too far from home. These likely warmer weather settlements probably reflect a balance between tending maize fields while still being able to harvest other important foods. And even with the appearance of these relatively fixed settlements, people still moved often; archaeologists often find smaller camps and even evidence of single families who moved away from the settlements to live in wigwams during colder weather (Murphy 1991). Archaeologists are also finding evidence that a borderland between the Western Basin tradition and the tradition to the east shifted west during this period. In fact, peoples related to each tradition may have even overlapped and shared space within this borderland.

By about 1400 CE, though, the nature of the boundaries between the two traditions may have shifted. There is evidence of defensive settlements, with more substantial enclosure walls and earthworks. The distinct archaeological patterns that we call Western Basin show up further west, while settlements that seem like the Ontario Iroquoian archaeological tradition are found well into southwestern Ontario. By around 1500 or 1600, Western Basin sites were present only in the extreme southwest of Ontario, such as along the Detroit River. Descendants of these late Western Basin peoples do not seem to have re-established fixed settlements in southwestern Ontario until later in the 1600s and 1700s.

From House to Landscape

Settlement patterns offer archaeologists a wealth of information and insight into the way past peoples lived and ordered their lives – in their homes, among their neighbours, and across the landscape. Understanding homes and broader landscapes helps provide the context that archaeologists need to gain insight into how people used everything from tools to buildings. Instead of merely describing artifacts, we can study how these objects are related to the many different contexts of living – cooking, eating, making, storage, waste disposal, and so on. The settlement patterns that archaeologists record at the household and village level also provide a glimpse of how families and communities organized themselves and defined space and place and how those sensibilities changed through time. Ultimately, settlements give us insight and a capacity to appreciate how life was experienced by those who were born, lived, loved, and died in a southern Ontario that was an extremely different place and homeland than what we know today.

7

Animals and Archaeologists

Suzanne Needs-Howarth

Animal bones are common in archaeological sites. For Aboriginal people, animals have spirits and are an important part of the cosmos; their bones are alive, even after they are buried. Archaeologists a century ago seldom kept animal bones from archaeological sites, not understanding just how informative they can be about past peoples' economies and ways of seeing the world. We now recognize, though, how much an archaeologist who specializes in animal bones – called a zooarchaeologist – can learn from these remains. The bones can tell us what people ate, to be sure, but they also show how, where, and when people hunted, fished, trapped, or collected different animals and how they used animal bones and hides as raw materials for tools, clothing, ornaments, and shelter.

People use different animals based partly on their availability in the environment and partly on cultural factors that influence how the animals are seen as potential sources of food, bones, and hides. For example, some groups do not eat animals that they consider sacred, although they may hunt them for their hides or to use in ceremonies (see Oberholtzer, chapter 11).

But when archaeologists interpret animal bones from archaeological sites, they have to contend with another complication – the many processes that affect animal remains from time of death to time of excavation. These processes, called taphonomy, include both natural and cultural influences. For example, people often break the long bones of larger mammals in order to get at the nutritious marrow inside the bone; this means that only fragments will be left for archaeologists to find. And for bone to survive being buried in the ground for hundreds or thousands of years the soil conditions have to be just right, with not too much moisture or acidity. Even if they survive being buried for so long, bones in archaeological sites usually are broken.

SIDEBAR 7.1

Working in the Bone Library Suzanne Needs-Howarth

When I receive bags with cleaned shells, bones, and teeth from the archaeologist who excavated them, I first sort them by zoological class (gastropod, bivalve, fish, amphibian, reptile, bird, and mammal). Then I try to figure out which part of the skeleton each fragment of each class represents. I check each bone against the same body part in a "bone library," a collection of recent skeletons that we use to identify bones. The oldest such bone library in Ontario, in the Department of Anthropology at the University of Toronto, was established by the founder of modern zooarchaeology in Canada, Dr Howard Savage. It now has hundreds of recent skeletons of all the animals likely to be found on an archaeological site in Ontario and beyond.

I also try to establish which species a bone represents. For birds and mammals, the absolute size of the bone will often guide me to a certain group of species. For example, bones of a deer are much smaller than those of a moose. Differences in anatomy can sometimes tell us what kind of animal we're dealing with. For example, sturgeon have instantly recognizable bony plates called scutes, instead of scales. And occasionally something unusual about the actual bone or tooth will indicate the group of animals it belongs to. For example, we can readily identify a national icon based on its long, curved, orange-coloured front teeth?

Bone can end up fragmented and distorted from being burnt during cooking or from being thrown into the fire before disposal to keep the smell down. All of these changes can make it difficult to figure out what the bone refuse means.

As a result of taphonomy and demographics, the largest, best-preserved collections of animal bones come from relatively recent sites in areas with less acidic soils. In practical terms, this means sites south of the Canadian Shield that date from the last 1,000 years. Even in the last 200 years, the landscape and animal communities south of the Shield have changed considerably through farming, livestock grazing, commercial hunting and fishing, and the construction of towns and cities. It can be hard to imagine what Ontario looked like before European explorers and missionaries settled here. The diverse environment contained many plants and animals that humans found useful, including many that are still used by First People today. Because there were so many choices available to them, different people had different lifeways even within the same environment.

So what kinds of animals did people eat? There were no cows, sheep, pigs, or chickens in Ontario until Europeans introduced them, so before that people had to find animals in the wild. In the next few pages, we will look at some of the animals that were important to Aboriginal people – and that you may not immediately think of as food – starting with those found on the land.

On the Land

For a short time after the last ice age, Paleoindian hunters may have taken down now-extinct types of elephants (see Ellis, chapter 2). The bones themselves show that mammoths were present in Ontario – some mammoth bones were even found in Toronto during excavation for the original Eaton's store at College and Yonge streets. Unfortunately, there were no human bones or artifacts along with those mammoths, so we can't be sure those particular animals were killed by humans. Aboriginal people also hunted four different species in the deer family: caribou, moose, wapiti (elk), and white-tailed deer. At the end of the last ice age, when caribou were found as far south as what is now Toronto, people stayed on the shores of lakes to hunt migrating caribou (Jackson 2000). Caribou follow the same migration routes year after year, so they were a predictable food for Aboriginal people. When you rely on hunting and gathering, predictable is good; it means spending less time and less effort to get the calories and nutrients needed to survive.

During the Woodland period, deer was often a major meat source. But the people valued deer as more than just food. They used deer hides for clothing and shoes. Antlers made good hammers and flakers for flint knapping. And the bones proved useful as the raw material for all sorts of tools, such as awls and netting needles (figure 7.1). White-tailed deer bones are plentiful on archaeological sites near prime deer areas, especially the Oak Ridges Moraine and the Hamilton area (Birch and Williamson 2013; Needs-Howarth and Williamson 2010; Stewart 2000). People hunted deer year-round, but particularly in autumn, when deer forage for acorns in open hardwood forests, and in winter, when their movement is hampered by snow and they gather in stands of hemlock and white cedar. The forest edges and vegetable gardens around Iroquoian villages attracted deer, so that sometimes they could be caught very close to home. Iroquoian people in areas with fewer deer may have made special deer-hunting trips to areas where deer were more numerous. They may also have traded for hides, essential for footwear and clothing, with Algonquian people. The effort to build hunting blinds, drives, and corrals (figure 7.2) for deer was well worth it – a single deer is a large packet of meat and hide, after all, and they often congregate in groups.

Between 4,500 and 2,900 years ago, weapons technology shifted from spears to smaller arrowheads (see Fox, chapter 9). These new weapons made it easier for Aboriginal hunters to target birds and smaller mammals. Even after Aboriginal people adopted arrows, they continued to trap animals such as beaver, muskrat, chipmunk, and squirrel, because trapping can be a very time-efficient way of securing food.

The Crawford Knoll Site, near Lake St Clair, yielded large quantities of muskrat bones. The degree of fusion of the ends of the long bones, which in younger animals indicates the biological age of the animal, suggested to the zooarchaeologist who analysed the material that these muskrat were caught in early spring. It seems that

Figure 7.1 *Above*
First Peoples made many different items from animal bone. A needle (two views in upper left) from the Mantle Site (early 1500s CE) may have been used to make and repair nets. The bone from a deer's foot (upper right) has a hole drilled in it, perhaps to use as a toggle fastener; it comes from the Antrex Site, a village in the Greater Toronto area that dates to the late 1200s and 1300s CE. The three tubes at the bottom of the photo are beads made from bird bone (New Site, 1350–1400 CE, Markham). (Courtesy of Archaeological Services Inc.)

Figure 7.2 *Left*
This woodcut depicts a communal deer hunt in Eastern Ontario. Although the image may not be completely accurate, it gives a good idea how fences helped funnel deer to waiting hunters. Champlain wrote that this blind, constructed in 1615, took 25 people 10 days to build but allowed the people to kill 120 deer in about 5 weeks. (Courtesy Project Gutenberg.)

Late Archaic (c. 1500–500 BCE) people at Crawford Knoll hunted them because they were plentiful and easy to catch in the lean season (Thomas 1988).

Once corn became the staple food, after about 1100 CE, people continued to hunt – sometimes right inside their villages. Keeping the rodent population under control in and around the village was a serious business, because deer mice and chipmunks could cause major damage to both the corn crop and the stored corn that was needed to feed a village during winter and as seed for spring. So people caught and likely ate these rodents – partly of necessity, partly because they were readily available and a good addition to the diet.

In some historic-period Neutral sites, it looks like villagers specifically targeted grey squirrels, likely to make squirrel-fur robes (see Prevec and Noble 1983). The villagers may have eaten the meat as well, but the prestige (and comfort) of having a squirrel-fur coat was probably the main reason.

Raccoon bones are very common on archaeological sites, and their meat was almost certainly eaten. They are in prime condition in autumn, and people could snare or trap them in hardwood forests near streams or lake edges – or even in their dens, which are in predictable locations. The people also hunted furbearing mammals such as mink and marten, but it is unlikely that they ate these members of the mustelid family – the meat would have tasted pretty strong. They were certainly valued for their fur, as occasional skinning marks show (figure 7.3).

Figure 7.3

This jaw bone of a marten has cuts on the bone that appear to be skinning marks. It was excavated from the Mantle Site, an Iroquoian village on Stoufville Creek, just north of Toronto, that dates to 1500–1530 CE. (Courtesy of Archaeological Services Inc.)

The only domesticated animal in Canada before European settlement was the dog. Dogs were primarily working animals rather than pets. They were a great help during deer hunts, were revered in Aboriginal cosmology, and were sacrificed and eaten during feasts. Their bones were often used to make beads or tools that may in turn have had ritual significance.

Bear was also both eaten and revered (see Oberholtzer, chapter 11). Archaeologists tend to find far more bear claws and canine teeth than other bear remains, suggesting that people kept and treasured the claws for ceremonial purposes, possibly as part of a pelt. Bears are best hunted just before they go into hibernation, when they are fat and sluggish and their pelts are in prime condition.

In the Sky

Aboriginal people hunted birds with bow and arrow and with nets. For some Aboriginal groups, birds were a good addition to a diet focused mainly on deer; for others, birds were part of a highly varied diet that included many different small animals and fish.

The passenger pigeon was one of the favoured foods of Aboriginal peoples. Now extinct, these birds were at one point so numerous that an estimated one in four birds in North America was a passenger pigeon (figure 7.4). They nested in the lower Great

Figure 7.4
Carolina parakeets and passenger pigeons were still alive in the early 1800s, when artist and outdoorsman John James Audubon created life-sized paintings of more than 400 species of birds in North America. These images are just part of his plates illustrating these two species.

Figure 7.5
A raptor (bird of prey) effigy pipe that was excavated from the Robb Site, a fourteenth-century Iroquoian village on the West Don River. (Courtesy of Archaeological Services Inc.)

Lakes in massive numbers, migrating south for winter. Aboriginal people hunted them extensively, but the pigeons were so numerous that the population was always able to recover. This balance was upset when European immigrants in eastern North America began to clear forests for farmland. Passenger pigeons needed large beech forests, for they were particularly fond of beech nuts and lived together in enormous flocks. As the forests declined, the birds started to move into the grain fields of the farmers, causing serious damage to crops. Farmers took to shooting the pigeons to use as food, selling the surplus at market. Soon the passenger pigeon population fell below the minimum number at which it could reproduce. In 1902, the last recorded pair in Ontario was seen near Penetanguishene. The last passenger pigeon in the world died at the Cincinnati Zoo in 1914.

In addition to passenger pigeon, Aboriginal people caught and ate other upland game birds, such as ruffed grouse and wild turkey. Jesuit missionary Jerome Lalemant reported in 1641 that the Neutral country had "multitudes of wild turkeys which go in flocks through the fields and woods" (Thwaites 1896–1901, vol. 21, 197). Many of these birds were year-round residents, available in all seasons.

Aboriginal people also hunted migratory birds, attracted to the many lakes and rivers. Trumpeter swans, for example, migrated through Ontario for a short time in spring and autumn, on the trip between their summer nesting areas and their over-wintering grounds. Other species, such as the passenger pigeon, nested and stayed in the area throughout summer, while several kinds of duck only overwintered. Archae-ologists can use the presence of these seasonally available animals to help determine when people made use of a site.

As with mammals, birds had value beyond simple food (figure 7.5). Iroquoian people frequently made beads from the long, straight wing bones of Canada goose, turkey, and sandhill crane (see figure 7.1). Zooarchaeologists also sometimes identify more unusual birds, which may have been caught for their feathers – the colourful woodpeckers, the raven, and the bald eagle, all birds that are revered in Aboriginal cosmology.

One zooarchaeologist found something even more exotic at a Late Woodland village called the Calvert Site (Timmins 1997): three bones of a Carolina parakeet (see figure 7.4). This bird has been extinct since 1918, when the last one died, also at the Cincinnati Zoo. In fact, the zooarchaeologist had to go to the Smithsonian Institution in Washington just to find a skeleton with which to compare the bones!

The bones were probably part of a complete parakeet skin, which archaeologists believe was used in pipe-smoking ceremonies (Prevec 1985; von Gernet and Timmins 1987). At first, researchers figured that the owner of this parakeet skin had traded for it with people farther south. But an until-recently-overlooked passage in the voluminous travel journals of Samuel de Champlain suggests that the bird may have been caught locally. On his travels in 1615, northwest of what is now Kingston, Champlain saw a bird that "had a beak like that of a parrot, and was of the size of a hen. It was entirely yellow, except the head which was red, and the wings which were blue, and it flew by intervals like a partridge" (quoted in Grant 1907, 299). This fits the description of a Carolina parakeet to the letter. Ornithologists think Champlain may have seen a so-called vagrant bird – one that was outside its normal geographic range.

In the Water

Aboriginal people made abundant use of the shellfish, amphibians, reptiles, and fish found in streams, rivers, and the Great Lakes themselves. Women and children probably were the ones who gathered or caught a lot of these animals, while men took care of the larger fishing expeditions.

Archaeologists often find whole or fragmented clam shells. People in the past knew that the meat inside them was nutritious, and they could conveniently gather clams when they were at a river or lake for fishing. The same goes for turtles and frogs. After all, a large snapping turtle provides a lot of meat, and even frog's legs have some nutritional value. At some sites, frog's legs are more numerous than other parts of the body, suggesting that people removed the legs to take home, having discarded the rest of the body at the catch site (where it is "invisible" to the archaeologist). Many turtle shell fragments are burned, indicating that people probably roasted turtles right in their shells. And some show signs of being polished or ground into decorative items or turtle-shell rattles.

Aboriginal peoples in Ontario valued fish of many different species, but their fishing was never intensive enough to deplete the fish stocks. As with the passenger pigeon, fish stocks became more depleted as a result of European farming and industrial activity (especially damming of spawning rivers) and commercial fishing. Eel and sturgeon, two fish prized by Aboriginal peoples (General and Warrick, in press), are now endangered in the province of Ontario. Landlocked Atlantic salmon became extirpated, or locally extinct, from Lake Ontario and its watersheds in the 1800s. A recent reintroduction project has started to show results; Atlantic salmon are once again reproducing in the wild (Merringer 2011).

Aboriginal people understood the need for a variety of fishing strategies and tools for fish living in different environments. They used nets and weirs during the spring spawning run to target cool-water fish living in rivers and lakes, such as sturgeon, suckers, walleye, and perch. They could use nets to catch lake trout and whitefish in large numbers during the autumn spawning runs just off the shores of large lakes, such as Lake Ontario and Georgian Bay. People also caught fish during the summer months, using spears, hand-held lines, and "passive" fishing gear such as fish traps to get brown bullhead and sunfish from marshes and shallow streams. Just as with mammals and birds, Aboriginal people needed a lot of knowledge of the local environment and climate to catch each type of fish when it was most plentiful.

Eels, for example, were seasonally available. The American eel is the only Ontario fish that migrates to the ocean to spawn. Aboriginal people caught adult eels in autumn when they swam down the St Lawrence River toward the sea, using weirs, fish traps, or pronged fish spears. A zooarchaeologist working on the Steward site in Morrisburg (about 1150–1550 CE) identified eel bones in quantities not seen before (or since) on an Ontario archaeological site (Junker-Andersen 1988). He argued that this site may have existed primarily to harvest eel. Eel is incredibly nutritious and can be smoked and stored for use over the winter.

Sometime during the Archaic period, people started to make and use nets to catch fish. Nets brought in large catches that could feed many people, but the method also required many hands to apply the nets and clean the catch before it spoiled. In the Late Woodland period, people used gill nets to catch huge numbers of autumn-spawning lake trout, lake herring and whitefish. They then dried or smoked these fish for the lean winter months (Sagard 1939, 186).

Aboriginal people often took advantage of river narrows for fishing. The Blue Water Bridge South site (about 140 BCE–660 CE) at the narrows on the St Clair River is a good example (Prowse 2008–09). Archaeologists working on the Middle Woodland site found fish bones and fishing-related artifacts that show the many methods that people used to catch fish: harpoons, spears, three-pronged spears (called leisters), fish-hooks, and nets. The great variety of different shapes and sizes of stone net sinkers suggests that people chose the equipment most suitable for a particular type of fishery and its associated water conditions. The site had a spring seine net fishery for spawning walleye and an intensive summer seine net fishery for spawning freshwater drum.

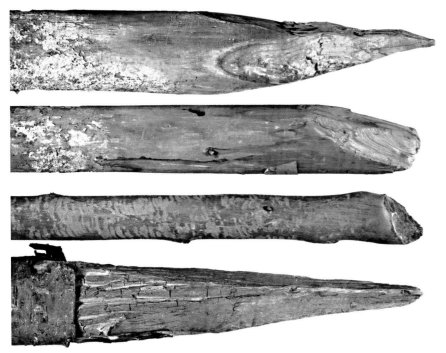

Figure 7.6
Archaeologists documenting the Mnjikaning Fish Weirs, near Orillia, collected examples of the wooden stakes used to construct the weirs. The stakes were made of local woods like sugar maple, white birch, and eastern white cedar; many of them were carefully shaped with axe cuts, though at least one (second from bottom) was a repurposed beaver-gnawed branch. (Photo by James Conolly and Kate Dougherty.)

One of the most striking finds of early fishing equipment is of one of the earliest fish weirs in North America, the Mnjikaning fish weirs, which date back to the Archaic period, about 5,000 years ago. The weirs were made of closely spaced wooden stakes, perhaps with interlaced material, driven into the bottom (figure 7.6). They stretched almost completely across Atherley Narrows, between Lake Simcoe and Lake Couchiching, directing fish to small openings, where they were captured with nets. The Mnjikaning weirs were still in use when French explorer Samuel de Champlain visited the area in autumn 1615 (Grant 1907). In his journal, Champlain noted that the Huron, using a number of weirs, caught large quantities of fish that they preserved for winter. The Mnjikaning weirs fell into disuse when the Huron left the area in the 1650s, but the water prevented the wood from rotting, helping preserve it.

The weirs were documented by underwater archaeologists in the 1970s (Johnston and Cassavoy 1978), then declared a National Historic Site in 1982. More recent monitoring of the site showed that contemporary fishing and currents were degrading the stakes of the fish weir, so they were excavated to record them (Ringer 2006). The local Chippewas, who are the First Nations people now living in the area, never used the weirs, but they value their traditional role as stewards of the weirs. To them, the weirs were much more than a fishing place. The area was a meeting place for treaties, trade, feasting, and ceremonies; it remains a sacred place.

The Promise of Fish Bones

Fish remains from the Peace Bridge Site provide a good reminder of what might happen to a bone before it gets to my lab (Needs-Howarth and MacDonald, in press). When I and other zooarchaeologists analyzed the fish remains from the site, located where Lake Erie flows into the Niagara River, we found that most of the remains belonged to walleye or sauger, two species that are difficult to differentiate based only on their bones. Measurements of the bones indicate these fish were adults, likely caught as they moved up the Niagara River during their spring spawning run. There were many vertebrae, or backbones, but few bones from the head – except for the dense, sturdy part of the lower jaw. The bone may have been trampled by people as they moved around the site, causing the more fragile parts to break and disintegrate.

Missing parts of animals are a real challenge for zooarchaeologists, because we need the bone to work backward to what types of meat and fish people ate. We often find lots of fish vertebrae, but no bones from the head, for example. On the face of it, this pattern seems to suggest that Aboriginal people gutted and smoked or dried the fish at the shore, bringing just the fillet back to the village to eat during the winter months. Even if people brought the heads back home, those bones may not have survived for archaeologists to find; the head bones of fatty autumn-spawning fish such as whitefish are very oily, so they break down quickly. In the worst-case scenario – boneless fillets – we find no bone at all. This causes us to underestimate the importance of these fish in Aboriginal diets. Certainly the early European explorers described the catching and processing of huge numbers of fish in autumn.

Zooarchaeologists can figure out a great amount of detail about the past, even from very mundane remains. For example, research that I did with a colleague revealed that people fishing at sites near Lake Simcoe dating between the late 1200s and the early 1500s appear to have varied their fishing strategies depending on the behaviour of the fish (Needs-Howarth and Thomas 1998). They caught fish such as sturgeon, walleye, and lake trout, which come together in large groups to spawn, during their spawning run. But fish that are more dispersed, such as pike, sunfish, and bullhead, were caught throughout the warmer weather.

How do we know? Fish grow throughout their life, so zooarchaeologists can use measurements of their bones to estimate their size and hence their biological age. We can also count and measure the growth rings on fish scales, fin spines and other bones (just like with trees) to tell the age of the animal (figure 7.7). The growth rings even tell the season of the year in which the fish died, because fish in a temperate climate, like Ontario's, stop growing in winter and then start growing again in spring.

When fisheries scientists and I looked at the scales of walleye from the Lake Simcoe sites under the microscope, we noticed that most of them showed just a little bit of new growth at the edge of the scales, suggesting that the fish had, indeed, been caught in spring. Similarly, very, very thin slices of the sturdy fin spines of bullhead indicated

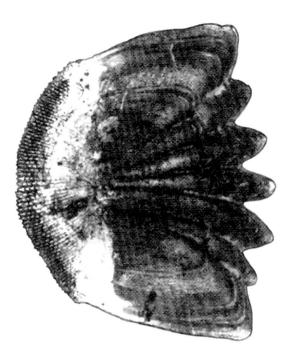

Figure 7.7
Fisheries scientists can use special software to count and measure the annual and seasonal growth rings. (Drawing by Marit Munson.)

these were likely summer catches (Needs-Howarth 1999). But the number of yearly growth rings revealed something else: tantalizing evidence of a small decrease in the age, and hence size, of brown bullhead over time in the local water sources – something I expected to happen with moderate fishing pressure. Unfortunately, as is often the case, I just didn't have enough bones to feel certain.

Choosing Animals

Archaeologists often have incomplete information, so we tend to suggest interpretations rather than conclude. Our research does show, though, that there was tremendous variety in how people used animals in their local environment. Some groups relied on animals that were both plentiful and amenable to mass capture, like deer and spawning fish. Sometimes people went for species that were not that convenient to catch or delicious to eat but were important for nondietary reasons, such as mink or bald eagle. Other times people made good use of a wide range of resources, such as clams, frogs, squirrels, muskrats, and raccoons – they may not have been prestigious foods, but they were just too available and convenient to pass up.

8

Plants and the Archaeology of the Invisible

Stephen G. Monckton

Popular representations of archaeology are almost all about pottery, stone tools, and bones. Why is it so rare to hear about the remains of plants? After all, it's hard to imagine any society not absolutely dependent on vegetation! When I was an undergraduate student at the University of Alberta, I was enthralled with the idea of doing archaeology. I finally got my big chance: a professor told me that I could to join a team of archaeologists who were about to embark on a Roman excavation in south Italy – but only if I was willing to do "this thing called 'flotation,' which is quite messy." It was messy, but it was also an amazing experience. Flotation involves mixing soil samples from an archaeological site with water. Little fragments of plant materials float up to the surface of the water, to be collected and examined under a stereoscope. Many years later, I did my PhD on native Canadian plant material in Ontario and found it tantalizing to marvel at what people were eating.

Studies of ancient plant use were relatively new at the time I began, and researchers were essentially botanists who understood some archaeology. On the other side, the archaeologists who asked for help with ancient plants were quite unaware of the strictly botanical issues involved. Now, happily, we have a group of researchers worldwide who are anthropologists interested in the interplay between human behaviour and the environment – the field known as paleoethnobotany. In this chapter, I'll explain what paleoethnobotanists do: how we make sense of plant use in the past, how knowledge of plant biology shapes our understanding of what we see in the archaeological record, and what we have learned about the interactions of plants and people through time.

SIDEBAR 8.1

Flotation Stephen Monckton

There are many methods of flotation (Pearsall 1989), but the one I prefer is the "double bucket method." It requires less water than other methods and uses inexpensive components available in any hardware store. The process involves two buckets, one half-filled with soil and the other filled with water. The water bucket is poured into the soil bucket and stirred to allow charred materials in the soil to float. The soil bucket, now containing water, is decanted gently through a 300-micrometre screen into the original water bucket. Good screens are a specialty item and are somewhat expensive regardless of the flotation apparatus. After several repetitions of recycling the screened water, all of the floating material is collected. Material that sinks to the bottom of the soil bucket is then passed through a coarse 2.00-millimetre screen to collect the "heavy fraction," which often contains small bones and artifacts. The double bucket method works well for processing small samples (i.e., 5–10 litres) over a wide area of the site. Larger devices, such as SMAP (Shell Mounds Archaeological Project) machines, are great for processing large sample volumes, though the machines also need cleaning between samples and consume prodigious amounts of water.

Nature of the Evidence

Plant remains come in two main categories: macrobotanical and microbotanical remains. Macrobotanicals are objects that are visible to the naked eye, such as seeds and pieces of wood. A stereoscope is useful in order to examine fine details of macrobotanical remains. Microbotanicals are smaller remains, including pollen and spores, that are invisible to the naked eye. Examining pollen, which requires a microscope, is known as palynology.

Analysis of plant remains, whether micro- or macro-, is in a way the archaeology of the invisible. Even the largest materials are extremely small. At one end of the scale, whole maize kernels can come from the ground in complete splendour. More often, we find only fragmentary pieces and have to learn to recognize the smallest physical characteristics of their structure – like identifying a car model from a fragment of its taillight. Items in the medium-size range, like raspberry seeds, are usually found complete due to their hard woody seed covers. At the other extreme, however, one often finds absolutely tiny but complete seeds of other plants, like strawberry or tobacco, which would fit comfortably on the head of a pin. There are even some, like cattail, that would fit on the pin's other end – and in huge numbers (figure 8.1).

Analysing such small pieces can be tedious, especially if one finds nothing. But there are rewards, not only in the anticipation of recovering what we expect, but also in the shock and exuberance of finding the unexpected. In the case of finding very small but rare specimens, I have learned to laugh inward so as not to blow away the evidence!

Figure 8.1
The familiar velvety brown head of the cattail is its flower; when the flower head breaks apart, the wind distributes as many as 250,000 tiny seeds. (Photo by Marit Munson.)

As tiny as plant remains may be, many of them preserve surprisingly well. Certain conditions help otherwise fragile plants survive: extremely dry conditions, wet oxygen-poor environments, or situations where plants were charred, or partially burned, in a fire. Even in these conditions, preservation depends on the age of the remains, given the tendency for local environmental conditions to change through time. In Ontario, most macroscopic plant remains are preserved through charring. Generally, this means that we find what people brought to the fire, although there were probably cases when plants that were of little or no interest to people burned accidentally. This means that the quantity of plant remains from a site is helpful in figuring out which plants were most important to the people who lived there.

The broad picture of plant use in Ontario's past shows that the earliest hunters – Paleoindians and Archaic peoples (see Ellis, chapter 2) – also gathered wild plant foods, beginning shortly after the last ice age, about 13,000 years ago. Ontario Early Woodlands people began to use maize around 500 CE, long after the plant was originally domesticated in Mexico, thousands of years earlier. Farming really took hold in Ontario about a thousand years ago; by 1300 CE, many farmers had settled into substantial longhouse villages, often with defensive palisade walls (see Williamson, chapter 3). Even with the increasing dependence on maize, however, the people continued to hunt and gather wild resources. By the time of European contact in the late 1500s and early 1600s (see Warrick, chapter 4), there were numerous large settlements, each with as many as 2,000 people who cultivated maize, beans, squash or pumpkin, sunflower, and tobacco. Thanks to the size of these settlements and their refuse deposits, we also gain insight into various other plants they continued to collect.

The Wild and the Husbanded

Collected plants included both "wild" and "husbanded" plants. Wild plants are those that grow without the benefit of any human actions. But there are many opportunistic plants that thrive in areas of human disturbance. Simply walking into a forest, cutting down trees, and making camp actually changes the composition of the plants in the area. "Weeds" (an unfortunate term) have seeds that are capable of long periods of dormancy. They can sleep for decades before germinating in the sunlight let in by new space in the tree canopy overhead.

When people see opportunistic plants as useful, they may encourage the plants to grow. This kind of husbandry is part of the transition from "wild" to "domesticated" plants. People tend husbanded plants, but the plants are still capable of independent reproduction. Domestication, on the other hand, is the interdependence of plants and people. Domesticates cannot reproduce without human help, because of the way the plants' reproductive structures have been altered. The large edible kernels on the maize cob are delicious food, but they are so densely packed that they seldom thrive if they fall to the ground themselves – people have to plant the seeds to make sure that they have enough room to grow into the next generation.

The relationship between people and plants is, and always has been, dynamic and highly interactive. Imagine, for example, collecting raspberries in a forest edge or open area, then happily eating them back in camp. Eventually, their seeds will pass through your digestive tract and go back to the ground. You have no real control over the redistribution of such seeds – you can't put them back where you found them, and it's likely that you would relieve yourself near your camp or settlement. Inadvertently, you have planted a host of fruit-producing plants where you live. The next season will bring a high concentration of the plants and, eventually, a bumper crop.

This artificial flora is known as "anthropogenic vegetation," or plant communities with human cause. In fact, Iroquoian archaeological sites dating to within the last millennium contain enormous quantities of raspberry seeds and the fruits of many other plant species. It makes one wonder what the expression "natural vegetation" really means.

Finding plants outside their natural geographical homeland is a strong indication that people encouraged the plants, extending their natural habitat through husbandry. For example, knotweed and chenopod are found in prehistoric sites in Ontario that are north of their natural distribution. The chenopod known as lamb's quarter is the common form in Ontario today and is of European origin. Indigenous little barley was last sighted in Ontario on railway tracks just north of the US border in the twentieth century. In the past, this plant grew at many Iroquoian sites in southern Ontario.

People continued to gather plants well into the historic period of pre-industrial European presence in Ontario. Ironically, it is only within the last ten or so years that historic plant materials have added to our understanding of First Nations and pre-industrial European food ways in nineteenth-century Ontario. This may be related to a bias against very recent archaeological sites, which some people feel are less important than what is known from historical documents. There is much that historical sources do not cover, however, if only because routine activities were probably considered unremarkable (or even indelicate to mention) at the time of their writing.

Greens, Grains, and Other Gathered Plants

The peoples of ancient Ontario had an enormous repertoire of knowledge about edible, medicinal, and otherwise useful plants. The remains of some of these plants simply have not survived to the present day; still, the range of plants recovered from archaeological sites is amazing.

Fruits

People in Ontario used dozens of kinds of fleshy fruits, represented in archaeological finds as charred seeds and other plant parts. These include bramble (a generic term for the raspberry), strawberry, plum, at least four species of cherry, hawthorn, blueberry, and elderberry. Remains of fruits are usually recovered from refuse deposits, or middens, located in or outside settlements, along with animal bone, stone tool fragments, and prodigious amounts of pottery.

Greens and Grains

Middens also provide the remains of herbs, or plants lacking woody stems, like chenopod, knotweed, and little barley (figure 8.2). These herbs provide leafy greens,

Figure 8.2
Plants now considered weedy, like goosefoot, provided greens and grains for First Nations. The species shown here, *Chenopodium album*, is a variety introduced by Europeans that has largely replaced the native species. (Photo by Marit Munson.)

as well as considerable quantities of nutritious seeds. Even today, we are surrounded by chenopod with its plentiful seeds. In the two-kilometre walk through Toronto from Robarts Library to my apartment building, I was able to fill a jar with seeds from European chenopod growing near the bases of maple trees lining Huron Street. This was without stopping, just grabbing the seed-bearing structures as I went, requiring maybe ten minutes. Even that is nothing compared to what you can find growing on temporarily abandoned construction sites, where soil is stacked high waiting for transport to distant lawns. The seeds make highly nutritious cakes, while chenopod leaves are a good replacement for spinach.

Other Useful Plants

Sumac, cattail, and spikenard, commonly found on many archaeological sites, had a variety of uses for aboriginal peoples. Sumac, for example, is a fast growing shrub that produces rather beautiful red clusters of fuzzy-looking fruits, high in vitamin C (figure 8.3). Early European observers noted that it was a common basis for making tea. Spikenard served medicinal purposes, helping to heal ulcers, wounds, and various other ailments. Cattail (not to be confused with bulrush) was apparently useful for food from its starchy roots and brown fruiting heads but also as a source of straplike leaves for weaving floor mats and roofing houses. Iroquoian longhouse settlements almost always include at least some cattail seeds.

Many other plants are found in good archaeological context, though they occur in such small numbers that it is hard to know how prehistoric peoples used them. These include poor-man's pepper, evening primrose, cleaver, ironwood, hornbeam, and bush honeysuckle, to name a few.

Figure 8.3
Staghorn sumac is a large shrub or small tree with distinctive clusters of fuzzy red fruits. Over the winter, the clusters begin to break apart into individual seeds. Still covered with red fuzz, the seeds are easy to identify based on their distinct size, shape, and structure. (Photo by Marit Munson.)

Nuts

The primary evidence we find of the use of nut-bearing trees is the remains of their nuts, both shells and meat. So far, archaeologists have found shell fragments of butternut, black walnut, hickory, oak, beech, and ironwood seeds. Of course, there are also many different trees whose remains are routinely identified in archaeological sites that are likely used as fuel for the fire. In fact, the remains of oak, beech, and ironwood may simply reflect the accidental inclusion of nuts along with firewood.

Cultivating Gardens

Prior to the arrival of Europeans in Ontario, Aboriginal peoples cultivated maize, bean, squash, sunflower, and tobacco. Of these maize is the plant food that is most often present in archaeological sites dating to the last 800 or so years in southern Ontario. The other cultivated plants, along with the husbanded plants discussed above, were useful foods, but maize was, by every scholar's estimate, the single most important food plant.

Cultivated plants in prehistoric Ontario began their journey to domestication in Mexico, by at least 3,500 BCE. As maize and other cultivated plants spread northward from their tropical origins, they became better adapted to higher latitudes. Maize arrived in this region by at least 500 CE, but archaeological remains suggest that it was not a major food source until about 900 years ago.

There is much debate about whether maize arrived with bean, sunflower, and squash, or if the three followed several hundred years later. The customary preparation of bean and squash may actually make it unlikely for very many examples to be preserved in archaeological sites. If beans or squash were soaked before cooking, for example, they might be less likely to char when brought close to the fire during the cooking process. Food preparation may bias our view of whether these plants were introduced into the lower Great Lakes region together as a complex of garden foods or in some sequence of introductions over time.

Looking at remains of cultivated plants in neighbouring areas actually makes the picture of food introductions into Ontario even more confusing. For example, both squash and sunflower show up to the south of us, in the Eastern Woodlands and Midwestern United States, much earlier than maize. On the other hand, beans seem to have arrived after maize in New York State, where researchers dated a bean at the Roundtop Site to about 1000 CE (Ritchie 1973). Another radiocarbon date later proved that it was no earlier than 1300 CE (Hart 1999), a time when maize and settled village life clearly went together. In Ontario, we have similar evidence of beans appearing as early as the 1200s (Smith and Crawford 1997). It will take more information to clarify this interesting sequence of events; the search for evidence and good solid radiocarbon dates continues.

Figure 8.4
This 1724 illustration from Jesuit priest Joseph
François Lafitau shows people working corn hills in
the background; in the foreground, they are boiling
down maple sap in iron kettles.

For years, researchers thought of beans as the perfect complement to maize. Beans are a legume, which help to replenish the nitrogen content of the soil that maize depletes. Also, maize lacks some key nutrients (niacin and the amino acids tryptophan and lysine) that help form protein essential for a balanced human diet. Aboriginal people, however, were fishing and hunting for millennia, and probably would not have needed beans to add this component to their diet. The popularity of beans was probably more a matter of cultural preference, with the benefit of maintaining soil nutrients in maize fields.

Early European accounts tell of the Huron growing maize, beans, and squash together on "corn hills," or piles of scraped-up soil into which the gardeners poked their seeds (figure 8.4). There are European references describing the people nurturing seedlings indoors before planting them in spring. More soil would be added during weeding and scraping. Writers frequently allude to the stalks of maize plants providing a kind of trellis or support for the vines of bean and squash. These corn hills may have also raised the crops slightly above the coldest air during spring, when there was a chance of late frost. The telltale lumps that such farming would have left on the land-scape no longer exist, mainly because of modern ploughing and forest growth.

Many researchers have assumed that people must have moved their villages every thirty years or so, as maize harvests declined due to soil nutrient depletion. Supplies of firewood also would become harder to locate within reasonable walking distance. Curiously enough, when villagers did move, they seem to have settled near their pre-vious locations, often no more than a few kilometres away (see Warrick, chapter 4). I believe that they would have depended on the previous settlement area for much of their collected fruits and greens, already burgeoning from the previous years of human waste and farming disturbance that are so beneficial to husbanded plants. New areas covered in gallery forests would have been relatively undisturbed, with almost nothing growing on the forest floor. Moving to an area not too far from their previous home would allow villagers to use already well-established wild plants from the home area, while acquiring new fertile soil and a fresh source of firewood. Indeed, the many settlements in both Ontario and New York State moved gradually along rivers, averaging two to four kilometres apart from earlier locations.

A Payload of Weeds

When Europeans arrived, Aboriginal farmers populated the entire Eastern Wood-lands of North America. The newcomers brought their own plants from the Old World, including wheat, barley, oats, peas, and, inadvertently, a payload of weeds. Growing European crops in a new climate proved a real challenge. In Ontario, the earliest evidence of European experimentation comes in the form of the remains of peas at Sainte-Marie-among-the-Huron, a settlement established by the Jesuits in the early 1600s, near what is now Midland. In written records, the Jesuits state that they were trying to grow wheat and various herbs, following written instructions on proper cultivation. Most of the plant remains in the archaeological record in this area were probably dried goods originally imported from the Saint Lawrence River area. As they experimented, the Jesuits were largely dependent on the local Aboriginal peoples for food.

As relentless waves of Europeans arrived from the 1600s through the early 1800s, they left abundant evidence of an increasingly wide range of imported and cultivated Old World plant foods, like wheat, barley, oats, peas, and figs – even coconut! Like the Huron and other Aboriginal people, Europeans collected prodigious quantities of local wild fruits. As one can imagine, the level of disturbance of the landscape was far greater than that caused by Aboriginal predecessors, and anthropogenic vegeta-tion grew at an unprecedented scale. By the mid-1800s, 80 percent of the forest cover in southern Ontario was removed. Hawthorn trees, which thrive in deforested areas, spread so widely that they have actually differentiated into new species within the last 200 years.

The story of plants and humans is complex and deeply rooted in time. For around 13,000 years, the many peoples of Ontario have depended on plants for life's necessities – food, medicine, shelter, and other items. People gathered and tended to plants, cleared land to farm and built villages. All of these interactions affected plant communities, in ways both intentional and unforeseen that shaped the environment of the past – and even of today.

9

Stories in Stone and Metal

William Fox

Stone-tool use is an ancient and longstanding tradition, stretching back millions of years and extending into the twentieth century. The working of stone by Aboriginal peoples throughout the Americas is not news to most Canadians who have visited a local museum to see a display of "Indian arrowheads"; however, few would realize the importance of stone tools to peoples of the industrialized world. As recently as the 1700s–1800s, the military in England, France, and Italy relied on millions of gunflints to fire their pistols and muskets in conflicts like the Napoleonic Wars. Master flintknappers used steel hammers to shape the gunflints by carefully flaking the stone. This flintknapping industry has been particularly well documented in the Brandon area of England. Stoneworking for tool production continued well into the twentieth century – Aboriginal peoples around the world relied on traditional stone tools to earn a living, and Europeans in countries like Cyprus and Turkey manufactured stone blades to make the threshing sledges used in harvesting grain.

Stone Tools in the Early Americas

Archaeological evidence suggests that some of the first people in the Americas arrived along the west coast some 20,000 years ago. They spread rapidly eastward across the continents, bringing with them a long tradition of stone-tool use. Despite this shared origin, the toolkits of the early peoples of South America and eastern North America have little in common. We have a great deal yet to learn about the first colonization of the Americas.

One specific stone tool, a very distinctive lancehead, serves as the "signature" of an early group known as the Clovis people (see Ellis, chapter 2). Highly mobile hunters and gatherers, the Clovis groups adapted to a wide variety of environments

SIDEBAR 9.1

Learning from a Modern Master William Fox

To learn more about making stone tools, I studied with one of the last remaining Cypriote master flintknappers, or *athkiakades technites*, during the 1980s. I brought Michales some cobbles of chert, a good tool-stone, from local riverbeds. He held the cobbles and tapped them with his hammer, listening to the sound that they made. Most made a dull "clack" and were discarded. Michales then directed me to his favourite chert source in a tiny valley hidden among the chalk hills. When I returned with a nodule freshly prized from the bedrock, he tapped

it, producing a ringing sound. This was the tone Michales wanted, for it indicated that the stone was without the internal flaws that would hinder flake production.

English flintknappers apparently did the same several centuries ago, determining the internal structure of large flint nodules quarried from the chalk in order to know how to split them, prior to the blade production stage in the manufacturing of gunflints.

Figure 9.1
These 11,000-year-old Paleoindian stone points would have been used as dart tips. The two on the left clearly show the distinctive flutes, or large flakes, struck from the bases of such points. The point on the right, enlarged to show detail, is a made from an unusual clear crystal material, quite different from the chert of the other points. (Courtesy of Archaeological Services Inc. [left and centre] and Dr Arthur Roberts, Simon Fraser University [right].)

across the Americas some 13,000 years ago. They were very skilled flintknappers, creating lanceheads with a channel or "flute" on each face (figure 9.1).

Paleoindians were selective about their stone, choosing only the best quality chert, often from distant sources as many as hundreds of kilometres away. They carried quality-tested chert with them on their travels, in the form of bifaces. They may even have valued the colour of their stone tools, perhaps seeing some colours as signatures of particular bands of people – *People of the Blood Red Stone* or, perhaps, *People*

SIDEBAR 9.2

Producing a Biface   William Fox

Archaeologists refer to stone tools flaked on both opposing faces as bifaces. These began as a large mass of stone, known as a core (figure 9.2). The flintknapper would strike the core with a hammerstone, driving off a series of flakes. Depending on the desired final product, he or she might work on shaping the original core into a rough shape (second from left), or could remove a large spall, or flake, and then switch to working on that piece. As the biface began to take form, the knapper would use a hammerstone or an antler tool to drive smaller flakes from the edges of the blank, refining its shape and thickness (second from right and right). This created a "biface preform," which could be used for cutting or could be further modified to produce a lancehead or drill. If the biface broke during production, due to an internal flaw or knapper error, it could be reworked into a smaller biface or simply discarded at a quarry workshop site. Either way, the bifaces carried away from the quarry had been quality tested.

with Snow White Lanceheads. They certainly held red ochre as full of special symbolic significance, for they sprinkled it over their dead, as do many peoples around the world.

As North America became ever more densely populated, groups settled into territories and began to use less exotic stone to make their tools (see Ellis, chapter 2). The local stone was useful for a variety of cutting, scraping, or drilling implements, although often of lesser quality for tool production. These more recent tools do not display the same care in manufacture, and the quality of workmanship declined as the millennia passed.

When the modern forest cover became established in regions like present-day Ontario, more groups had access to large trees. They began to use the trees to make dugout canoes, creating heavy new woodworking tools like axes and adzes. Shaped from igneous and metamorphic rock, these heavy-duty tools were formed first by flaking and pecking, then ground into their final shape (figure 9.3) (Ellis et al. 1990).

These Archaic stone toolkits looked quite different from those of the Clovis peoples and other early groups. Stones cobbles heated in a fire were even used for cooking and probably for sweatlodges as well. During this period Aboriginal people in Ontario discovered native copper, or nodules of pure copper, along river and lake shores, which they found to be malleable using fire and hammer stones. Aboriginal groups were making metal tools before the peoples of Europe (figure 9.4)!

Figure 9.3 *Left*
This grooved axe, shaped by grinding, comes from a private collection in Dundas, Ontario. It dates to the Middle Archaic period, around 6,000–2,500 BCE. (Photo courtesy of Archaeological Services Inc.)

Figure 9.4 *Below*
Early copper artifacts, dating to the Archaic period, include a range of tools. The curved hook on the left is a gaff, used for fishing, while the solid piece (above centre) is a gouge used in woodworking. The curved piece at the bottom is a chopping tool. The spear point (at right) would have been hafted onto a wooden shaft. (Courtesy of the Royal Ontario Museum.)

Durable Goods

The last several thousand years were a dynamic period of Native history, witnessing the ebb and flow of ideas to and from what is now the province of Ontario (see Williamson, chapter 3). Stone tools provide one of the primary types of evidence in reconstructing these past events, by studying their distribution across the land. Stone is durable in any form – as finished tools, tools in production, debris from manufacturing, or simply as raw material transported for use in the future. Tools and toolstone are widely distributed across the landscape, providing evidence for the location of a wide range of human activities right up until at least the late 1800s. Hunters re-sharpened chert arrowpoints and knives; artisans produced ground stone pipes. Traders transported chert, native copper, and native silver, and grieving relatives placed stone tools in graves with their deceased kin (see Spence, chapter 14).

No other class of archaeological items speaks as clearly and consistently as do stone tools. The origins and the endpoints of the raw materials and tools reveal stories of the long distance transportation of goods over a period of two and a half millennia. Raw materials like slate or schist, used to produce birdstones, ornaments, and other ground stone tools, are distributed in the bedrock across the Canadian Shield and are found in widespread gravel deposits to the south, courtesy of the continental glaciers. Some cherts and native copper and silver are much more specific in their distribution, originating in limited areas of bedrock. Still, the advancing continental glaciers also transported these materials considerable distances, making it possible for Native peoples to get these stones and metals from glacial deposits rather than bedrock sources – a factor that complicates our understanding of their distribution in the archaeological record.

Even when archaeologists are able to determine that a particular stone tool was produced near its primary source, it can still be difficult to identify the exact source. Most native copper, for example, looks essentially the same, whether it came from such far-flung sources as the west end of Lake Superior or the southern Appalachian Mountains. The only exception is native copper that contains a visible quantity of silver, which strongly suggests that its source is in the area of Keewanaw, Michigan (Griffin 1961).

If you cannot tell the source of a raw material simply by looking at it, how can a stone tool tell you about Aboriginal lifeways in the past? Well, the form of a tool, plus the type of material from which it was made, can tell you a considerable amount about its former owners. And even when it is impossible to identify a specific source of a stone visually, scientists can perform tests that sometimes provide an answer. A geologist, for example, might use a microscope to inspect a thin section, or very fine slice of material cut from a stone tool, while a physicist can use specialized equipment to identify the trace elements in stone. These and other chemical tests can assist in narrowing the search for a specific primary source (see Ellis, chapter 2). These tests can be expensive, though, and time-consuming – after all, a single archaeological site might include thousands or hundreds of thousands of stone artifacts, including tools and manufacturing debris. Fortunately, some archaeologists have enough experience studying stone tools and stone from primary deposits to be able to identify the source of most materials.

What do these stones tell us about Ontario's past? One of the stories speaks to 13,000 years of quarrying a particular chert adjacent to the eastern Lake Erie shore. It is called Onondaga chert, after the name of the geological formation in which it is found. Flintknappers quarried and worked this toolstone for thousands of years, exporting it, probably hand-to-hand, to groups throughout the Northeast. They traded the stone as finished tools, and also as unfinished pieces known as blanks and cores – quality-tested pieces of stone, ready to be worked into a variety of tools, such as knives, scrapers, drills, and points (see Williamson, chapter 3).

About 2,800 years ago, residents of the Niagara and lower Grand River region developed an entire industry, using Onondaga chert to make tens of thousands of thin, elegant biface blanks. Some, they used locally; others they exported to locations as far away as New Brunswick and northern Ontario, as well as adjacent states like Michigan, New York, and Ohio (Taché 2011a and b).

For about 500 years, the Onondaga chert blanks were a highly desirable commodity. Then, about 2,300 years ago, a major industry centred in what is now Ohio displaced the Ontario trade. Groups known as the Adena and the Hopewell peoples traded stone, copper, and native silver, in the form of tools and ornaments, on a continental scale. They facilitated trade in silver from Cobalt, Ontario, all the way to what is now the state of Mississippi. They also established a manufacturing industry at Flint Ridge, Ohio (Mills 1921), making chert biface blanks (figure 9.5) from massive deposits of colourful cream, blue, red, yellow, and green chert from the Vanport Formation. Their flintknappers produced hundreds of thousands of blanks, distributing them for hundreds of kilometres in all directions. As demand for Onondaga

Figure 9.5
These roughly oval-shaped bifaces are made out of Flint Ridge chert, which was widely traded throughout northeastern North America. (Courtesy of the Royal Ontario Museum.)

chert decreased, the Ontario industry declined and disappeared. The Hopewell groups also imported copper, some from northern Ontario, and exported manufactured goods like ear spools to Aboriginal peoples in what is now southwestern Ontario. (Sounds familiar, in terms of modern trade, doesn't it?)

By about 1,200 years ago, the widespread influence of Aboriginal groups to the south had declined considerably. Manufactured goods from Ohio become rare in the archaeological record from Ontario. Local interest in stone ornaments, such as polished slate gorgets, pendants, and soapstone pipes, had also declined. Aboriginal groups in Ontario settled into hunting and gathering territories across the Canadian Shield, or along river valleys in southern Ontario that were suitable for tending newly arrived corn plants, along with other exotic plants like gourds and tobacco (see Monckton, chapter 8).

Flintknapping was no longer an art for the few, but became a generally practiced skill for survival. Knappers worked flakes of various toolstones – chert, quartz, quartzite, taconite, rhyolite – into small knives, scrapers, gravers, and arrowpoints. Schist was useful for the adzes and chisels needed to clear the forest and make utensils out of wood. People made these tools expediently, when the need arose, and often discarded them when the tools became worn, rather than attempting to sharpen or repair them. Local soapstone served well for the occasional plain elbow-shaped pipe or disc-shaped bead. While the people had previously buried their dead with ornaments of stone, copper, or silver and sprinkled them with red ochre paint, by 1000 CE, burial traditions changed to simple, individual interments, devoid of accompanying stone tools or ornaments (see Spence, chapter 14).

This pattern of locally produced expedient stone tools continued throughout Ontario until the 1500s. The ancient Onondaga chert quarries were the only exception to this trend; around 1200–1300 CE, people along the eastern Lake Erie shore began to make many more chert biface blanks, knives, and arrowpoints than they needed for their own use (Bursey 1996). They exported the blanks and finished tools to adjacent Iroquoian speaking groups in southern Ontario until the mid-1600s.

Throughout the 1500s, Iroquoian villagers began importing native copper from the Lake Superior region in increasingly larger quantities (Fox et al. 1995). Most of the copper came in the form of small rolled sheet copper beads, rings, and raw nuggets, along with a few highly symbolic large copper knives (figure 9.6). All of the larger items were interred with the dead, as burial ceremonialism once more elaborated by the end of the century. Long-distance exchange of stone continued through the mid-1600s at southern Ontario villages of the Petun, Huron, and Neutral Iroquoian groups. The Aboriginal people of Ontario were not unique in this regard, as there is evidence for the long distance movement of goods and people throughout eastern North America at this time.

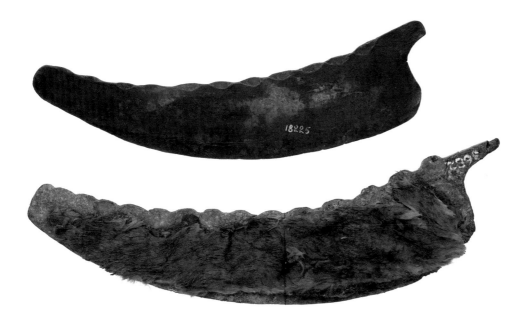

Figure 9.6
Late Woodland peoples shaped copper into many different forms, like these large copper knives, that combined practical functions with symbolic meaning. Copper salts leaching from one knife have preserved a piece of organic material – in this case, animal fur – that was in contact with one side of the knife.
(Courtesy of the Royal Ontario Museum.)

Historic Stories in Stone

The "stories in stone" for Ontario continue into the historic period. Stone tools tell of the continuing warfare between Iroquoian- and Algonquian-speaking peoples in southwestern Ontario. They track trade connections between the Odawa of Georgian Bay with Algonquian- and Siouian-speaking groups to the west and the Petun/Huron Iroquoians to the east (Fox 2002). The distribution of stone tools even documents the diplomatic connections between the Neutral Iroquoians of the Hamilton/Niagara region of Ontario with the proto-Shawnee in the Ohio Valley and, further south, the proto-Creek of Alabama (Fox 2004).

Some of the stone tools in Ontario's past were pedestrian; others were beautiful and full of symbolism. All have stories to tell, from ancient peoples' movements across the land, to long-distance trade and industry, to the dynamic inter-tribal relations of more recent centuries.

10

Pots and Pipes: Artifacts Made from Clay

Mima Kapches

When Europeans first travelled to Ontario in the early 1600s, they encountered Iroquoians making clay pots and clay smoking pipes employing a technology of unparalleled sophistication; it was a ceramic tradition that was to decline, as Aboriginal pots were quickly replaced by European-made copper and brass kettles and Aboriginal pipes were replaced by European-made pipes. By the 1650s, Aboriginal production of clay artifacts in southern Ontario was in disarray and soon disappeared, bringing to an end a tradition that had been flourishing in Ontario for over two and half millennia.

In this chapter, I'll start by looking at the clay-pot-making tradition when it was at the height of its technical expression among Ontario Iroquoians in the southern part of the province, and then I'll explore its Ontario origins. Although I mostly focus on the production and significance of pots, any discussion of clay arts must also include the manufacture of clay smoking pipes, one of the most spectacular clay artifacts made by Ontario Iroquoians. I'll address pipes in the final part of this chapter.

Ontario Iroquoian Clay Pots

Pottery, after stone tools, is by far the artifact that is most studied by Ontario archaeologists. Why? Ceramic is durable and is the most numerous artifact on many sites. If you break a cup it shatters into many pieces; clay pots when broken shattered into hundreds of pieces, which we call potsherds or just sherds. The inhabitants of a single village might produce many hundreds of thousands of sherds over the lifespan of their village. It is not the quantity of these sherds that is important, though – it is their different shapes and designs that make them important artifacts for archaeologists. We study them to determine how and when they were made, how they were used, and who made them. The study of changes in pottery over time can answer some of those questions.

Making Pottery

In 1623, Friar Gabriel Sagard (1939) observed Huron Iroquoian women in southern Ontario making, firing, and using clay pots. At that time the Huron had been in contact with the French, starting with Samuel de Champlain, for nearly fifteen years. But so few French had visited the Huron in their homeland that their way of life, as observed by Sagard, was relatively unaffected by the introduction of European goods and European ways. Sagard's description is the only one we have of Huron women making clay pots. I've taken pottery classes, and the basic steps that he describes are little different than those still employed by modern potters who hand-build their wares.

Sagard said that the women collected the clay that was the "right kind of earth" from naturally occurring sources of fine clay along creek or river banks. They then washed the clay, picking out rocks and twigs and other impurities. After kneading or "wedging" the clay to remove air pockets, they added temper, a small amount of little quartz grains. (One reason potters add temper is to prevent the pot from shattering when it first shrinks as it dries and then expands from the heat as it is fired.)

The Huron potters of the 1600s then formed the kneaded mass of clay into a ball, which they shaped by putting their fist into it. Using this as their starting point, they pulled and enlarged the ball. To assist in the pulling and shaping, they used a small wooden paddle – called an anvil – inside the pot and likely used a larger paddle on the exterior of the pot to shape and pull the clay. This is called the paddle and anvil technique.

Most pots were round in shape, with no feet or handles, except for the mouth or the rim where there was a small projection forming a collar. Sagard said that to make a pot took as long as was required to make the pot of the chosen size, so apparently small pots took less time to make and larger pots longer. Once the pots were dried they were fired in what Sagard called an oven, though it was not an oven or kiln in the sense that we know today. Instead the pots were placed in a shallow pit, more like a hearth or fire pit, where they were covered with brush and wood that was lit on fire and burned away, thus firing the pots. These fire pits were usually situated away from the villages, out of fear that the fire could become uncontrollable and spread with devastating results to the village.

Firing took a short period of time – just a couple of hours – with the maximum temperature of about 900°C reached quickly (Rice 1987). The open pit firing method never really gets too hot, so the pots were not as hard as those of modern potters firing their pots today. But the finished vessels were relatively strong and did not break when set on the fire, although moisture and cold water eventually took their toll and pots sometimes disintegrated or shattered when too damp or wet. Pots were so valued that when cracks appeared holes were drilled on either side of the crack and a lace was tied tight to keep the crack from expanding, thereby extending the life of the vessel.

For the Huron and other Ontario Iroquoians, we know that pots were made by women of the community. It is possible that there were women who excelled at the manufacture of pots, and as specialists they produced more than they needed and these extra pots were exchanged for other goods, such as robes. Some archaeologists have tried to identify these individual potters (Martelle 2002). But in general women produced the pots needed for their own household and mothers taught their daughters how to make pottery. Sometimes crudely made small pinch pots are found on sites, showing that young girls played with clay, much the way kids play with modelling clay nowadays.

SIDEBAR 10.1

Models and Interpretations, or How Do We Know?   Susan M. Jamieson

Archaeologists are stuck in the present, but we are interested in the past. In order to make the leap from our "here and now" observations of sites and artifacts to what happened centuries or even millennia ago, archaeologists draw on information from many different sources. We might use historic records, like Sagard's writings from the 1620s, or perhaps studies from around the world on how people farm, make pottery, and cook their food. These sources provide basic principles that archaeologists assemble into models, which ideally help simplify and render intelligible the complex human past.

Not surprisingly, archaeologists have many different models that might explain the same sets of "here and now" observations. Each model relies on slightly different assumptions and principles – and each can lead to different interpretations of the past. For example, archaeologists disagree about who exactly made Woodland pottery. Some archaeologists suggest that every family made their own pottery, drawing on a model of a simple economy where every household was self-sufficient (Trigger 1990a, 40–1). Other archaeologists question this model (Martelle 2002 and 2004), pointing out examples from around the world that suggest that most economies are more complicated than they first appear; they believe that some Woodland individuals specialized in making pots, which they could have traded to others.

There are also competing models for other aspects of ancient pottery. Did each Iroquoian tribe decorate their pottery in truly distinctive ways, as models of pottery style as showing ethnic identity suggest? Or do styles of pottery decoration actually reflect social interactions well beyond the tribe? When women were kidnapped or adopted into a new community, did they continue to decorate their pots with their traditional designs? Or would they have adapted to their new lives in part by learning the designs of their new community? Each of these possibilities reflects the assumptions of different models – of why people decorated pots and of how people interact and relate to each other.

Ultimately, the test of any particular archaeologist's explanation rests in how well it agrees with our ever-changing knowledge of the social and natural world. The better the model at any given point in time, the better it explains what we know about the past. As we gather new information, some of our previously useful models prove to be a poor fit with what we know; when this happens, archaeologists modify the existing model, or even reject it in favour of a new way of thinking about the past.

The Importance of Decoration

Understanding how the pots were made is an important aspect of archaeologists' study of pottery, but it's also important to study the pot decorations, because each Iroquoian tribe decorated their pottery in different styles. We know that Iroquoians did not paint designs on their pots. Instead, they scratched or stamped designs on the clay when it was still wet or when the clay was nearly dry, at what is known as the leather hard stage. Potters used bone, stone, or wooden tools to add their designs on the surfaces of the collars, necks, or shoulders of the pots. The bodies of the pots are usually undecorated. The decorations were simple or complex geometric designs put on the collars and the necks of the pots.

Huron potters preferred a simple pattern of oblique designs on the upper rim (figure 10.1), while St Lawrence Iroquoians liked complex rows of sets of lines and deep notches on the collar (figure 10.2). Neutral potters often decorated their vessels with simple incised oblique lines, or simply left them without any decoration at all.

Figure 10.1
This Huron-style pot uses simple incised lines to create a design at the rim and shoulder. It also has punctates at the shoulder, as well as a single castellation, visible at the upper right of the pot's rim. The pot is 14 cm high and 17 cm in diameter. (Courtesy of the Royal Ontario Museum [976.191.1417].)

Figure 10.2
This St Lawrence Iroquoian pot uses a fairly elaborate pattern of incised lines and punctates on the collar, with a similar incised design on the shoulder. It is 20 cm high and 20 cm in diameter. (Courtesy of the Royal Ontario Museum [NS3142].)

Sometimes archaeologists find pots decorated in a "foreign" style at a village oc-cupied by a different Iroquoian group. For example, St Lawrence Iroquoian style pottery is sometimes found on Huron Iroquoian sites. Many researchers think that the presence of this "foreign" pottery shows that St Lawrence Iroquoian women were brought into the Huron village through marriage, or adoption, or even kidnapping (see Warrick, chapter 4). Chemical analysis of clay sources indicates that these new-comers used local clays to make pots but used their traditional designs to decorate the vessels.

Pots for All Reasons

The shapes of pots offer some clues as to how they were used (figure 10.3). Some pots probably had very specialized uses, such as large several-litre-size pots for feasts (see Jamieson, chapter 12) and small pots used for storing seed corn or possibly by women who were not supposed to eat food from the communal pots when they had their periods. Large pots were very rarely used as burial urns for infants. In early his-toric times, when Europeans lived in Ontario Iroquoian villages, there are even exam-ples of stemmed goblets of clay made by Aboriginal people to mimic those used by the Europeans.

Most Iroquoian pots were rounded in shape, with some that were flat-bottomed. One of the most distinctive features of many Iroquoian pots was a protuberance at the rim, where the potter enhanced the collar with clay so that it jutted out like a jaw. These overhanging projections, called castellations, are sometimes at opposite ends of an oval-mouthed pot. Some researchers have suggested that the castellations were used as spouts or as places to allow a cord to be tied underneath the collar so that the pot could be suspended over a fire. I have my doubts about this latter suggestion because there are no wear marks on the necks of the pots suggesting this happened. Also, the collar is a weak point in the construction of the pot – it is hard to believe that a cook would risk losing both the pot and dinner into the fire.

The Earliest Ontario Pottery

The earliest pottery in Ontario is found about 800 BCE. At the time, making and using pottery was a novel idea that was shared among many people around the lower Great Lakes and northeast North America, all experimenting with this new tech-nology. These people already had the means to store, carry, and cook in containers before the introduction of pottery. They made wooden bowls and wooden cooking troughs, string or mesh bags, birch-bark containers, and skin sacks. The earliest pot-ters experimented with shaping vessels by adding coils of clay one on top of the other. This coil construction, as it is called, sounds easy, but I can say from experience that it's far more challenging than it seems!

Figure 10.3
This small conical pot is just 10 cm high and 13 cm in diameter. The texture on the outside of the vessel was produced by pressing the wet clay with a cord-wrapped wooden paddle. (Courtesy of the Royal Ontario Museum [NS 40717].)

The early pots were thick – thick-walled, thick-bottomed, with large pieces of grit for temper and large coils. The pots had bases pointed like a cone and were heavy because of the thickness of the coils. They had no real decoration except for the impressions of cords, pressed into their interior and exterior while the clay was still wet. In fact, some archaeologists think they were formed by being shaped in a mesh bag that burned off when fired. They were fired at low temperatures, far below the 900°C of Iroquoian pots, which meant that they broke easily and did not work very well for holding water or cooking (figure 10.4).

So what was the attraction to this new type of container? Initially there probably wasn't much of an attraction; pots were probably more a status object, a curiosity item, and an interesting technological challenge. The people who made this pottery were hunters and gatherers; they moved throughout their territory over the year, hunting, fishing, and collecting wild foods, such as nuts and wild rice.

Even though the earliest vessels were inefficient they did offer one important advantage: food could simmer in a clay pot. This made it easier to prepare foods that needed a long time to cook. In today's modern kitchen, wild rice takes about an hour to cook – just imagine cooking it over an open fire in a small clay pot! Collecting and preparing plant food and cooking were probably women's chores in these societies, along with making pots. Developing pottery provided women another way to cook highly nutritious meals that they could not have cooked before. Even so, the poor firing, the fragility, and the heavy weight of these early pots made it unlikely that anyone carried them on the yearly seasonal round – the pots were probably made for only a short period of use at temporary campsites.

Figure 10.4
This Early Woodland pot has the thick walls typical of some of the first pottery in Ontario. The potter roughened the exterior of the pot by pressing it with cords, perhaps wrapped around a paddle, while the clay was still wet. The interior has a similar texture. (Photo courtesy of Jean-Luc Pilon.)

Over time, potters improved their craft; the pots that had once been ungainly and cumbersome became well made. Between 300 BCE and 900 CE, potters began to use smaller particles of grit temper and thinner coils to build their pots. They skilfully smoothed the coils, probably using a paddle and anvil, into seamless walls, making larger pots. Higher firing temperatures meant that the pottery was more durable. Potters also made major changes in the shape of the pots, adding a filet of clay (a flattened coil) below the lip to thicken the rim into a collar.

By far the greatest change was the increased variety of decorations on the pots, including patterns of oblique lines that covered the whole pot or in some cases just the rim. Potters used a variety of new tools to add decoration. Toothed implements of bone, wood, or possibly slate created dentate (or "toothed") stamped designs, while wavy edged implements produced designs reminiscent of scallop shell impressions. Sometimes a potter wrapped a stick with a cord and rolled it over the surface of the pot, creating a textured pattern. In other cases, potters used sticks to push holes into the wet clay, making a small circular depression or pit called a punctate; the clay displaced from the pit created a raised bump on the other side, known as a boss. Sometimes these bosses show the fingerprint of the potter as she held the wet rim to prevent the stick from breaking through the surface. Already in these early times there were differences in the way designs were applied between eastern and western Ontario, perhaps foreshadowing the development of different First Nations in Ontario (see Williamson, chapter 3).

Around 1000 CE, Ontarians began living year-round in small permanent villages, growing corn and other crops (see Williamson, chapter 3). The examination of the baked-on food residues in cooking pots tells us what Iroquoians ate – often a fish stew with corn added, akin to corn chowder. Archaeologists can even tell that Iroquoian dogs ate these stews, too! Stable village-life gave women potters time to perfect their craft, and over the next 700 years, they did exactly that. By the time Sagard arrived in Huronia in 1623, the manufacture of Iroquoian pottery was at its technical and artistic peak. But since I have already described what Sagard saw, let's turn our attention to perhaps the most important clay artifacts produced by Ontario Iroquoians: the clay smoking pipe.

Ontario Iroquoian Clay Pipes

We know from historic records that Iroquoian men smoked tobacco in clay pipes. Men also planted and tended the tobacco plants. They smoked on canoe trips to dull their hunger and passed around pipes during political and religious ceremonies. Sharing a smoking pipe during a political event created trust and cemented alliances, while smoking during religious ceremonies was one way of communing with the spirit world. Interestingly, there are no references to women smoking. We know that Iroquoian women were the potters, but, if women didn't smoke, then did they make the clay pipes? One eyewitness account seems to suggest that men made them: in 1637, Pierre Boucher saw Ontario Iroquoians making "calumets or pipes" (Boucher 1883, 55). This statement is somewhat misleading, though, and the word calumet is important; what he actually describes is men making stone pipes. Calumets are made of stone, not clay, and they often lack stems – they are just bowls to which a wooden stem is attached. Archaeologists often find small, poorly formed clay pipes on some archaeological sites, which may be examples of inexperienced potters learning to make pipes (Kapches 1992). But there are also well made miniature pipes, less than six centimetres in length, that researchers believe men gave to other men as gifts in order to cement alliances among different tribes. So who made the clay pipes? For now, we just can't say for sure. What we do know is that Ontario Iroquoians were quite skilful makers of clay pipes.

The pipes are modelled from clay with very small quartz crystals or fine sand as temper. The pipe-makers created the hole in the stem by rolling reeds or a piece of cord in the clay, which burned away when the pipe was fired. The exterior of the pipe is often smooth, and some are burnished. Burnishing is a long process of smoothing of the leather-hard exterior with a stone or shell, then putting on a fat that is absorbed into the clay, rubbing again, and then firing. The result is a lustrous shiny exterior.

Just as the form of pots changed over time, so did the shapes of the pipes, stems, and bowls. Early pipes have the bowl at right angles to the stem, while later examples have the bowl dropped back a bit at an obtuse angle. The stems of early pipes

Figure 10.5 *Right*
Early Iroquoian pipes, like this one, are usually straight-sided and have simple decorations, like the horizontal stripes on this pipe's bowl. The pipe is 5.2 cm high and 7.25 cm long – just the right size to cradle in one's hand. (Courtesy of the Royal Ontario Museum [979.306.1].)

Figure 10.6 *Below*
The distinctive shape of this pipe's bowl provides its name – a collared or coronet pipe. It is just under 8 cm high and is 11.4 cm in length. (Courtesy of the Royal Ontario Museum [NS25547].)

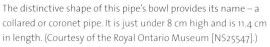
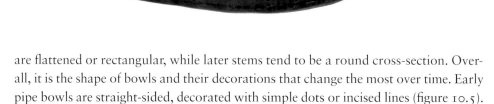

are flattened or rectangular, while later stems tend to be a round cross-section. Overall, it is the shape of bowls and their decorations that change the most over time. Early pipe bowls are straight-sided, decorated with simple dots or incised lines (figure 10.5).

About 1300 CE, there was an explosion in the varieties of bowl shapes: trumpets, apple bowls, vase-like or vasiform shapes, and collared bowls, called coronets (figure 10.6). The pipes might be plain, or were decorated with finely incised opposed oblique decorations, which researchers think might be copies of the complex decorations on pottery vessels of the same time. Just as archaeologists do not know for sure why complex designs exist on pots they aren't certain why they are found on pipes either.

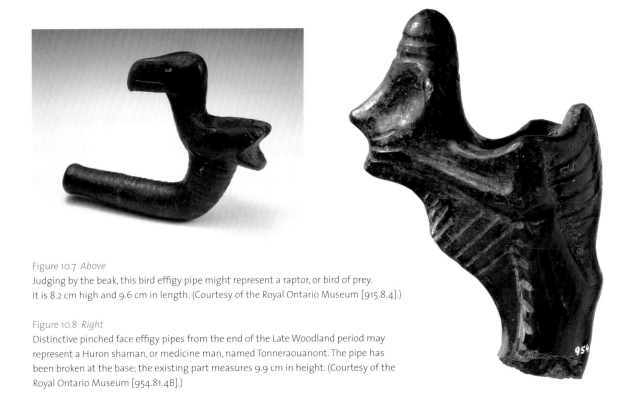

Figure 10.7 *Above*
Judging by the beak, this bird effigy pipe might represent a raptor, or bird of prey.
It is 8.2 cm high and 9.6 cm in length. (Courtesy of the Royal Ontario Museum [915.8.4].)

Figure 10.8 *Right*
Distinctive pinched face effigy pipes from the end of the Late Woodland period may
represent a Huron shaman, or medicine man, named Tonneraouanont. The pipe has
been broken at the base; the existing part measures 9.9 cm in height. (Courtesy of the
Royal Ontario Museum [954.81.4B].)

The most dramatic change in pipe varieties arose in about 1500 CE, when a new and unusual type of pipe, the effigy, became very popular. Effigy pipes were occasionally made in earlier periods, but they were not well made nor were they common. Effigy pipes include representations of a wide range of human faces, animal-human combinations, and animals such as owls, hawks, loons, parrots, bears, dogs, salamanders, fish, and snakes (see Needs-Howarth, chapter 8) (figure 10.7). Some human effigy pipes have holes in the ears for earrings; others have holes in the nostrils so that the effigy appeared to be smoking when the pipe was being smoked. Some effigies have rattles in their heads. Most effigies were placed so that they faced the smoker of the pipe. One of the most unusual and distinctive smoking pipes, made by Ontario Huron Iroquoians from about 1620–1650 CE, is called the pinched-face effigy (figure 10.8). These large, barrel-chested and hunched-back pipes show a man with a face with pinched cheeks and skeletal ribs incised on the body. They probably depict a hunchback Huron shaman named Tonneraouanont (pronounced Ton-neh-rah-wan-nont), who was very vocal in his opposition to the Jesuit missionaries who were trying to convert the Huron to Catholicism (Kearsley 1997).

As with the tradition of making clay pots, the manufacture of clay smoking pipes ceased in Ontario after 1650 when Ontario Iroquoians left the province. Stemless stone calumet pipes continued to be made into the 1700s by Mississauga peoples, but the Aboriginal clay pipe tradition disappeared.

Pots and Pipes

Clay artifacts offer a truly unique medium for artistic expression as well as for cultural identifiers. Potters and pipe-makers created beautiful and useful objects, each working in their own distinctive style. Archaeologists studying ancient peoples now use the variation in the form and decoration of these artifacts to track changes through time and changes over a region. In contrast to stone artifacts, clay, as a malleable and flexible medium, allowed rapid change and alteration. The clay tradition in Ontario was truncated by European intrusion, but it left a lasting presence in the archaeological record. The ancient pots and pipes of Aboriginal peoples provide a tangible and intriguing reminder of the arts and cultures of a time before Ontario.

11
The Living Landscape

Cath Oberholtzer

Step back in time and imagine walking along a trail through the woods, the sun creating dappled patterns as it filters through the green canopy, the white birches radiant where the sunlight touches them. You catch an occasional glimpse of a lake shimmering in the distance. The solitude is punctuated by the shrill raspy call of nesting eagles, and perhaps by the melodic chant of human voices drifting toward you on the breeze.

Suddenly, the trail widens and you walk into a clearing. There, before you, sloping gently southeastward toward the rising sun, stands a rare outcrop of crystalline limestone. The stark luminosity of the white rock contrasts with the surrounding lush forest, while a subterranean stream burbles below the rock's surface. Moving closer, you notice that this rock serves as a "canvas" for several hundred distinct images engraved, pecked, and abraded into its surface (figure 11.1). The artists intentionally incorporated the many fissures, cracks, crevices, and coloured seams of the natural surface into the images of sun figures, boats, turtles, serpents, birds, and more.

This rock serves as the interface between each of the layers of the cosmos. Blessed by the rays of the morning sun above, some figures display themselves to the light, while others slip down crevices into the underwater world below. The faint voices you heard while on the trail are those of a shaman, or spiritual leader, who is using the images to teach his protegés about the spiritual energy inherent in this spectacular setting and how to communicate with those spirits. Close to this teaching rock, a rare jade green lake outlined with grey-white marl, one of just twenty-five such lakes in Canada, enhances the sacred mystique of this natural setting. Now known as the Peterborough Petroglyphs, this site on the southern boundary of the Canadian Shield combines cultural meanings and spiritual activities with the physical attributes of this location to create a living landscape.

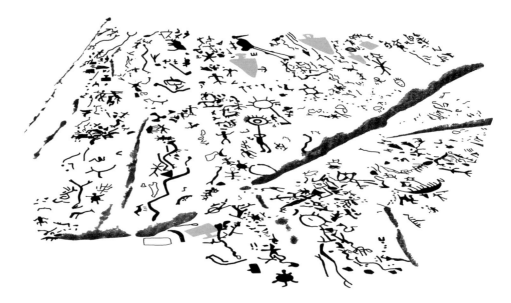

Figure 11.1

The Peterborough Petrogylph Site includes images of hundreds of "persons" in human and animal form. The petroglyph artists often incorporated the natural cracks and fissures of the rock surface as they pecked the images. For example, notice the large crack running diagonally across the image from the upper right, which has been transformed into a horned serpent by the addition of two curving lines pecked at its lower end. Another crack in the lower right has been similarly transformed. A few of the prominent images at the Petroglyphs (shown in grey) were actually added by vandals in the early 1900s. (Drawing by Marit Munson.)

The petrogylph site is just one example of many physical locations that Aboriginal peoples find full of meaning. Through their understanding and experiences, the post-glacial landscape, punctuated with rugged rock outcrops, lakes, and roaring rivers, became transformed into cultural phenomena. When the people moved through this landscape, they followed routes defined by unusual or prominent natural features, which they acknowledged as being inhabited by, or providing access to, spiritual powers. Features such as hill tops, cliffs, eccentric rock formations, caves, springs, waterfalls, rapids, and marshes all held the potential of being sacred sites. As a consequence, certain locations connected the sacred with the living and the ancestors, with individuals and the group, and with the animate and inanimate. By 2,400 years ago, recognition of these sacred sites became formalized to the extent that some Aboriginal groups deliberately built sites, such as mounds, to replicate natural elements in the landscape.

The Many Persons of the Three Worlds

An overview of the beliefs of Aboriginal groups helps in grasping the meaning that these landforms held for their people. Aboriginal cosmology recognizes three cosmic planes of Sky, Earth, and Water (or Underwater) worlds, each characterized by specific

Figure 11.2
This sun design was incised just below a series of short slashes that mark the shoulder of a Late Woodland pot. The circular designs inside the rayed sun seem as if they could be a pupil of an eye; combined sun/eye symbolism is fairly common in Native cosmology. (Drawing by Marit Munson.)

spiritual powers. In concert, these powers serve as the defining forces behind human behaviour. In general terms, the inhabitants of these cosmic zones form a community of "persons" that includes animals, humans, and other-than-humans, or what we might call supernaturals (Fox and Pearce 2005). The Sky World is the home of the celestial luminaries: sun, moon, and stars, the four winds, and thunder and lightning, the latter two represented by the iconic Thunderbird, a super-eagle. Of these manitous, or spirit powers, the sun was paramount, revered as the omnipotent life-giver and life-sustainer with powers of regeneration (figure 11.2).

In all likelihood the practices of the ancient Woodland peoples were similar to those of the Algonquians, recorded by travellers (Kohl 1985 [1860]), ethnographers (Densmore 1979 [1929]; Flannery and Chambers 1985; Landes 1937; Rogers 1962) and Aboriginal people themselves (Bird 2005 and 2007). These accounts describe how people emphasize the power of the rising sun by situating shelters with east-facing entrances, performing certain rites of passage at dawn, and ensuring that the sun's rays bless the equipment of hunters and shamans. Sun veneration played a prominent role in historic Iroquoian society as well. For these farming people, the sun possessed two aspects: one beneficent, the other warlike. The people dedicated rituals to this deity on behalf of the growing of crops and for the protection of warriors.

Images relating to the sky world occur on pottery, human bone, on the underside of scalps, and as sun disc wands. The bolder Thunderbird, capable of transforming into a human at will, creates lightning by flashing its eyes and thunder by beating its wings (figure 11.3). Displaying warriorlike aggression, the Thunderbird battles its perpetual enemy, the mighty Mishipizhiw (pronounced Mih-shih-PEH-shu), the Underwater Lynx or Panther. As the Thunderbird consumes only snakes, the battle prize consists of eating the Horned Snakes, guardians of Mishipizhiw, and ultimately the

Figure 11.3
Archaeologists excavating at the Peace Bridge Site recovered a fragment of a slate gorget that bears two incised Thunderbird images. They found the piece in an archaeological feature associated with the historic Neutral or New York Iroquois, from about 1650 CE. (Courtesy of Archaeological Services Inc.)

protectors of humans. Thunderbirds are believed to nest in isolated areas, in nests made of rocks on the top of cliffs or of sticks in the upper reaches of tree tops.

The Water World, the source for both food and healing waters, was the domain of Mishipizhiw (figure 11.4), supported by two horned serpents. Mishipizhiw controlled large bodies of water, causing storms, high winds, and turbulent water if not properly appeased. Aboriginal people interpreted the turbulence in Lake Superior and other rough waters as reflecting the constant battles between this underwater power and his mortal enemy, the Thunderbird. To calm the water, people made offerings, throwing tobacco (or kinnikinnick, a mixture of dried bark and leaves) on the water or even sacrificing dogs and hanging them on poles angled over the water.

Spirits also inhabit other water sources, from the mighty roaring falls at Niagara to transitional areas between water and land, such as shallower rapids or marshy areas (figure 11.5). These latter examples played significant roles as points of access to spiritual forces. Humans could also initiate contact with other-than-human persons through the reflective surface of small pools of water, used to divine the location of game. Thus, the Water World quenched thirst, provided food, supported watercraft, purified and healed bodies, was the source of shells, and created a means to see into the future.

Figure 11.4 *Opposite*
This moose antler comb comes from Teiaiagon (Baby Point), a Seneca village near the mouth of the Humber River in Toronto. Dating to the 1680s, the comb has depictions of significant Aboriginal religious symbols including Mishipizhiw, the long panther-like being at the bottom with its head to the right and tail curled under its body to the left. (Courtesy of Archaeological Services Inc.)

Figure 11.5
This impressive waterfall, on the Canadian Shield in Manitoba, is named Pisew (Lynx) Falls. The name comes from the growling, hissing noise of the water as it pours over the rocks, giving voice to the mighty Lynx. (Photo by Susan Jamieson.)

The composition of the Earth World is somewhat more complex. It is inhabited by animal-persons (animals), human-persons (men, women, and children) and other-than-human-persons (spirits or supernaturals). It also supplies the raw materials used to fulfill obligations to everyone in this community. Many of the animal-persons served as food sources (see Needs-Howarth, chapter 7), while others played signifi-cant roles in the spiritual aspect of this cosmic plane. For instance, Grandfather Bear's ability to transform into human form attests to his spiritual powers, as does his gift of healing people. As a respected elder, he is entrusted with guiding human-persons in their social behaviour. On the other hand, the role of the keen-sighted high-flying eagle includes carrying earthly messages to the Sun. Human-persons especially revered the animal-persons who were able to move from one cosmic plane to another, like wa-terfowl, amphibians, and water-dwelling mammals. Creatures such as geese, turtles, otters, and beavers played mediating roles between two or more worlds (figure 11.6).

Numerous plant species clothed the Earth. Of these, the people accorded special re-spect to medicinal herbs and aromatic plants such as sweet grass, kinnikinnick, and later, tobacco. These latter two serve as votive gifts left at specific sites throughout the landscape; when burnt, they carry blessings and invocations skyward with their

smoke. Tall trees also hold special significance. With roots bound to the Earth and branches extending into the Sky, the tree serves as a cosmic axis connecting humans with the Sky powers. Stripped of branches and bark, the tree becomes a display pole draped with offerings to the other-than-human persons, such as Grandfather Bear.

The earth also yields useful and distinctive materials, like chert, quartz, copper, galena, and red ochre (figure 11.7), while the boundary between land and water offers up shells. By drawing upon information found in historic documents and more recent studies of First Nations, archaeologists conclude that ancient peoples held these substances from the earth and the water sacred. Archaeologists interpret the locations, contexts, or situations in which they find these materials as being ceremonial in nature. Less tangible in nature are the four winds of the Sky World, which determine the four directions of the Earth World. Human-persons address these four directions, plus the zenith (Sky World) and the nadir (Under [water] World), offering them tobacco smoke when praying to the other-than-human-persons.

The survival of human-persons in the southern Ontario landscape required more than just physical prowess and group rituals. These strengths were augmented with spiritual power, which individuals gained through dreaming or vision quests. The people taught children to be aware of their dreams; when youths reached puberty, they deliberately sought visions from spirit helpers. The vision seeker chose an isolated location, close to waterfalls or fast-moving water, near the Sky powers and ready to be blessed by the rising sun. Preferred sites included hill tops, rocky ledges, platforms in trees, and occasionally caves. The spiritual powers gained through dreaming often

Figure 11.7
Archaeologists recovered this copper celt or axe head from the Pea Hill Site in Hamilton. It dates to some time between the Late Archaic and the Early Woodland period (around 2,500–800 BCE). The surface of the celt is pitted from corrosion and shows a distinctive greenish patina of copper oxide. The bit end (to the right) is covered with red ochre. (Courtesy of Archaeological Services Inc.)

inspired decoration on clothing, hunting equipment, personal ornaments, and rock faces. In other cases, they are recorded in the naming of vision sites.

An individual might also gain spiritual power by demonstrating respect during and after killing a bear. Wearing accessories made with the bear's claws, teeth, and chin skin provides one way of absorbing the creature's power. A hunter might also please the spirit of the bear by offering tobacco to a slain bear, or by sharing the meat in a communal feast. Ultimately, people might hang the de-fleshed and decorated skull facing eastward on a tree (as cosmic axis) by the water's edge, thus bridging the three cosmic planes. Or, alternatively, the skull might be made into a mask for interment with human burials to identify the shamanic powers of the individual and his ability to transform from human into a bear and back again.

Images on the Rocks

Rock art, too, expresses the complex cosmology and social relationships of human-persons with the worlds around them. Rock art includes images painted on rock, known as pictographs, and those pecked into the rock's surface, called petroglyphs. These markings are found in remote regions of the Canadian Shield, in an east to northwest swath across northern Ontario (Conway and Conway 1990 and 1989; Dewdney 1962; Rajnovich 1994). Pictographs are most frequently placed on the perpendicular face of monumental rock cliffs with bases deep within the water and crests that reach the sky. As natural canvases, these rocks support images showing food an-

Figure 11.8
The famous pictograph site on Agawa
Bay, Lake Superior, shows Mishipizhiw, the
Underwater Lynx or Panther. One of the
serpents who accompanies him is visible
below. (Drawing by Marit Munson.)

imals, such as deer and caribou, clan totems or signs, shamanic elements, dream symbols of individuals, depictions of cosmological personages, and some historic events.

The painters created the images by mixing red ochre (or occasionally white, yellow, or black pigments) with grease from Grandfather Bear. Painted onto the dark grey rocks, the pictographs are reflected by the water, evoking a changing and ongoing dialogue between the natural landscape and the social environment, between the other-than-human persons and the human-persons. It was difficult for an artist to obtain images through vision seeking and dreaming; it was equally arduous to master the physical aspects of painting. In many instances, the artists painted the pictographs while standing balanced in a canoe when the water was relatively calm. Others painted pictographs in remote areas on cave ceilings, reaching the caves by paddling a canoe and then crawling through small openings. The inaccessibility of many of these pictograph sites, and the fading memories of the people, lend credence to their belief that the images were painted by Maymaygwayshi, or the "little people," who lived behind the rock faces, coming and going through crevices in the rock.

The depiction of Mishipizhiw, the Underwater Lynx, at Agawa Bay on Lake Superior is one of most recognized – and most powerful – of these images (figure 11.8) (Conway and Conway 1990). The mythological animal appears to rise out of the water next to a canoe. Below the horned and scaly-backed creature are its two guardian spirits, the Great Horned snakes of the Underwater World, food of the thunderbirds. And indeed, the thunderbirds believed to be nesting on the crest of the rock would be drawn into the perpetual battle. At other sites, images of the mythological thunderbirds can be seen soaring up to the sun or, when reflected on the water, to be diving into the water in search of their archenemy. Thunderbirds in bird and human forms, shamans, bears, animals in the process of transformation, snakes, and other more abstract images reiterate the sacred nature of the pictographs across Ontario's north.

At the Peterborough Petroglyphs site described above (see figure 11.1), the images carved into the stone face by the shamans and their apprentices evoke a different sensibility (Vastokas and Vastokas 1973). Comprised of female figures, isolated vulvas, phallic male figures and images of symbolic copulations, these glyphs underscore the importance of fertility in humans. Images of turtles and snakes in association with eggs make a similar reference for animal-persons. Snakes are often associated with powers of regeneration, exemplified by the shedding of old skin and by their – and turtles' – "rebirth" each spring when the sun once again warms the Earth and they emerge from their winter torpor.

Some snake images at the site seem to emerge from or disappear into natural crevices in the rock, positions that reveal their role as intermediaries between the Earth World and the Underwater World. Other snakes are shown with stubby horns, representing the guardians of the Underwater Lynx. With the number of snake images the carvers engraved into the rock, it is interesting that there are only six glyphs of thunderbirds and of those three are in their human form. The explanation may be, as researchers Romas and Joan Vastokas (1973, 105) suggest in their book *Sacred Art of the Algonkians*, "that the animals engraved upon … [the rock] may depict those species controlled by the *manitous* of the rock." However, with eagles nesting in the trees at the site there may have been no need to carve their images into the rock. Other individual images at the site may represent clan totems, spirits acquired during visions, and other symbols that were meaningful to Algonquian-speaking groups.

Serpent Mounds

The symbolic importance of snakes is reflected in Aboriginal peoples' construction of earth mounds at various locations on the north side of Rice Lake. One of these, known as Serpent Mound, is an artificially constructed mound nearly sixty metres in length, situated between two rivers flowing into the marshy shores of Rice Lake (figure 11.9; see also figure 1.5). The mound, named for its similarity to a larger serpentine mound in Ohio, zigzags across the land, with round or oval mounds nearby (figure 11.9). The shape of the serpent mound calls to mind the serpent's place in Aboriginal cosmology. Snakes are able to move from the Earth's surface into the ground or into the water, attesting to the role they play as mediators between the Earth World and the Under World. On a deeper level of meaning, snakes refer to the Aboriginal concept of death and rebirth by shedding their old skins and regenerating themselves anew.

In addition, the zigzag shape of the mound can also be interpreted as the lightning bolts emanating from Thunderbird's eyes, serving as a reminder of the mortal battles

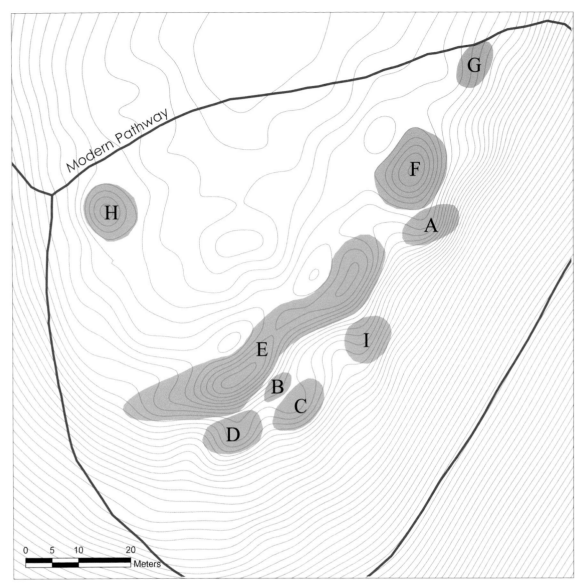

Figure 11.9
Serpent Mounds, on the north shore of Rice Lake, includes a series of mounds, shown here in grey. Archaeologists from Trent University recently completed this contour map of the site, which shows the large zigzag mound (E) of the serpent's body as well as a series of smaller oval mounds that some believe represent the eggs of the serpent. (Map by James Conolly.)

between these Upper World creatures and the serpent guardians of Mishipizhiw. The ambiguity of the zigzag shape with its layers of meaning, coupled with the mound as place for human burials, subtly creates a holistic metaphor by combining death and the Underworld with regeneration or rebirth in the Upper World.

The long Serpent Mound served as a place of burial, associating it with mounds at Cameron's Point and in other parts of area around Rice Lake and the Trent River (see Spence, chapter 14). As a whole, these mounds suggest a link between the Woodland people of what is now Ontario and the Adena-Hopewell people in what is now Ohio. The style of burial in two nearly circular mounds on East Sugar Island, in Rice Lake, is reminiscent of more southern burials, and goods placed with the dead also suggest that outside influences reached Ontario during this Woodland Period (see Fox, chapter 9). At the same time, the construction of these artificial burial mounds also suggests that the people were intentionally recreating the earlier practice of burying the dead in glacial kames, those ridges of gravel deposits left by retreating glaciers. These later people believed that the ancestors had created the kames, thereby rendering the mounds sacred and appropriate places to bury the dead. The liberal use of red ochre and the inclusion of galena, artifacts of copper, banded slate, marine shell, and bear skulls in these burials reflect a cosmology including elements of the Earth, Water, and Sky Worlds.

The Living Landscape

The landscape is not merely an assemblage of lakes, rivers, rocks, and hills. It is a dynamic backdrop, which Aboriginal peoples recognized as the sacred places of vision quests, as points to contact the other-than-human-persons, as the homes of particular spirits, and as the locations of rituals to ask and thank other-than-human-persons for favours. The red soil of the hills in Halton County, quarry sites for chert, quartz, and copper, Niagara Falls, springs and rapids, the rock canvases of pictographs and petroglyphs, the legendary giant of Thunder Bay, the turtle-shaped islands and rocks - all are honoured and respected as sacred sites. For the Woodland peoples, the land, especially certain physical features, held deep cultural meanings. It was – and still is – indeed a living landscape.

12
Social and Political Lives

Susan M. Jamieson

Archaeologists tend to concentrate on physical objects in order to explain what people did in the past – how they made pots and stone tools, how they built their houses and what their villages looked like, what they ate, and so on. In fact, my colleagues focus on many of these questions in their chapters of this book. This chapter, though, is about two of the more abstract aspects of human society – the ways in which people organized themselves into groups and governed themselves in the past. These are especially difficult to infer from archaeological remains. So how do archaeologists learn about these things?

The most straightforward approach for archaeologists is to rely on historic records that describe social organization and politics in a particular geographical area, then to project these records back into the *recent* archaeological past for that area. That is why there is so much emphasis in this book on documents by the French missionaries and explorers who worked in Ontario during the 1600s (e.g., Grant 1907; Sagard 1939). As we move farther back in time, though, it becomes much more difficult to learn about social and political organization. After all, human societies change over time. The farther back in time archaeologists go, the less certain we are that the organizations that we study resemble those described in the historical records.

Fortunately, archaeologists are able to draw general conclusions about the complexity of social and political organizations in the distant past by using studies of social and political change in historic and present-day societies from around the world. For example, we know the more that social distinctions between individuals, households, and communities show up in the materials of everyday life, the greater the degree of complexity in that society.

Evidence of trade connections, either within a society or external to it, provides clues to social and political organization, as does large-scale feasting, which offers a chance for public display of good leadership qualities. It is burial sites, though, that provide some of the best clues as to the workings of past societies. Archaeologists often assume that people who were treated differently in life are treated differently in death, because this is often the case in recent societies (see Spence, chapter 14).

The Importance of Being Earnest

In the early 1600s, Aboriginal people in Ontario were organized primarily around gender, age, kin, and community relationships (Day 1978; Day and Trigger 1978; Dickason 1997; Hickerson 1962, 1970; Sioui 1999; Speck 1913 and 1915; Tooker 1967; Trigger 1976; Trigger and Day 1994). Depending on availability of food and other factors that affected the size of the population, these societies ranged from perhaps a hundred people in the north to tens of thousands of people in the south.

Northerly societies were organized into fairly small groups made up of a number of families. Their leaders, who typically were men, relied on experience and personal traits as the basis for their authority. Leadership, which could be transitory in nature, was by consensus. All individuals were more or less social equals and group membership was fluid (see Hamilton, chapter 5).

In contrast, more southerly social groups were usually larger, with leaders appointed from families that held higher status and special knowledge – and therefore had greater social, political, and ceremonial authority. The leaders were always men but were appointed by women. Even in these societies, leaders were still bound to act as spokesmen for their groups. That is, power was of the "bottom up" communal variety, not the "top down" individual type with which most Canadians are familiar.

As the French missionary Jean de Brébeuf expressed it in 1636, "these positions are servitudes more than anything else" (Thwaites 1896–1901, vol. 10, 233). The ideal leader was persuasive, courageous, and wise – but, above all, generous (Herman 1956; Thwaites 1896–1901, vol. 10, 179–81, 233, 279–301). He was highly adept at networking within and among groups, was skilled in planning, had an astute sense of timing, and was knowledgeable about natural resources. In short, he exhibited balance, connection, and holism. At the same time, he was quite capable of manipulating circumstances when opportunities arose (Jamieson 2011; Thwaites 1896–1901, vol. 8, 91–3; Trigger 1990b, 139–42).

In all societies, individuals have certain rights, privileges, and obligations. Some are assigned at birth, without regard for individual qualities or differences; others are achieved solely through personal effort. Sometimes, privileges and obligations are a combination of assigned and earned. How one uses these assets in interpersonal relationships is critical to prestige and influence. If others are positively impressed, one's standing is enhanced; if others' impressions are negative, one's standing suffers accordingly. In Native American societies, for example, anyone who is generous is meeting a moral obligation to others and thus receives public esteem – the more generosity, the greater that esteem (Gallivan 2007; Hantman 1990; Herman 1956; Potter 1993). With esteem comes prestige and an increased ability to influence the behaviour of others (Ethridge 2009, 6–7; Feinman and Neitzel 1984). In this setting, political activity involves achieving agreement within the group. No one is obliged to support a decision against their will; the leader's success depends on his ability to find ways to make a positive impression on his constituency.

Because leaders had no authority to force their will on anyone, they held office by virtue of their ability to redistribute community-owned wealth – gifts that simultaneously maintained a harmonious relationship with all even as they created indebtedness (Herman 1956; Tooker 1967; Trigger 1990b, 143, and 2003, 40). Leaders also held ceremonial knowledge, an important source of authority and prestige (Sioui

---

SIDEBAR 12.1

Reckoning Descent Susan M. Jamieson

Lineal descent groups having a real or mythical ancestor in common are like a very large extended family. They are an important means of social problem-solving because they provide a labour pool larger than a single household can muster, maintain communal resources, and permit even distant members to claim and expect assistance from one another. Yet, not all societies have such descent groups. Most Canadians, for example, handle the social problems indicated above not through a descent group per se, but through the kindred, a group that has a living relative in common. In contrast to a descent group, the kindred is not perpetual; its membership does not operate efficiently because it is not clearly defined. The kindred is not as strong as a descent group.

In Canada, too, most of us are assigned our father's surname at birth, a practice that acknowledges the father's side of the family as the most important in terms of descent, confering greater authority on men than on women. In much of historic and present-day Ontario, First Nations were and are organized into kindreds rather than descent groups, and the father's family side was acknowledged as the most important in terms of descent. In contrast, though, early French mission-

aries and explorers described some southern Ontario peoples as being organized into descent groups that reckoned descent through their mother's family, the most important in terms of descent and kin relations. These descent groups included (Sahlins 1968):

- lineages, or people known to be actually descended from a common ancestor;
- clans, or a category of people sharing a common identity based on perceived descent from a common ancestor;
- phratries, or groups of clans considered as a single group for ritual purposes; and
- moieties, or two large kin groups based on common descent that together make up a society.

Because descent groups are not simply a form of personal affiliation but also are a political ideology, wherever descent was reckoned through the mother's family, older women held familial authority; they were the ones who selected which boys or men of the family had the best personal qualities to speak on behalf of their group and to be groomed as a future leader.

1999). They could increase their prestige by being more generous, sharing cosmologically charged objects and knowledge within or even beyond their social group. Archaeologists have long recognized that trade and alliances through marriage or adoption can be powerful political transformers (e.g., Jamieson 1999; Nassaney and Sassaman 1995; Spielmann 2002), as royal families in Europe will attest.

The Entrepreneurial Leader

Within this general framework, a particularly entrepreneurial leader could enhance his prestige while acting on behalf of his constituency. In 1627, the French missionary Joseph de la Roche Daillon wrote about the farming peoples known as the Neutral, who lived to the south of Lake Ontario (see Warrick, chapter 4). According to Daillon, their leader Tsouharissen (pronounced So-ha-EE-sen) was a "chief of the greatest credit and authority that has ever been in all these nations, because he is not only chief of his town, but of all those of his nation" – a nation that included some 40,000 people living in around 40 towns, villages, and hamlets (Noble 1984 and 1985, 133). Daillon writes that Tsouharissen, unlike other chiefs, had absolute authority, having acquired his honour and power in war. In earlier, more peaceful times, the Neutral had been able to express interests in other peoples, ideas, and objects, which promoted external alliances and trade (e.g., Fox 2004; Jamieson 1999). In times of war, however, their loyalties were first to their own group, their leaders, and allies. In these circumstances, Tsouharissen was evidently able to garner considerable prestige, even within a social system that limited and discouraged selfish status-seeking behaviour.

Individuals or groups could gain prestige and influence by hosting communal ceremonies, such as those designed to reduce infighting or to build political alliances (Spielmann 2002). The more lavish the feast and the better and more numerous the gifts, the greater the host's prestige and status, much as many of us today might seek to impress by serving guests a lavish Christmas dinner.

Feasting was an opportunity to impress potential followers by outdoing other potential hosts (Hayden 1997, 129) – although always with permission of the group. In Native American societies, it is considered immoral to be stingy; it endangers the welfare of the community, as well as affecting the health of others (Sioui 1999). Archaeologists infer that this belief extends into the past, too. Thus, any individual who attempted to raise his prestige and status solely for his own benefit and without group permission would be seen as acting in an inappropriate way. He would no longer receive support from those for whom he had been selected to speak. Feasting, generosity, and gift-giving required hard work by the leader – and by his supporters, who had to acquire the wherewithal to enhance their leader's reputation.

At the same time, aspiring leaders may have used large-scale ceremonial feasting and ceremonial payments of rare and exotic valuables as one tactic for outdoing rivals, hence for attracting followers (Hayden 1997, 129). Ceremonies provided a platform from which certain individuals or groups could display and distribute their generosity, while obligating others to consume it and become indebted (Hastorf 1990, 150, 174–75). Such ritual exchanges of food and goods tended to even out disparities in the things different individuals ate and possessed, while at the same time enhancing the reputation of donors, producers, and their spokesman. Tsouharissen must have given many lavish feasts on behalf of his constituency.

The Feast of Souls

In southern Ontario in the early 1600s, the most important ceremony for promoting social solidarity was probably the Feast of Souls (Trigger 1990a). Also known as the Feast of the Dead, the feast was a mortuary ceremony given every eight to twelve years by a group of related Huron villages in Simcoe County (figure 12.1). The ceremony was intended for all those who had died since the last such feast. The Huron notified neighbouring allies of the ceremony so that they, too, might attend and mourn those relatives being buried in the large, communal grave. All were welcomed and

Figure 12.1

The Huron Feast of the Dead, illustrated from Father Lafitau's description from the early 1700s. The picture shows the ossuary pit, in the centre, surrounded by folded back beaver robes; more beaver robes are displayed on posts in the background. In the foreground, people carry the recently dead on their backs, while skeletons of the previously dead hang from scaffolding around the pit. This picture is rather fanciful, showing the important parts of the event but not depicting everything literally. In reality, the bones of the skeletons would have been de-articulated, or no longer attached in anatomical position, and the bodies of the dead would have been wrapped.

Figure 12.2
European trade goods, such as these glass beads, were valued for gift-giving. These beads were found on the Grimsby Site, a Neutral cemetery along the Niagara Escarpment, dating from the 1640s-1650s. Notice the flat faces on the large bead (inset), where someone ground away the blue outer layer of the bead to expose more of the desirable red colour inside. (Illustration by Marit Munson.)

feasted for ten days. In addition, there was dancing, competitions of skill, and much gift-giving. Through this ceremony, friendships, alliances, and obligations were created and reaffirmed.

People deposited wealth with the deceased and also shared with others – much of it with the old and with important men, who used it in ceremonial presentations to express their generosity to others through giving. French documents record symbolically and cosmologically charged items of exchange including fur robes, beads of glass (figure 12.2) and marine shell, and an array of metal objects, which came from distant places, important in terms of beliefs and worldview. These valued items, kept in relatively constant exchange through ceremonial presentation, were amassed and stored by the community well in advance. Archaeologists believe that these needs could only be met through careful long-term planning involving increased trade with distant allies.

SIDEBAR 12.2

Trade Susan M. Jamieson

Archaeologists' thinking about trade and exchange in the past has shifted recently. We used to assume that trade was a simple matter of commercial relationships, based on a desire for material gain. Now, we recognize that the transfer of material goods and ideas is tied up with the giving of gifts and the diverse relationships, privileges, and obligations that go with them (Oka and Kusimba 2008). These social and political factors, in turn, are derived from the friendships or marriage alliances that underlay and facilitated all encounters involving trade and exchange.

For Aboriginal peoples, profit and other commercial motivations were always moderated by specific social, political, and environmental ideologies that included the exchange of gifts, services, or favours. Among other things, these ideologies discouraged gouging and hoarding and promoted more complex forms of sociopolitical development.

Foods served at feasts included the meat of deer, bear or dog, large fish, and thick corn soup, cooked in large communal vessels or roasted over the fire, as appropriate. As is true of luxury foods from around the world, these were usually reserved for special occasions, either because they were difficult to obtain or were labour-intensive to prepare – much like good quality caviar today, which is expensive and increasingly difficult to find in shops as stocks of the right sort of sturgeon decline.

The Jesuit missionaries in Huronia describe the great quantity of food served at feasts in 1635 (figure 12.3) (Thwaites 1896–1901, vol. 10, 177–9). One feast included 25 kettles that held 50 huge fish, plus another 120 that were only slightly smaller. At another feast, the Jesuits tell of 30 kettles, holding 20 deer and 4 bears. The Feast of Souls required even larger amounts of food, as both the living and the souls were fed. Massive quantities of maize were necessary to make the corn soup eaten by the living and to provide the corn piled in a thick layer over the dead so that they, too, could feast. Feasting created demands not only for enormous amounts of food but also for large cooking and serving vessels, all of which had to be collected and specially prepared well in advance of any ceremony.

Figure 12.3
This early image of a feast is from Father Lafitau's 1724 book, which documents his five years of travel among Iroquoian speakers in what is now Canada. Notice that the illustration shows women, in the foreground, preparing food within a ritual context.

Fragile Ties

The farther back in time one goes from written accounts, the more difficult it is to know exactly how leaders maintained their authority. Still, what we know about how small societies operate around the world suggests that Ontario societies were smaller and less integrated the farther back in time one looks, but that the qualities of what made a good leader were probably always much like what their historic descendants admired in the 1600s.

This means that for the thousands of years, leaders performed the delicate political processes that balanced the distribution of gifts and specialized knowledge in order to support their prestige and authority. That they were not always successful can be seen in evidence of infighting, such as violent deaths among early farmers living north of Lake Erie around 1350–1500 CE (Wintemberg 1939, 58; 1928, 49; and 1948, 41). These societies were composed of a number of communities bound together by rather fragile ties; cohesiveness was a constant negotiation. In fact, infighting was only one way to check overly ambitious leaders: people could quite literally vote with their feet, walking away from a self-serving and unpopular leader. The split of communities would have resulted in social change, as new communities were formed or as existing groups accepted the disaffected into their numbers (see Warrick, chapter 4).

Communal Ritual at Rice Lake

Communal rituals – especially burial ceremonies – were another important means to bind together fragile communities. Rituals provided a context for people to come together, facilitating the political alliances that helped to unite a society both internally and externally. Mortuary rituals in the Rice Lake area between 2,000 and 1,400 years ago provide an excellent example of ritual's social and political importance (Spence 1967 and 1986; Spence et al. 1968, 1979, 1984). Community members built large numbers of imposing mounds, clustered along the north shore of the lake (see Spence, chapter 14). The largest of the mounds, at the outlet of Rice Lake, measures 21 metres long by 4.4 metres wide and is over 14 metres high (see figure 14.5). Archaeologists believe that a single social group built each mound, creating burial places for the dead, marking group territories, and signifying the linkage between the earth, the Creator sky, and the ancestors (see Oberholtzer, chapter 11).

Most mounds are elongated in shape and many show evidence of having been gradually built up or added to over a period of time as people returned time and time again to bury their dead in these sacred places. The Rice Lake mounds contained concentrations of ritually charged and skilfully crafted valuables exchanged from distant regions (Johnston 1968a; Spence et al. 1990). Copper quarried along the shores and islands of western Lake Superior was formed into embossed plaques, beads, pendants, panpipe covers, and a large adze, weighing almost 1.5 kilograms. Ore deposits from near Cobalt, Ontario, provided silver for beads and the covers of panpipes. The marine shell that was shaped into beads, pendants, and an effigy all originated from the Atlantic Coast of the United States or perhaps even the Caribbean, as did a shark's tooth pendant. In most cases, the Rice Lake people obtained these items through hand-to-hand transactions, rather than by long-distance trading trips.

The burials surely also included valuables such as woven mats, masks and other wooden items, fur robes, basketry, and quillwork. These items, more perishable than stone or teeth, are largely irretrievable. A worked piece of wood excavated from a mound at Cameron's Point more than a century ago is a sad case in point – it crumbled when exposed to air (Spence and Harper 1968).

Despite the presence of rich goods in the mounds, only certain individuals were buried with valuables (see Spence, chapter 14). Most people were buried in the mound fill without goods. This suggests that the building of a mound enhanced group solidarity and cohesion by bringing families together on a periodic basis. At the same time, the uneven distribution of socially valued exotic items within the mounds expressed the prestige and power of some and the exclusion of others.

The exotic materials found in mound burials rarely turn up in nearby settlements, and then only as scrap left over from making things. In contrast to the repeated ceremonial gifting during the Huron mortuary ceremony, these valuables seem to have been important primarily as offerings for the souls of the deceased.

Each of the Rice Lake mound clusters shows evidence of large-scale feasting in connection with the burials. Here, archaeologists have encountered tell-tale deposits of ash from cooking fires, large deep fire pits, rock cracked in the fire during the cooking process, and charcoal (Jamieson 2011). The pottery includes those of the considerable size needed to feed large numbers of people. Food remains suggest that the primary foodstuff at the feasts was freshwater mussel, fish, and deer meat. Wild rice, which was present in the lake at this time, was probably also served, even though direct evidence for this has not preserved (see Monckton, chapter 8).

Like all other communal consumption, feasting would have been a way to achieve balance, connection, and holism of the individuals who attended as well as the group. It would have been critical to creating social relationships and alliances, pulling together scattered family groups into united communities. Feasts also were opportunities for individuals to forge and mark their identity, to signal notable occasions, and to amass prestige through acts of generosity.

But how far back in time do archaeologists see evidence for such large scale feasting in Ontario? Some 7,500 years ago, people at the McIntyre Site, located a short distance west of Serpent Mounds, dug more than thirty large conical fire pits to a depth of as much as one metre below the ground (Johnston 1984) (figure 12.4). Archaeologists who unearthed the pits in the 1970s found that they contained fire-blackened soil, fire-cracked rock, and disintegrated charcoal – good evidence for cooking and, given the large number of these pits, for cooking on a large scale over a period of time. Such symbolically charged valuables as copper blades, points, pins, and adzes were found nearby. The copper reflects ritual activities; it originates from the distant end of Lake Superior and is both of the earth and earth-coloured (see Oberholtzer, chapter 11). As at the later Rice Lake mounds, offering and consuming foods at McIntyre would have been significant acts of generosity, promoting mutual well-being and bringing prestige to those individuals or groups who hosted the ceremonies. The scale of feasting at McIntyre strongly suggests that quite sizeable groups may have been involved, with a need for some sort of socially integrating ritual.

Figure 12.4
Excavations at the McIntyre Site uncovered more than thirty large pits. The pits initially appeared to be large dark stains in the earth. (A) Students dug out the contents of each pit by carefully following the contour where the darkened soil met the lighter surrounding earth (B). The rocks piled up behind the excavated pit were identified as fire-cracked rock, based on the way that the stones fractured after heating. The size of the pits, along with the rocks and other signs of burning, suggests that they were used to roast foods such as game and roots.
(Photos by R.B. Johnston)

Luxury Goods, Maize, and Politics

As the Neutral, Huron, and Rice Lake examples show, archaeologists have found marked differences through time and from one region to another in the way that Aboriginal peoples in southern Ontario made and used valued goods. I have focused here on some of the more obvious signs available to us from Ontario's long history, but there are other examples I could have chosen. In this chapter I noted that people obtained valuables through trade networks that involved mutual flows of information and objects. These exotic goods and materials were likely used in relatively large-scale prestige-building activities, based on acts of generosity. As we move further back in time, evidence for this sort of behaviour becomes increasingly rare. Although a pattern of gift giving is evident at all time periods, prior to about 7,500 years ago most people seem to have used valuables mostly in local, small-scale gifting. Typically, these gifts were used until they were no longer serviceable and then were discarded. In a few cases, they were deposited as part of a ritual. As part of this persistent early pattern, people quarried chert or flint from the places on the land that were important parts of Aboriginal worldviews, then traded the stone widely hand-to-hand throughout southern Ontario (see Ellis, chapter 2).

Some archaeologists have made the case that there is a connection between farming and the demand for luxury foods used in communal feasting. In southern Ontario, gathering and hunting peoples living along the Grand River, near Hamilton, and in the Rice Lake area, south of Peterborough, may have initially imported maize around 500 CE as a feast food which was used to cement social ties. If so, its gradual incorporation into the everyday diet over a period of several centuries (see Keenleyside, chapter 13) was an outgrowth of its importance as a feast food at a time when societies were becoming more politically complex. In this scenario, archaeologists think that feasting created a demand for maize that ultimately could only be met by adopting a farming lifestyle. Interestingly, early maize is commonly found at camp sites located in areas where wild rice grew (Crawford et al. 2006; Lee et al. 2004); even today, Ontario's First Nations regard both wild rice and maize as sacred plants.

Over time, Ontario's political systems varied in their degrees of integration. For thousands of years, people lived in small, family-centred gathering and hunting groups, moving about within their communal territories. These family-centred groups selected their leaders for specific short-term purposes, based on an individual's experience, personal traits, or knowledge of ritual, curing, or hunting.

Eventually, environmental change and improved techniques for getting food made it possible for larger groups to come together seasonally where resources were particularly plentiful. The Rice Lake area was one such location where family groups began to congregate during the warm seasons of the year, around 7,500 years ago. The plentiful food created seasonal surpluses, prompting generosity through sharing foods, as well as valued objects and knowledge gleaned from distant locations.

It may have been generosity itself that led the people to adopt maize, valued as a luxury food for feasting. As they settled into farming communities, family hierarchies and relatively permanent leadership began to emerge among certain groups. The prestige and status of leaders became something subject to negotiation, with the approval of the group they represented. By the time the French first came into Ontario in the early 1600s, they found Aboriginal groups with developed social and political hierarchies.

13

Skeletal Evidence of Health and Disease among Iroquoians

Anne Keenleyside

Health is the product of a complex interaction between biology, the environment, and behaviour. People who study the health of modern-day populations examine a wide range of factors: lifestyle, diet and nutrition, cultural background, physical fitness, socioeconomic status, employment, education, and access to medical care. Bioarchaeologists who investigate the health of populations that are no longer living take a similar approach, looking at the interaction of biological, environmental, and social factors. We have much more limited information, however, and we rely to a large extent on key sources like early historic accounts, archaeological evidence, and the physical remains of the once-living people themselves.

With respect to Ontario Iroquoian peoples, the Jesuits' eyewitness accounts provide us with general comments on the people's health, describe the health hazards that these communities faced, and document outbreaks of disease during the 1600s and 1700s (Thwaites 1896–1901). Archaeological data such as the size and number of longhouses tell us something about the size and density of these populations (see Ferris, chapter 6) – important factors in terms of the spread of disease. Finally, human skeletal remains provide direct evidence of diseases and other ailments that afflicted Iroquoian peoples.

Despite these varied sources of information, reconstructing the health of populations that lived hundreds or thousands of years ago is no easy task. Eyewitness accounts recorded by the Jesuits make only brief references to health. Their descriptions of symptoms associated with outbreaks of disease may apply to a number of different diseases, creating uncertainty about what exactly caused the outbreaks. In the case of skeletal remains, acute diseases such as measles and influenza do not affect the skeleton. Thus only chronic diseases leave traces in bone. Even then, some diseases affect bone in only a small percentage of cases, or individuals may die before they develop lesions, the physical signs of disease that are left on bones. Even when lesions are present, it can be difficult to diagnose which disease was responsible, as different disease-causing microorganisms may produce similar bone changes. Incomplete and fragmentary skeletal remains also pose a challenge to reconstructing the health of past populations. For instance, lesions may not be present on the bones that archaeologists find. In some cases, bones that have been damaged by disease may be more likely to decay.

Studying Ancient Bones

Constructing the health profile of a population that lived long ago requires knowledge of the age and sex of the skeletons from a given site or area. We can often determine the sex of an individual and estimate the person's age-at-death by looking at certain characteristics of his or her bones and teeth. Knowing the sex and age of individuals can help us more accurately diagnose skeletal lesions, determine the life expectancy at birth, and calculate the sex- and age-based prevalence of disease.

Creating a demographic profile of Ontario Iroquoian populations, however, is greatly hindered by the biased nature of skeletal samples – that is, the collection of bones recovered from a particular burial or site does not necessarily reflect everyone who lived in the area. Skeletal remains from ossuaries (see Spence, chapter 14), communal graves that contain the remains of individuals who have been reburied, are

SIDEBAR 13.1

Sexing and Aging Skeletons Anne Keenleyside

Bioarchaeologists can get a great deal of information from human skeletal remains, including the sex and age-at-death of the deceased. One of the most common methods used to determine sex is to look at features of the pelvic bones. For example, the opening of the pelvis (the pelvic inlet) is larger in females than it is in males in order to facilitate childbirth. Sex differences are also reflected in the skull. In general, males have larger, more robust skulls with heavier muscle attachments and larger brow ridges. They also tend to have a more square-shaped chin in contrast to females, who have a more rounded chin. Since sex differences in the skull and pelvic bones do not become readily apparent until after puberty, it is usually impossible to

determine the sex of individuals below this age.

The age of an individual when he or she died can be estimated for both children and adults. In the case of infants and children, the stage of formation and eruption of the teeth and the length of the long bones can provide an approximate age-at-death, within a range of a few years. For young adults and older individuals, however, age estimation becomes more difficult and is based primarily on degeneration of the skeleton. Methods include examining changes in the appearance of the rib ends and the joint between the pubic bones (the pubic symphysis), closure of the cranial sutures, and the degree of wear on the teeth, which is also linked to diet.

Figure 13.1

This remarkable bone pit, known as the Teston Ossuary, was full of the bones of up to 400 individuals, carefully placed there by community members after the flesh had decayed away. The pit was uncovered in 2005, when construction crews working on widening a road cut into it with heavy equipment, shattering the bones. Archaeological Services Inc. was called in to document the remains, which were eventually reburied through the efforts of elders of the Huron-Wendat of Quebec, the Mississauga of Scugog Island, and Six Nations of Grand River working with officials from Vaughan and York Region. (Courtesy of Archaeological Services Inc., used with permission of the Huron-Wendat Nation.)

especially tricky. Remains from ossuaries are often commingled with bones from multiple individuals mixed together, making it difficult or impossible to identify individual skeletons (figure 13.1). Sometimes archaeologists are unable to recover all parts of the skeletons. The bones of the very young and the very old tend to be more poorly preserved due to their fragile nature. As well, sometimes the living excluded certain individuals from the ossuary for various reasons.

Despite these limitations, the age and sex distribution of such skeletal samples may offer clues to the health of the populations from which these individuals were derived. For instance, bioarchaeologists have compared remains from two different ossuaries: one from Moatfield, a village site (1300 CE) located in Toronto, and the other

SIDEBAR 13.2

The Ethics of Studying Human Remains   Anne Keenleyside

The collection and study of human remains have long been surrounded by controversy and debate (Buikstra 2006; Walker 2008). The manner in which Aboriginal remains in Canada are studied is determined separately by various institutes, municipalities, provinces, and territories. Some communities consider taking photographs of Aboriginal human remains for publication or other purposes to be disrespectful to their ancestors, and bioarchaeologists wishing to take such photographs as part of a scientific study are typically required to seek permission from the relevant First Nations to do so. Other individuals are interested in learning more about their ancestors, including information that can be recovered by examining or testing their bones (see Spence, chapter 14).

Bioarchaeologists need to balance the desires and rights of descendant communities with their professional obligations to gather knowledge about the past and publish their work for the future. The authors of this book collectively discussed whether or not to include images of bones. Ultimately, we decided that it was important to show readers examples of ossuary burials and the types of information, such as evidence of disease, that we can learn from ancient bones.

from Uxbridge (late 1400s CE), located 100 kilometres northeast of Toronto. A greater proportion of older adults interred at Moatfield suggests that inhabitants of that area had better health and a longer lifespan than the people interred at Uxbridge (Merrett 2003). In contrast, a high proportion of young adults in some samples may reflect epidemics to which this segment of the population succumbed.

It is rarely possible to determine an individual's cause of death from his or her skeleton. Nevertheless, a wide range of ailments suffered during life may be recorded in an individual's bones and teeth, and these indicators of stress, as we call them, provide valuable information on the health, diet and nutritional status, and behaviour of that individual.

We know from studies of skeletal remains that nutritional deficiencies were a common occurrence in the past. Porous lesions that appear as pitting on the vault of the skull and on the roof of the eye socket have been linked to several forms of anaemia, including childhood episodes of iron deficiency anaemia resulting from a low dietary intake of iron, poor intestinal absorption of iron, or loss of iron due to infectious diseases. These lesions may also result from other nutritional deficiencies such as scurvy (vitamin C deficiency) and rickets (vitamin D deficiency), as well as tumors and eye infections. Nutritional stresses or infectious diseases during childhood can also disrupt the growth of the skeleton, leading to defects known as Harris lines, which are visible in X-rays as white lines in the long bones of children's arms and legs.

Traumatic injuries can also affect bone. The most common of these are fractures, and numerous examples have been observed in ossuary samples. Such injuries can provide insight into the lives of past peoples. Many of the traumatic injuries recorded

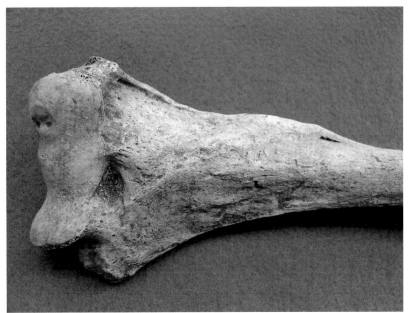

Figure 13.2
Bioarchaeologists use their knowledge of skeletal anatomy to identify signs of illness. This humerus, or upper arm bone, shows signs of a healed fracture. A normal humerus would taper neatly from the elbow joint (left of photo) toward the other end of the shaft. The thick, misshapen section of this shaft shows where new growth repaired the break. This example is from an ancient Greek burial. (Courtesy of Anne Keenleyside.)

in ossuary samples consist of fractures to the ribs, bones of the hands and feet, clavicle (collarbone), and vertebrae (neck and backbones). The location and nature of these injuries suggest that many were caused by accidents during day-to-day activities.

Fractures can also tell us something about the level of interpersonal conflict in the past. Unhealed fractures to the skull and facial bones, for example, are often a sign of violent encounters. The manner in which fractures have healed can also provide clues to a community's knowledge of medical treatment. A fractured bone that is poorly set (figure 13.2), for instance, suggests a lack of knowledge about how to properly treat a broken bone. Complications resulting from a fracture can have implications in terms of an individual's ability to survive on his or her own. Severe fractures, for instance, may have meant a loss of mobility, making it difficult to obtain food.

A variety of infectious diseases can also leave their mark on the skeleton. Some of these diseases are nonspecific in nature, meaning that they can be caused by a variety of different disease-causing microorganisms, many of them bacteria. The lesions resulting from these infections typically take the form of a buildup of new bone on the outer surface of the affected area, or lesions extending into the marrow cavity inside the bone. They can be caused by a localized infection, such as an overlying skin ulcer, by an infection that has spread through the bloodstream from another location in the body, or from a wound. In addition to nonspecific infections, a host of specific infectious diseases, such as tuberculosis and venereal syphilis, can also alter the skeleton. The presence of these diseases in bone reflects chronic conditions that may or may not have been the immediate cause of death of the affected individual.

Figure 13.3
Cavities were a potentially serious problem in the days before fillings and antibiotics. This photo shows several of the upper molars of an individual from an ancient Greek colony in Bulgaria. At least two of these teeth have cavities, including the gaping hole visible on the right side of the largest tooth. (Courtesy of Anne Kennleyside.)

A study of dental disease can reveal aspects of the health and diet of a population. Teeth provide information on the type and nature of foods consumed and the level of oral hygiene (figure 13.3). They may also reflect nutritional and disease stress (and even the use of the teeth as tools). The level of tooth decay is an important indicator of diet. Cavities are associated with the consumption of carbohydrates, especially sugars. Individuals in farming societies, for example, often show high numbers of cavities because of their heavy reliance on carbohydrate-rich corn and other cereals, which break down into sugars when digested. High rates of tooth decay may eventually lead to the loss of teeth in an individual's lifetime, either from the complete destruction of the tooth or through intentional extraction of the tooth to reduce pain. Tooth decay, trauma, or heavy wear can also end up exposing the pulp cavity of the tooth, allowing bacteria to infiltrate the crown and root, causing inflammation and the formation of an abscess. This was no small matter in the days before antibiotics, for abscesses could cause blood poisoning – and even death – as the bacteria spread through the person's body.

Nutritional stress or infectious diseases can also disrupt the formation of the enamel on the teeth, causing permanent defects on the surface of the teeth. Such defects provide a permanent record into adulthood of episodes of stress from early childhood. High levels of tooth wear can result from eating a diet of uncooked and unrefined food items such as coarse cereal grains. Eating poorly washed foods or foods like grains, ground with grinding stones, also creates wear on teeth by introducing particles of grit into the diet.

Osteoarthritis, or degenerative joint disease, also reflects the health and lifestyle of people from the past. Just as many elderly people today experience the aches and pains of arthritis in their hips, knees, and other joints, so too did people who lived hundreds of years ago. The prevalence and distribution of arthritic bone changes can tell us something about activity patterns and workload. Congenital abnormalities, such as cleft palate or club foot, are also visible in skeletal remains. The survival to adulthood of some individuals with such conditions suggests that they may have received care and assistance from other members of their group.

High-Tech Analyses

In recent years, bioarchaeologists have used more sophisticated analytical techniques to study human skeletal remains, drawing out more information about the health of past peoples than was previously possible. The chemical analysis of bones, for instance, can reveal a great deal of information about the diet of past peoples. Traditional sources of dietary information provide an idea of the range of foods available, while analysis of collagen, the protein found in bone, shows which foods a person actually ate. For example, studying stable isotopes of carbon and nitrogen in bone collagen can tell us something about the types of plant foods eaten and the proportion of marine versus land-based foods in the diet. Such studies have helped detect the introduction of maize agriculture and are used to investigate changes in diet over time. The extraction and analysis of DNA from archaeological remains can also tell us something about the types of diseases that afflicted early peoples of Ontario.

Health before the Europeans

Studies of bones from ossuaries dating to the pre-contact period have played a significant role in assessing the impact of European contact on the health of Aboriginal peoples. A great deal of debate has surrounded the health status of these populations prior to contact, and many have long held the belief that Aboriginal peoples enjoyed a virtually disease-free existence. Indeed, some historic accounts from the early contact period include references to Iroquoians as being healthy. French missionary Jean de Brébeuf, for example, described the Huron in the 1600s as being "more healthy than we" (Thwaites 1896–1901, vol. 38, 257). Within the last fifteen years, however, researchers have amassed a considerable body of data indicating that Aboriginal peoples in Ontario and elsewhere in North America were by no means disease-free prior to contact (Verano and Ubelaker 1992). Rather, they suffered from a variety of ailments, some of which made them particularly vulnerable to diseases introduced by Europeans.

Studies of the distribution and determinants of disease in modern situations have shown that the presence of a disease-causing microorganism is not enough in itself to cause disease. Instead, social and environmental conditions dictate whether or not exposure to such organisms leads to disease. It is therefore essential to consider not only the type of disease-causing organisms that may have been present in the environment but also the cultural and behavioural factors that may have facilitated the transmission of these organisms to humans.

We can gain insight into the types of health problems that likely afflicted Iroquoians by examining disease in modern-day groups who get much of their food by hunting and gathering. We know from archaeological evidence that Archaic and Early Woodland peoples used a wide range of plants and animals (see Needs-Howarth, chapter 7, and Monckton, chapter 8). Close contact with animals would have placed people at risk of infections that can be transmitted to humans. For example, parasites such as pinworms and tapeworms can infect people who eat raw or undercooked meat, or who handle carcasses during butchering. Insect or animal bites may also have transmitted infectious diseases from animal hosts to humans. In addition, the early inhabitants of Ontario would have been exposed to a variety of bacteria, such as those that cause strep throat today, and food-borne pathogens like salmonella.

The Draper Site, a village in Pickering, offers a good example of the health problems that plagued Iroquoians in the 1400s. Jesuit accounts from the early contact period describe longhouses such as those found at Draper as crowded, smoke-filled environments (see Ferris, chapter 6). The Iroquois used central hearths to cook food and provide heat, but those same fires also meant chronic exposure to smoke that could have contributed to the development of respiratory and sinus infections. Biological anthropologist Shelley Saunders and her colleagues (1992) have argued that as the size and density of Iroquoian populations increased during the 1400s, crowded living conditions both within the longhouses and within villages would have facilitated the spread of airborne infections. In addition, refuse dumps located close to living quarters would have attracted rodents, dogs, and insects such as mosquitoes and ticks, which are known to carry diseases that can be transmitted to humans. The existence of widespread trade networks along which large numbers of people would have moved, would also have allowed for the transmission of diseases from one community to another.

While some infectious diseases require a large number of individuals in order to be maintained in a population, others can be maintained for long periods of time in small groups. A good example is tuberculosis, a disease that has been documented in both pre- and post-contact Ontario Iroquoian skeletons. Tuberculosis is sometimes visible in the form of destructive lesions of the vertebrae or lesions on the inner surfaces of the ribs. Bioarchaeologists have documented such lesions in remains from one part of the Serpent Mounds Site (900–1300 CE) near Rice Lake and in a number of pre-contact ossuaries, including Uxbridge and Moatfield, mentioned earlier, and those associated with the fourteenth-century sites of Glen Williams in Halton region and Fairty in Markham. Uxbridge in particular shows a very high frequency of bone lesions characteristic of tuberculosis. In fact, DNA analysis of two vertebrae from the ossuary has confirmed the presence of the disease in this region by the mid-1400s (Braun et al. 1998). Tuberculosis affects the skeleton in only 5–7 percent of cases, so its substantial presence in the Uxbridge bones suggests that a high percentage of the people had the disease (Pfeiffer 1984).

Bioarchaeologists have also documented non-specific bone infections in ossuary samples. For example, researchers have found lesions, perhaps from meningitis, on the inner surface of several skulls of young people from the Moatfield ossuary (Dupras 2003). A large number of individuals buried in the Moatfield and Uxbridge ossuaries have lesions in their sinus cavities, suggesting that they had sinus infections caused by respiratory illnesses and chronic exposure to smoke from wood fires (Merrett 2003; Merrett and Pfeiffer 2000).

Traumatic injuries are also common in many pre-contact skeletons. Most of these are healed fractures resulting from accidental injuries. Others resulted from interpersonal violence, attesting to the presence of warfare among Ontario Iroquoians. For example, at the fifteenth-century Quackenbush Site located near Peterborough, Ontario, archaeologists found nine individuals with cranial fractures (Helmuth 1993). The skeleton of one unfortunate adult from the twelfth-century Miller site in York region had the tip of a projectile point embedded in one of its vertebrae (Ossenberg 1969) (figure 13.4).

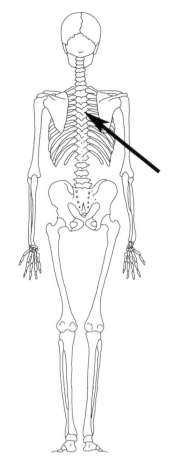

Figure 13.4
Bioarchaeologists studying human remains from the Miller Site discovered that one individual had a stone projectile point embedded in one of his or her vertebrae. (Drawing by Marit Munson.)

Chemical analyses of pre-contact ossuary remains indicate that maize was introduced into southern Ontario by 500 CE (see Monckton, chapter 8) and that its consumption peaked around 1300 CE or slightly earlier (Katzenberg et al. 1995). Despite being a good source of dietary fibre, protein, vitamins, and minerals, a heavy reliance on maize has been linked to numerous health problems, including nutritional deficiencies resulting from the lack of key nutrients, and infectious diseases to which malnourished individuals would have been more susceptible. Increased rates of tooth decay from the Early to Late Woodland period point to the increased consumption of carbohydrates, corresponding with chemical evidence for a greater reliance on maize in the centuries leading up to contact. The common occurrence in pre-contact skeletal remains of porous lesions on the roof of the eye socket, possibly reflecting iron deficiency anaemia and nonspecific infections, may also reflect, in part, the increased consumption of maize. Nutritional or disease stress also had an impact on individuals' growth, as evident by the presence of Harris lines in X-rays of immature long bones (figure 13.5).

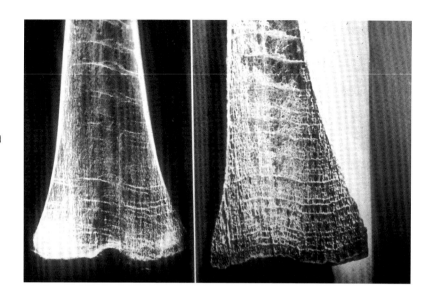

Figure 13.5
These X-rays clearly show a series of lines, known as Harris lines, that mark places where this individual's growth was delayed due to periods of nutritional stress while his or her bones were growing. (Copyright BARC, Archaeological Sciences, University of Bradford.)

Post-contact Health

Few dispute the devastating impact that infectious diseases introduced by Europeans had on Aboriginal populations in Ontario and elsewhere in North America. Most notable among these were measles and smallpox, diseases that were common childhood afflictions among Europeans, whose recovery from such ailments rendered them immune for life. Aboriginal people, who had never been exposed before, therefore lacked immunity or resistance to these diseases. The first recorded outbreak of European disease among the Huron occurred in 1634, when an epidemic of what may have been measles killed approximately 20 percent of the population. From 1634 to 1640, subsequent outbreaks of smallpox and other diseases decimated Huron communities and those of their neighbours (see Warrick, chapter 4), reducing the population from an estimated 30,000 to 12,000 (Warrick 2003). As noted earlier, acute diseases such as these leave no evidence in bone, though bioarchaeologists have documented bone lesions interpreted as resulting from smallpox in a Neutral skeleton dating to shortly before 1650 (Jackes 1983).

In addition to acute infectious diseases such as measles and smallpox, Ontario Iroquoians were also afflicted with a variety of chronic ailments in the contact period. Lesions suggestive of venereal syphilis and tuberculosis have been documented in remains from a number of early contact period ossuaries. These diseases would have had consequences not only for the overall health of afflicted individuals but also for their fertility. Venereal syphilis and other types of sexually transmitted diseases such as gonorrhea, for example, can lead to infertility if untreated. Similarly, genital tuberculosis is a major cause of infertility in developing countries today.

Warfare and famine also exacted a heavy toll on Iroquoian communities (see Warrick, chapter 4). The Jesuits remarked that war, famine, and sickness had been particularly prevalent among the Neutral during the early 1640s (figure 13.6). In 1643, famine linked to unusually harsh winters was recorded among the Huron and neighbouring groups. Aside from reduced fertility and the risk of starvation, individuals whose health was compromised by malnutrition may have been particularly vulnerable to outbreaks of disease. Malnutrition would also have had an impact on an individual's ability to engage in physical labour. The removal of the most productive members of society through illness and death would have had a significant impact on the ability of those left behind to feed themselves.

Bioarchaeological studies have much to tell us about the health of past populations and can provide us with an important perspective on that of modern-day populations as well. The integration of historic, archaeological, and skeletal evidence provides valuable information on patterns of health and disease in pre- and post-contact Iroquoian populations of southern Ontario. It is clear from these sources that the health status of many of these communities was already compromised prior to contact. As a consequence, they may have been even more susceptible to diseases introduced by Europeans.

Figure 13.6
Father Lafitau's 1724 manuscript includes this depiction of warfare among First Nations, including the defenders within a palisaded longhouse village. Such conflicts likely caused some of the fractures seen in their skeletal remains.

14

Death and Burial in Woodland Times

Michael W. Spence

The dead do not bury themselves. It is the survivors, the living members of the community, who plan and conduct funeral rites. They are the ones who determine how to treat the body, where to place the burial, and what things to put with it for the afterlife. When archaeologists examine an ancient burial, we are likely to learn at least as much about the society that the person lived in as we do about the deceased person in particular. In the small traditional societies that lived in southern Ontario, death would have had a profound impact on the community, in the personal grief felt by those closest to the deceased as well as the wider social dislocation caused by the death. Relationships had to be readjusted, duties and roles reassigned.

Death was one of the principal and most disturbing events in the social life of a community, so the people often marked it with elaborate rituals. In fact, many early Ontario societies had what seems to us a bewildering variety of mortuary practices. People were buried in the ground, exposed on platforms, cremated, stripped of their flesh, dismembered, or prepared in a variety of other ways. In some cases, the rituals for a deceased person continued over a decade or more. To complicate matters further for the archaeologist, there is no universal link between any particular mortuary practice and the facts of the deceased person's life or identity. Cremation, for example, may be reserved for high-ranking people in one society, for low-ranking people in another, and for people who died in a particular way in a third – or it may simply be a practical way to reduce the body to a more manageable package for transport to a distant burial place.

SIDEBAR 14.1

Primary and Secondary Burial Michael Spence

Here we encounter a complex distinction that – although it seems rather strange to us – was an important component of ancient Ontario mortuary programs: primary versus secondary burial. Primary burial occurs at or shortly after death. It may involve burial in the ground, exposure on a platform, storage in some sort of container or structure, or even cremation. The archaeologist excavating a primary burial can often expect to find a fully articulated skeleton, with all of its bones present and in their proper positions.

In many cases, though, primary burial was not the end of things. After some time, whether weeks or several years, people might exhume the body (or parts of it) and bury it a second time – the second-

ary burial. The archaeologist will then encounter a skeleton that is at most only partially articulated, as the body would have decomposed and fallen apart in the primary burial. Secondary burials are often missing some body parts, either because they were overlooked when the primary burial was exhumed or were simply discarded as unimportant. Secondary burials also frequently hold the bones of more than one person. This prolonged mortuary process was usually meant to ensure that the dead of the community received their final burial together, so they could continue to dwell together in the afterlife – just as each of us, at death, hopes to be buried with our family.

Understanding Burial Practices

To bring some order to this rather chaotic picture, archaeologists try to tease out the standard set of procedures in a society's handling of death – its mortuary program. We also consider alternative mortuary tracks, the less common practices that are reserved for individuals who held some special position in the society – chief, criminal, newborn infant – or who died a certain kind of death, or in some other way stood apart from the rest.

Understanding a society's mortuary program can provide important insights into their beliefs and social structure. Still, there is little about this endeavour that is straightforward (Carr 1995). The ancient people of Ontario, just like us today, sometimes manipulated burial rituals for their own advantage. Funeral rites usually involved most of the community, so they provided an ideal venue for this sort of social manoeuvring (see Jamieson, chapter 12). Individuals may have put forward personal claims and tried to revise social facts.

Huron society in southern Ontario in the 1600s is a good example. After the intrusion of French missionaries and traders disrupted Huron society, aspiring leaders seeking to attract supporters became involved in periodic large funeral ceremonies (Cannon 1989). Large amounts of wealth changed hands in these ceremonies, in the form of local materials like furs and hides, as well as European trade materials like glass beads, iron axes, and copper kettles. The ostentatious displays of generosity (and, we suspect, quiet acquisition of wealth and power) by Huron leaders worried

Jesuit observers, who feared that some families were impoverishing themselves in these exchanges. They did not realize that this apparently profligate expenditure was really a form of political investment (Jamieson 2011).

Despite such examples, social manipulations of Ontario burial practices may have been fairly limited. For one thing, the social independence and status competition that often underlie them may have been of less importance in these societies, at least until the arrival of the Europeans (see Jamieson, chapter 12). After all, most individuals in the small bands of the Early and Middle Woodland periods (900 BCE–800 CE) would have had frequent face-to-face contact. When an individual is well known, there is little room for claims that seriously distort the facts. It would be like a man from a small Ontario farming community insisting he was the illegitimate child of the British royal family. His fellow villagers would know to just nod and smile when he claimed to be in line for the throne.

In the larger and more socially complex Late Woodland (800–1650 CE) societies, this intimacy might have been less of an obstacle. Members would have had less direct contact and personal knowledge of one another. Late Woodland peoples seem to have balanced this opportunity for personal aggrandizement with burial practices designed to mute the individual identities of the deceased, removing the basis on which the living might make extravagant social claims. Instead, Late Woodland burial practices seem to emphasize larger groups, like the lineage and community, over the individual.

Early Woodland Cemeteries

The Meadowood people of the Early Woodland period (900–400 BCE) were one group who used secondary burial as a way to keep their deceased together. The Meadowood people lived in small mobile bands of twenty-five to fifty individuals. They moved seasonally, settling for a period of weeks or months at prime spots to harvest local wild foods (see Williamson, chapter 3). Their most favoured place was the location of the band cemetery. Over the course of a year, one or two people in the band might die – of old age, accident, or health problems in infancy or childhood. If they died near the cemetery, they would receive a primary and final burial there. If, however, they died at some more distant place, their relatives would keep their bodies – store them, in effect – until they could be brought to the cemetery. Many of the burials in the cemetery would be secondary burials, the bodies having already suffered some decomposition (or even deliberate reduction for ease of transport) before arriving at the cemetery.

This pattern of secondary burials shows up clearly in the Meadowood cemetery known as the Bruce Boyd Site (Spence et al. 1978), on the north shore of Lake Erie. The cemetery as a whole may have included the band dead from a decade or two. Most of the individuals buried there were at least slightly disarticulated – some of

SIDEBAR 14.2

The Social Functions of Cemeteries   Michael Spence

Cemeteries made their first appearance in Ontario in the Terminal Archaic period (1500–900 BCE). As areas devoted exclusively to the burial of the band dead, they reflect a developing communal ethos. Some archaeologists believe that their major function was to establish a claim against rival bands to a territory and its resources. Certainly they did that – what better land claim than the burial of your ancestors there? However, at this time populations were small and dispersed, with more than enough land for everybody and no evidence of conflict.

More likely the socially potent aspect of cemeteries lay not in their message to outsiders but rather in the rituals performed within their boundaries. In these small societies burial rituals would have commanded the attention of everybody, either as participants or as audience. The ceremonies would have become the venue for the social readjustments made necessary by death. Others would have to take over the deceased's duties – providing for the family, conducting special rituals, or manufacturing particular items like pots or knives. As part of the ceremony these roles would be reassigned, other members of the band publicly accepting responsibility for them. The community would be reaffirmed, redefined, and ultimately strengthened through its ritual management of loss.

their bones were out of place or missing. Some were almost completely disarticulated and about one-quarter of them had been cremated. Several had been painted with red ochre. The survivors had placed offerings with many of the bodies, but most often with the adult men. These included copper beads, a stone pendant, iron pyrites used to strike a spark to make fire, a stone axe, flint arrow- and spear-points, and preforms or blanks of flint ready to be made into points (figure 14.1; see also Fox, chapter 9). The grave of an elderly man and an infant, who probably died in the same year, had offerings of many different foods: parts of at least six deer, a dog or wolf, a fox, a woodchuck, three wild turkeys, and sixteen fish of nine different species. These offerings clearly represent the hunting and fishing efforts of many individuals.

The Bruce Boyd cemetery includes other evidence of group rituals beyond the burial rites associated with the individual dead. When I excavated there, I found two caches of stone tools and blanks ready to be made into finished tools. One cache included several flint items (ten points, two drills, and seventeen blanks), an iron pyrite fire-making kit, and two distinctive and beautifully made stone gorgets (figure 14.2). The presence of the gorgets – let alone the location of the caches in a cemetery – suggests that this was not just storage of materials for the future (figure 14.3). Neither cache was associated with any particular burial; instead, they may have been communal offerings to the collective band dead, materials that they could all draw upon in the afterlife.

Figure 14.1 *Right*
These Meadowood projectile points (top) and flint blanks (bottom) are typical of the kinds of tools found placed with burials in the Early Woodland period. These artifacts come from the Bruce Boyd Site. (Photo by Christopher Ellis.)

Figure 14.2 *Below*
The Bruce Boyd Site, near Long Point, included a Meadowood offering that contained an iron pyrite ("fool's gold") fire-making kit, and two beautifully finished trapezoidal gorgets, and more than two dozen flint points, drills, and blanks. (Courtesy of Archaeological Services Inc.)

Figure 14.3
This slate gorget, one of two recovered from the offering shown in figure 14.2, has a series of fine scratches on its dark surface – marks left from the abrasive used in shaping and smoothing the piece. The person who made it drilled the two central holes using a hollow bone or reed, along with grit as an abrasive. Archaeologists believe that the gorgets were probably suspended from a cord tied through the holes, though it is not clear exactly why. Such gorgets could have been worn as jewellery, or perhaps were suspended from a wooden staff and carried as a badge of office. (Photo by Christopher Ellis.)

0   2cm

The Middle Woodland and the Rice Lake Mounds

Aboriginal people in the Middle Woodland period (400 BCE–800 CE) continued to bury their dead in cemeteries, but with some changes (Spence et al. 1990). At the Donaldson Site on the Bruce Peninsula, for example, most of the people in the two small cemeteries were in primary burials, fully articulated (Finlayson 1977; Molto 1979; Wright and Anderson 1963). The Donaldson people, like other Middle Woodland bands in southern Ontario, were somewhat more settled than their ancestors, so more deaths probably happened within reach of the band cemetery. Grave offerings at the Donaldson Site accompanied women and children, not just adult men. In fact, in the later of the two Donaldson cemeteries only the infants and children had offerings, often strings of small shell beads that had been traded in from the Atlantic coast. This may mark the first appearance of more widespread social groups, the lineages and clans that became common in the later Late Woodland societies (see Warrick, chapter 4, and Jamieson, chapter 12). These kin groups provided a broad safety net for individuals and families, a wide network of relatives who aided and supported one another. One of their main concerns was always to maintain and increase their membership through the production and raising of children. Women, and especially children, were thus of crucial importance to these groups, and their deaths were a matter of great communal concern.

Middle Woodland people living in the Rice Lake area created one of the most complex mortuary programs of their time (about 1–200 CE). Like their contemporaries at the Donaldson Site, the Rice Lake people placed precious goods in the graves of women and children: carved stone pipes, beads of shell, copper and silver, shell pendants, and copper and silver sheaths for reed panpipes (Kenyon 1986) (figure 14.4). The shell came from the Atlantic, the copper from the Lake Superior region, and the silver from the Cobalt area some 400 kilometres to the north – a testament to the remarkable breadth of Middle Woodland trade networks.

The mortuary cycle of the Rice Lake people was considerably longer than that of their neighbours. The burial mound at Cameron's Point (figure 14.5), which contains the remains of at least sixty-nine people, provides a clear view of this emerging pattern (Dougherty 2003; Spence and Harper 1968). Eleven adults and children were placed in pits dug into the original ground surface beneath the base of the mound. They were either fully or partially articulated and often had grave offerings. The rest of the bodies were placed in the fill of the mound as it was being raised. These fill burials were extensively or completely disarticulated, and only two of them had offerings.

The human bones in the fill were clustered in five distinct concentrations through the mound, generally above corresponding clusters of sub-floor burials. It seems that the contributing community – those who buried their dead at Cameron's Point – consisted of five subgroups. Three adults in one of the bone concentrations had a very rare, genetically based trait, relating to the way that the bones of the upper forehead knit together. This trait only occurs in 0.4 people per 1,000, and only one or two cases are known from elsewhere in early Ontario. This suggests that each of the concentrations of burials represents the dead of a group of closely related people, like an extended family or small lineage within the larger community.

Figure 14.4
Copper from the shore of Lake Superior was a valued offering in Middle Woodland burials. This copper sheath for panpipes came from Cameron's Point Mound C in the Rice Lake area, south of Peterborough. (Courtesy of William F. Fox.)

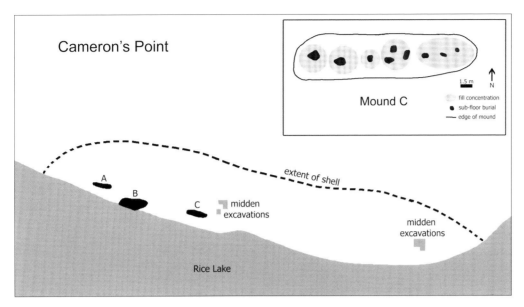

Figure 14.5
The Cameron's Point Mounds are located on the east end of Rice Lake, where the Trent River flows out toward the Bay of Quinte. The mounds were first reported in the late 1800s; by the 1960s, erosion from the lake had claimed mounds B and C. Archaeologists who examined the site in 1964 noted a broad area littered with shell fragments – presumably the remains of a large midden or trash deposit. The inset image is a map of mound C, with black marking the location of burials in the "floor," or original ground surface, of the mound. The larger grey ovals indicate burials that were placed in the mound fill. (Drawing by Marit Munson, based on Spence and Harper 1968, figure 2, and Dougherty 2003.)

The sixty-nine people in Cameron's Point Mound C clearly represent the accumulated dead of many years, but the mound itself was built in one continuous effort, rather than a series of additions over time. We can suggest a plausible reconstruction of the burial event: when the people decided that it was time to build a mound, all of the community's deceased were retrieved from their primary graves and carried to the construction site. Those who had died recently enough to still be largely intact were buried first, in pits in the ground. Then the community raised the mound over them, placing the rest of the dead in the fill as the mound grew. Each lineage used a particular part of the structure for their dead. Several years, or perhaps decades, might pass between episodes of mound construction.

This marks a new turn of events, the appearance of a significantly different mortuary program in Ontario. The ritual treatment of the dead continued over a generation or so, not just a single year. The community was more stable and durable, perhaps even a more formally defined group. Except for the most recently deceased, most of the individuals buried in the mound were mixed and anonymous. If any aspect of their previous identities persisted, it was only their membership in larger and longer-lasting kin groups. This shift marks the first appearance of a less individualistic and more inclusive emphasis in Ontario societies.

Late Woodland Ossuaries

In the Late Woodland period (800–1650 CE), mortuary practices shifted along with changing social dynamics. A growing reliance on farming allowed a more stable lifestyle, with long-lasting villages housing hundreds of inhabitants (see Warrick, chapter 4). In the smallest and earliest Late Woodland communities, final burial was still an annual event (Spence 1994). Villagers exhumed those who had died over the course of the year from their original graves, burying them together in a secondary burial pit. Each pit might hold anywhere from a couple to around a dozen incomplete individuals, depending on how large the village was and, perhaps, on what sort of luck the year had brought. No great care was taken to keep the skeletons separate in the pit, and no offerings were left with them. These early farming villages seem to have had an egalitarian and communal ethos, with the identity of the individual absorbed, at least after death, into the larger collective.

As village life became more settled, the major disruption in the community's social life changed. In earlier times, people moved camp seasonally or annually, to take advantage of resources. With more settled villages, the major event was the movement of the whole village to a new location – something that occurred only every decade or so, when the local soils finally became exhausted and unproductive (see Williamson, chapter 3).

As might be expected, the mortuary cycle followed suit in some regions. The community exhumed their dead from their primary graves when the village was abandoned. The final joint burial pit, holding about a decade of accumulated dead, would include dozens or even hundreds of individuals. These larger collective pits are called ossuaries (see figure 12.1). As before, bodies were mixed, or at least not painstakingly separated. The rare instances of offerings seem to have been intended for the collective, rather than for any single individual. For example, at around 1300 CE, people placed a remarkable ceramic pipe with a turtle effigy at the base of the Moatfield ossuary (figure 14.6) (Williamson and Pfeiffer 2003) and parts of a golden eagle were laid on the floor of a Serpent Mounds ossuary.

The Serpent Mounds Site has a lot to tell us about the evolution of burial practices in Ontario (Anderson 1968; Johnston 1968b). It is on Rice Lake, just down the shore from the Cameron's Point Mounds, and was occupied from the Middle Woodland into the Late Woodland periods. Its early features, dating to around 1–200 CE, include burial mounds like those at Cameron's Point. Later mounds at the site date to about 500–800 CE and seem to represent a further evolution of the pattern seen at Cameron's Point. Each mound covers a large pit that contains a multiple burial. Most of the people in it are secondary burials, but the bottom level of each of the pits contains a few complete primary burials. This suggests a longer mortuary cycle, like that at Cameron's Point, though the subgroups that had been separated there were now blended in death. The individual distinctions previously reflected in separate

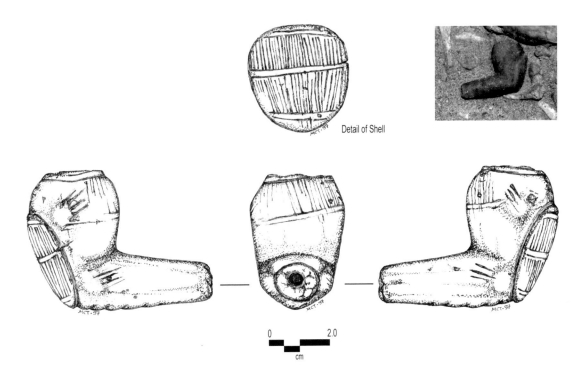

Detail of Shell

0   2.0
cm

sub-floor burials with offerings were no longer recognized. The later mounds were, in effect, ossuaries with mounds over them.

A series of more recent ossuary pits at Serpent Mounds, dating from 900–1300 CE, continued this basic pattern but without the mounding. The Ontario tradition of ossuary burial, with its long mortuary cycle, seems then to have had its earliest appearance in the Rice Lake area, even before the development of stable farming villages. This leaves us with a rather perplexing question: if the prolonged mortuary cycle was not based on village movement (as was the case later), then what did trigger these major burial events?

In other parts of Ontario, Late Woodland burials follow the older pattern of multiple secondary burial on an annual basis. For example, most burial features at the Libby-Miller Site (1500 CE) in Wallaceburg included from two to eight disarticulated and often cremated individuals – with an important exception, discussed shortly. A burial pit at the Dorchester Village Site (1300–1400 CE) near London held eight secondary burials. At a 1400 AD cemetery in Windsor, the burial features each contained from one to nine secondary individuals.

Exceptions to the Late Woodland Rule

The more abundant evidence available for Late Woodland burial practices makes it possible to see some of the exceptions to the rule, the alternative mortuary tracks mentioned earlier. The French traders and missionaries who lived among the Huron

Figure 14.6
A pottery pipe from the Moatfield ossuary depicts a turtle with a grooved shell. The inset photo in the upper right shows the excavation of the pipe. (Courtesy of Archaeological Services Inc.)

Indians in the 1600s mentioned some of these. For example, the Huron often buried infants in houses or other areas that people frequented. Instead of then travelling to the Village of the Dead with those villagers who had been exhumed from their primary graves and then reburied together in the ossuary, these infants would be reincarnated in the wombs of women who passed by their graves.

Beliefs about the reincarnation of infants may have considerable time depth. Of the eighty-seven people in the earlier Moatfield ossuary, only six were infants – far fewer than expected given the high infant mortality that these societies usually suffered (Williamson and Pfeiffer 2003). At the Keffer Site, a Huron village from 1500 CE, I found several infants who had been buried in the village but never exhumed for the ossuary (figure 14.7). Most of their graves were in houses where they would have been exposed to regular traffic, increasing the likelihood of their reincarnation. Two infants, however, were placed in the narrow and virtually inaccessible space between the two parallel palisade rows that encircled and protected the village, a location that ensured no woman would pass near their graves. Their burial treatment was designed to thwart their reincarnation and to exclude them from the ossuary and the Village of the Dead. I can only guess at what led to such drastic treatment, but suspicion centres on the sins of the parents – an incestuous relationship, or an inappropriate liaison? Might these infants have even been victims of infanticide?

Missionaries recorded another alternative mortuary track, the primary and final burial of those who had died a violent death. These unfortunates were denied access to the ossuary, and so to the Village of the Dead, because the Huron believed that their spirits must have been angered by the manner of their death and would have been disruptive influences in the afterlife community. One of the individuals buried in the Draper Site, a Huron village, had clearly died violently – a flint point was embedded in his thigh – and had never been moved to the village ossuary. The Van Oordt Site was a cemetery from 1400 CE for men who had died violently and in some cases had been tortured to death. The area was well beyond any village and the dozen or so burials there were primary burials, though the men had been dismembered.

The earliest case of violent death in Ontario, our oldest cold case, is the Lafarge discovery. The police asked me to investigate a find of human bones from the edge of London, and after a brief study I determined that they represented a single, isolated burial. A more detailed analysis revealed that the Lafarge skeleton was of a man in his early twenties, dating to about 800–1000 CE. He had been struck from behind by four arrows (one of which pierced his heart), stomped on the chest, and then scalped. His burial was primary, unexhumed, and not near any settlement. He may be our earliest indication that, as communities became larger and more formally defined, hostilities sometimes developed between them, and a violent death became a worrisome possibility.

Another alternative mortuary track may have involved individuals with power in the supernatural realm. One early example of this, from 1000 CE, is the "Shaman of

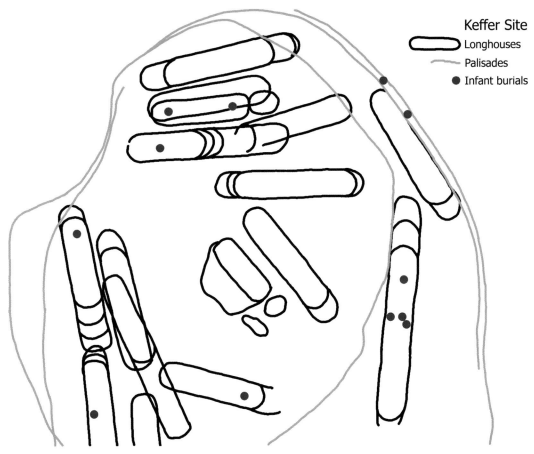

Figure 14.7
This map shows the Keffer village, including remodeled longhouses and expanding palisades. The dots mark the locations of burials of newborn infants. Note that most are in houses, where women would pass them frequently, while two are between the palisade rows at the northeast edge of the village (upper right). (Courtesy Michael Spence; redrawn from Finlayson, Smith, and Wheeler 1987.)

Long Point," the isolated primary burial of a man with several items that suggest ritual power, including the lower jaws of three bears (see Oberholtzer, chapter 11). Evidence from the nearby living site suggests that multiple secondary burial was the usual pattern there.

Much later, around 1500 CE, an adolescent at the Libby-Miller Site was given a single primary burial with a partial deer cranium. This stands apart from the usual pattern of annual multiple secondary burial with no grave offerings, raising the question of why this adolescent was treated this way. The answer may lie in a series of congenital disabilities apparent in the skeleton: a hip joint that suffered frequent dislocation, muscular torticollis ("wryneck"), and a developmental failure in the lower back. The effects of these would have been quite visible in the adolescent's posture and gait, and may have suggested to the other villagers some special relationship with the supernatural world. But whether their differential treatment of the adolescent reflected favour or fear, honour or ostracism, is not at all clear.

A Message from the Ancestors

Neal Ferris and I recently excavated a burial pit at the Johnson 1 Site, on the land of Walpole Island First Nation. The feature had been disturbed by modern ploughing and the residents of Walpole Island wanted it excavated so that it would not suffer further damage. However, they also thought that the discovery of the burial was not just an accident. They believed that the ancestors had wanted to be found, that they wished to communicate something to their modern descendants. When Neal and I excavated and studied the burial, we found that the feature was actually a *reburial* pit. About 1,000 years ago, the ancient people of the Johnson 1 Site accidentally intruded on a burial pit from centuries earlier. They then collected the bones that they had displaced and reinterred them in a new pit, carefully placing a box turtle with them as an offering. This, then, was their message to their descendants, and perhaps to all of us – how to properly treat the disturbed burials of the ancestors. We should do no less.

SIDEBAR 14.3

Scientific Research with Respect Michael Spence

In earlier years archaeologists excavated burials with virtual impunity. Eventually, however, First Nations complaints reached a large and sympathetic audience and severe restraints were placed on burial excavation by the government (see Nahrgang, chapter 14). Now in Ontario no Aboriginal burial can be exhumed without the prior consent of both the owner of the land where the burial is located and the First Nation community designated by the Ontario government to act on behalf of the deceased person, as a sort of next of kin. The selection of that First Nation is decided on purely geographic grounds; it is the community nearest to the burial. This has the advantage of resolving any uncertainties about which First Nations people should have the responsibility even in cases where the burial is so ancient that it cannot be archaeologically linked to any modern group. Furthermore, the conditions imposed on the excavation and the ultimate disposition of the remains are determined by that First Nation community.

As an archaeologist I at first bridled at these constraints on my "pursuit of scientific truth." However, I have come to realize the benefits of this new process. I now work in collaboration with First Nations traditionalists and heritage officials and have gained new ideas and insights from them, some of which would never have occurred to me while I was operating under the archaeological paradigms of an earlier day. First Nations interest in their ancestral societies and their desire to know more about them is as great as my own. They are also generally willing to allow some analysis of the skeletons, within the limits of their traditional requirements of respect and reburial. The process is not just a compromise between respect for the ancestors and scientific research – it is a fusion of both.

Part III
The Last (But Not Final) Word

Marit K. Munson

Most of Ontario's past is Aboriginal. Almost 600 generations of Aboriginal people were born, lived, and died since people first moved onto the land at the end of the last ice age; another 15 generations met, fought, married, and traded with European explorers and colonizers.

In the last century, Ontarians of all walks of life have become increasingly interested in the province's past, eager to learn about the multitude of generations who came before. Some stories about the past come from First Nations, who maintain longstanding oral histories of their people. Other stories come from archaeologists, who have spent a century or more digging into archaeological sites from the most ancient Paleoindians to fur-trade-era posts and camps.

Some Ontarians, including some archaeologists, have a bad track record – of freely digging into Aboriginal burials yet treating Euro-Canadian graves with respect, of destroying ancient village sites without a second thought, of damaging or desecrating sacred sites with careless actions, of discounting oral histories and privileging written records. As a result, many First Nations are, at best, wary of archaeologists' fascination with the past. This final section of the book presents two perspectives on the relationships between First Nations and archaeology. The first, a deeply felt critique of archaeology, comes from Kris Nahrgang, chief of Kawartha Nishnawbe First Nation and himself a licensed archaeologist. Nahrgang is one of a few individuals in Canada who can claim both perspectives. As readers will see, Nahrgang is simultaneously bitter about how archaeology affects First Nations and interested in using archaeology's tools to learn more about the past. The second perspective, a sidebar by Scott Hamilton, describes how archaeology can be of use to First Nations, especially in the context of contemporary political and legal issues.

Taken together, Nahrgang's and Hamilton's statements demonstrate both the challenges and the promise of archaeology for First Nations. Their messages are important and all of us – archaeologists, landowners, developers, governments, and First Nations – can learn from them, if we are willing to listen.

15

An Aboriginal Perspective

Kris Nahrgang

The chapters in this book have been written by some of the most respected experts in the field of Ontario archaeology. Working diligently, these archaeologists have gathered an incredible amount of knowledge about the pasts of First Nations. Yet we need to realize that none of this information was written by a single First Nations person. It is sad to think that there are fewer than ten archaeologists of Aboriginal ancestry in all of Canada, and that our history must be gathered by others from the footprints that we left in the past.

In this chapter, I offer you a different perspective on Ontario archaeology, as seen through the eyes of a First Nations person. This perspective is based on personal experience and, for some of you who read this chapter, my comments may seem to be political, subjective, interpretive, and disturbing: in short, overly human. I do not apologize for this because my objective is to make archaeologists more self-conscious and self-aware of the larger societal implications of what they do, to make them realize that for First Nations their work is not only colonial but also an intrusion and a catalyst for conflict. Once archaeologists understand this then maybe we can start to work together.

I have been on council for twenty-three years, with more than thirteen years as the elected chief of my community. My first experience with archaeology happened more than a decade ago when I found an Aboriginal pot deep under water, while scuba diving. I was told at that time that I had to give the pot to the government to keep, as there was no inherent right for a First Nations person to have ownership of artifacts. Since that time I have done everything in my power to ensure that our people are involved in the archaeological process.

An Honourable Profession?

When I first became involved with archaeology, I thought that it was something done by rich explorers, professors, and doctors – daring experts seeking and recording the history of this continent. I was under the impression that when I met an archaeologist I would be meeting an Indiana Jones or a Lara Croft character, secretive yet honourable. I wonder if everyone else out there thinks an archaeologist is someone always looking for treasure or the Holy Grail? This is far from reality (figure 15.1). What I found was a discipline that began more than a century ago as a gentlemen's club.

I also thought that the professors and other archaeologists would have answers to all of my questions. Instead, I found myself frustrated with archaeologists' interpretations of Aboriginal pasts. Because the actions of past peoples cannot actually be observed by archaeologists, it seemed to me that they must be guessing about how we used our items and how we lived and carried out ceremony. It seemed to me that archaeologists forgot that these peoples were fathers, mothers, sons and daughters, and lovers. It also seemed wrong to me that much of the history that we think we know about Aboriginal customs was written by missionaries, who were here for one reason only: to turn our hearts to their God and remove our customs from the face of the Earth. Fortunately, today's archaeologists are aware of bias in early documents and do question the validity of the missionaries' interpretations.

Experiences with Archaeologists

For First Nations, our first experience with archaeologists always seems to be after an important site is found or a machine has dug up one of our ancestors. Did you know that until the 1970s there was no legal obligation in Ontario to consult with First Nations when the bones of our ancestors were found? Even today, we have to fight for the legal right to be consulted when the homes and belongings of our ancestors are disturbed. This is changing with the rulings of the higher courts, but why should the courts have to mandate that developers and government – and especially archaeologists – respect First Nations peoples? They are disturbing our former homes, belongings, and burials, and places where spirits still live.

First Nations peoples in Ontario have been sitting on the outside looking in, as our heritage is repeatedly ploughed up, dug up, and built over. Try to imagine how First Nations peoples feel when we see scenarios like this played out before us. After all, whose heritage is this? It may seem as if we are asking for more than people feel that we are entitled to, but I hope that I can shed some light on this subject and on the history of our involvement to date.

Remember, the First Nations peoples of Canada never ceded any land by war and, in fact, were instrumental in protecting this country from invading US forces. We were offered treaties, which are contracts between First Nations and white governments.

Figure 15.1
Archaeologists Kris Nahrgang (left) and Susan Jamieson examine an artifact recovered by students during an archaeological fieldschool on the Clark's Bay Site, on Stoney Lake to the north of Peterborough. (Courtesy of Susan Jamieson.)

We were given certain rights for signing these Treaties. We continue to work at ensuring these rights are upheld.

Recently, I worked with Ontario's Ministry of Culture and others to help design better guidelines for archaeologists to follow when working with our First Nations history. One of the most significant changes would *require* archaeologists working on an Aboriginal site to contact the affected group, or groups, as a part of their duty and responsibility. Yet, a minority of archaeologists – somewhat surprisingly in this day and age – continue to dispute any need for this sort of consultation.

Rights and Fears

Our people say that we have always been here. Archaeologists propose varying dates for when they believe that we arrived, usually somewhere in the range of 12,000 to 15,000 years ago, around the end of the last ice age (see Ellis, chapter 1). Because there have been many different groups living here over these thousands of years, it is impossible to say which modern First Nations are their direct descendants (see Ferris, introduction). But you can rest assured that they are the ancestors of peoples that are still in existence. We are unsure of the language or languages the first peoples spoke, but it is archaeologists who have named them Paleoindians and who have told us what artifacts they left behind and how they lived.

Archaeologists have named and described most of the groups that have walked on these lands. As a First Nations person, I ask why there is so much history available about our past, yet we are not asked to comment upon any of it? Some of the old people may well know how our ancestors used the things that archaeologists find, how the people lived, and how they did their ceremonies. The degree of resistance to our involvement suggests to me that some archaeologists think that they know our own past better than we do.

Every year in Ontario, 500 to 1,000 sites are destroyed by development. Why is it that archaeologists still avoid contacting our people when they are working on our ancestral sites? What harm could be done by involving our Nations in the process of archaeology? To me, it is clear that people are afraid that we will claim ownership of artifacts and real estate and that finds of our heritage and history equate with ownership or rights that have never been extinguished by treaties.

I think that, as descendants of the creators of this heritage and history, First Nations people have a special right to be involved in the process of archaeology. And I believe that the Government of Canada has an obligation to protect the history of the peoples whom they hold under treaty and thus that the law requires consultation with us (Ferris 2003).

These questions run through my mind when I look at how archaeology is practiced in Ontario. As First Nations, we have the right to control how archaeology is being done on First Nations' sites (Rosenswig 1997; Wylie 1997). However, this control infringes upon the rights of the public and the developer, so we need to work together. If we don't start working together soon, there will be nothing left to protect. The time has come to take the lead in this area to protect our fragile and decimated heritage. If all parties consult, in good faith, with the affected groups this will lead to a better system, one that could expedite development while protecting rights. I do not see this consultation as being more onerous, but rather as an obligation upon us all to protect the heritage and history of those who lived here before us. There are some good examples of this sort of beneficial consultation from the United States and elsewhere in Canada (Hansen and Rosen 2007; Lyons et al. 2010; Watkins 2003; Yellowhorn 1996).

The Perfect Scenario

If I could imagine the perfect scenario, it would be doing archaeology on every occasion when there is major disturbance of the ground. There are countless unmarked sites – many of the grave and village markers that were of relevance to our people no longer standing, but the areas of concern still remain in the ground. As many as 80

Northern First Nations, Land Use and Occupancy, and Archaeology
Scott Hamilton

Natural resource development is beginning to drive great change in far northern Ontario, and First Nations residents view it with mixed feelings. Will development provide jobs, revitalize the local economy, and improve community infrastructure, health, and education? Or will it degrade the environment, erode treaty rights and traditional lifestyles, and leave northern communities with few economic benefits?

This debate occurs at a time when the courts are increasingly reaffirming that the Crown has a duty to consult with Aboriginal people and to accommodate their concerns when natural resource development impacts Aboriginal and treaty rights. It seems likely that procedures for managing land and resources in northern Ontario will shift in favour of greater local First Nations control. With adversarial legal proceedings and politically contentious negotiations on the horizon, though, documentation of traditional land use and occupancy has become an important priority for northern communities.

For many contemporary northern Aboriginal communities, traditional hunting, trapping, and fishing lifestyles are matters of "living memory," and continued harvest activities contribute a significant part of local food to most families. But having traditional knowledge is not necessarily enough; communities are faced with developing local technical capacity needed to collect, manage, interpret, and store that knowledge to protect their interests in face of emerging industrial natural resource harvests. Many individual First Nations require outside technical assistance. Some communities engage the services of outside specialists to either conduct the work or develop local training programs. Some communities also recognize the importance of archaeological and historical research to document cultural heritage dating back beyond the elders' memories.

These collaborations can raise difficult issues. Few First Nations are prepared to unreservedly share Aboriginal knowledge with provincial authorities or consultants employed by natural resource developers. This reflects both tactical and spiritual considerations. If non-Aboriginal regulators and developers gain control of traditional knowledge, then what would motivate continued Aboriginal engagement? This is a central issue in a climate of distrust and unequal power. Elders holding information also face a dilemma. Some knowledge is sacred, and sharing it with outsiders risks defiling or trivializing it. However, not documenting sensitive places leaves them unidentified and unprotected within the planning and regulatory process.

There is also a general distrust of current environmental assessment processes, as most communities lack the financial and technical resources needed to participate proactively. Aboriginal knowledge is often collected in a hurried and ad hoc fashion, without documented methodological standards, nor with explicit recognition that many elders have died without sharing their knowledge. This results in spotty and incomplete values mapping; information "voids" may be used to develop legal arguments that a First Nation has no interest in specific regions. This is particularly a problem in adversarial court cases, and there is a growing recognition that land use and occupancy data collection must reflect a high methodological standard to prevent inappropriate use (Tobias 2000 and 2009).

Land use and occupancy documentation also tends to focus on the relatively recent past. Researchers might deliberately collect only information that reflects individuals' personal experiences, fearing that knowledge deriving from past generations will be challenged as "hearsay" evidence. But this focus upon "living memory" may fail to

continued on following page

include traditional knowledge reflecting the spiritual relationship with the land that was passed down from the distant past or data reflecting the pace and direction of culture change. In my view, a more overtly anthropological or ethnohistoric perspective can help provide the necessary cultural, spiritual, and historical framework for traditional knowledge.

Archaeologists are increasingly part of the process of documentation, as First Nations commission them to document archaeological sites and to participate in collecting information on land use and occupancy. Aboriginal people might take part in interviews, participate in designing archaeological surveys and constructing map biographies, or visit archaeological sites. In turn, the detailed knowledge that Aboriginal people contribute furthers archaeological insight by providing seasonal use information, individual agency, and "intangible" heritage values to which archaeologists are usually oblivious. This may well contribute to the development of an "Indigenous

Archaeology" perspective that will profoundly transform conventional archaeological "ways of seeing."

Such applied research differs from past archaeological practice, as many communities insist on retaining information control. This has obvious implications for conventional reporting, publication, and dissemination of heritage knowledge. Many communities are also reluctant to deal with outsiders with no "track record" of past research with First Nations. This will prove problematic for archaeological consulting firms without a long-standing practice in the region or who have not yet invested time in developing such relationships. It is also challenging for consulting firms working under contract for natural resource developers with difficult relationships with First Nations. Conducting northern Ontario archaeological research will increasingly require a significant investment of time and effort in developing grassroots relationships and in careful negotiation of perilous political waters.

percent of our sites are still undisturbed in this province and have yet to be found. Why not make sure that developers look for archaeological sites and plan around them to ensure their protection as we develop more land? Would it be so hard for municipalities to demand that archaeological evaluations be done before anyone can disturb the spirits of our ancestors? What lies in the ground cannot be replenished after it is removed; it is a nonrenewable treasure. If we allow the destruction of our sites, we are destroying a direct link to our heritage and history and forever leaving a gap in the story of those who came before us.

The Founding First Nations Circle

In an effort to protect our history and our heritage, some of the main Nations still in existence came together in a group called the Founding First Nations Circle. The group includes the Huron/Wendat, Six Nations groups, other Iroquois, and the Algonquian Nations that still hold Treaty in southern Ontario. The idea was to gather the legal representatives of many Nations to sit at one table and to represent our individual and

common heritage. First Nations politics are similar to those of any other system governing a community people; each party or group is protective of the issues and territories over which it has perceived jurisdiction. Boundaries of treaties, past use of lands, and traditional use areas often intersect, overlap, and are sometimes the same. This sets up competition and potential conflict between perceived interests.

Members of the Founding First Nations Circle agreed on rules designed to help all participants feel comfortable with issues under discussion and our achievements in the heritage arena. The rules are simple and binding for all. First, there is to be no fighting over the artifacts, history, or the bones and resting places of our ancestors. We do not provide ownership, only protection and stewardship. In this manner we deal only with the immediate archaeological issues, not the rights of the individual First Nations that need to be dealt with by the government.

Having representatives from these First Nations deal with heritage and history issues makes a great deal of sense. For one thing, the law requires consultation with us. What better way to start than to be able to call the people that speak for the area? No one group can handle every issue that comes forward, but we can deal with most of them and can refer particular issues to other groups that need to be involved.

In order to ensure that we are properly represented, we need to exclude impostors who pretend to represent First Nations for their own gains. It is amazing how many people fraudulently claim to represent our communities and, in doing so, have duped both government agencies and First Nations. We have had enough of people trying to save us; we are not in need of any more saviours. It is important for all of us to ask these people, "Whom do you represent?" We need to make them prove who they are. These are a few of the reasons why our people must be involved in decisions about our heritage and history.

Bones of Our Ancestors

The bones of our ancestors have been a major source of contention. In the past, archaeologists who found human remains, following government guidelines, deposited the bones for the closest First Nations to look after. I am not sure who thought this was a good idea. Our Nations are not all the same. We have important differences in ceremony and other customs. When a box of bones from an ancestor shows up at our communities, it triggers a multitude of feelings and emotions. Over the thousands of years that we have been in southern Ontario, hundreds of thousands or more of our people have died here. Although we know that they are of a common thread, we also know that our elders had differing ceremonies for the ones that passed before us.

Many First Nations peoples believe that we as humans have two souls: one that goes to the Creator and the spirit world, and another that stays with the body. When these people are dug up, more than just bones are disturbed. Spirits are disturbed as well. When someone arrives at a community with bones, they bring the soul of the person with them. Spirits may be angry at having their journey disrupted, or may be the spirits of traditional enemies, and so on. This is a problem for our people. Our people are still superstitious. Bringing an angry soul or the soul of a past enemy back to our communities should not be taken lightly. For this, and a multitude of other reasons, it is preferable that we leave the bones of our people where they are found. But that cannot always happen.

When the bones arrive in a community, the first reaction is to begin a mourning process for the ancestor. It is amazing the grief that passes through us as we try to do what is best for this person. Although most people think of bones as someone of the past, we wonder if they are our great-great grandfather or great-great grandmother. Most whites wrongly assume that we have a ceremony ready for this type of interruption of an ancestor's journey. When our ancestors chose a site as their resting place, it was a place of meaning. For us, it is a still a place of meaning, a sacred place, a place linking past, present, and future generations. Dealing with the issue of reburial has been a real challenge for our communities, both emotionally and financially. In some cases this leads to great anger and confrontation with the government.

Artifacts are also a point of contention. We often don't know precisely why specific objects were created. Was the pot that has been taken from the ground made for a burial ceremony? Was it a wedding pot? Was it part of a sacred ceremony created by an elder? In any of these instances, that pot needs to stay in the earth or the sacredness of the ceremony of which the pot was (and still is) a part, will be destroyed. That is because for us, the ceremony is seen as still being active and not something solely of the past (e.g., Baugher 2005).

We use pipes to talk to the Creator – our version of prayer, as we speak in our own manner and custom. Some pipes were used and then put into the ground as part of ceremonies by our holy people. Is it any wonder that we are disturbed when the pipe leaves its intended resting place to end up in a box on an archaeologist's shelf, thereby breaking the sacredness of that ceremony?

Finding Ways to Fix Discontent

In this new world of technology and unimaginable change from those times of my ancestors, perhaps people think that that we should give up our interest of protecting the past. People may believe that it is time to join the rest of the country in the development of the lands that we live upon. These ideas have ruled Canada for centuries, in the form of attempts to eradicate our people through disease and assimilation (such as residential schools). If these issues of which I speak seem to be unrelated to archaeology, know that in First Nations' eyes it is all connected to white colonialism. Archaeology goes hand-in-hand with development and the physical eradication of our heritage. The hijacking of our history is very real. We see this as just one more system that will remove our rights and our past.

Yet despite these issues that create so many tensions between our Nations and archaeologists, we may be able to fix the discontent that so often is the catalyst for confrontation. Imagine, if you will, a development going into your neighbourhood, one that requires an archaeological evaluation before any building plans are finalized. Say that during this process a site is found, and archaeologists learn that it has been used by Aboriginal people for thousands of years. Imagine that at this point in the process archaeologists contact the relevant First Nations group(s) to let them know that something that may be of importance to them has been found. This would mean that First Nations are already involved in the process, not just added as an afterthought if any bones are found or contentious issues arise. Maybe discussions with the affected groups would lead to changes in the project design, using some simple planning to leave the site undisturbed. The project would stay on track, with minimal cost to the developer, virtually no impact upon our heritage or history, and no impact upon spirits or First Nations communities.

I believe that it would be easy to include our people in such a process. If the government were to legislate our involvement into the archaeological process as it is carried out on a day-to-day basis, we would create a working relationship with each other and with archaeologists that would allow all parties to help create solutions when issues arise. We cannot afford to destroy our heritage and to erase our history any further. Archaeology must be the first part of the process when developments are being contemplated.

As First Nations, we ask that if you are going to dig in the breast of Mother Earth, please have the courtesy to have an archaeological evaluation completed for the area that you are going to disturb. This could be seen as due diligence by the government and as respect offered by the archaeologists who have been become the caretakers of our First Nations' histories. It is time for us to make a concerted effort to work together to protect this history for all the people of the world. It is a duty that should be imposed upon us all, Aboriginal and non-Aboriginal alike. If nothing else, it is simply a matter of respect for those who lived on the lands before others arrived. It is long overdue.

References

Adams, N. 1989. "The Geological Formation of the St Clair River Delta and Its Implications for Archaeological Research on the Walpole Island Indian Reserve." *KEWA* 89(2): 2–17.

Allen, W.A. 2002. "Wa-nant-git-che-ang: Canoe Route to Lake Huron through Southern Algonquia." *Ontario Archaeology* 73: 38–68.

Anderson, Jake. 2009. *The Archaeology of the Lawson Site, Special Publication Number 2.* London, ON: Museum of Ontario Archaeology.

Anderson, James. 1968. *The Serpent Mounds Site Physical Anthropology.* Toronto: Royal Ontario Museum.

Anderson, T.W., and C.F.M. Lewis. 2002. "Upper Great Lakes Climate and Water-Level Changes 11 to 7 ka: Effect on the Sheguiandah Archaeological Site." *The Sheguiandah Site: Archaeological, Geological and Paleobotanical Studies at a Paleoindian Site on Manitoulin Island*, edited by Patrick J. Julig, 195–234. Hull, QC: Canadian Museum of Civilization.

Barnett, P.J. 1992. "Quaternary Geology of Ontario." *Geology of Ontario*, edited by P.C. Thurston, H.R. Williams, R.H. Sutcliffe, and G.M. Scott, 1011–88. Sudbury, ON: Ontario Geological Survey, Ontario Ministry of Northern Development and Mines.

Baugher, Sherene. 2005. "Sacredness, Sensitivity, and Significance: The Controversy over Native American Sacred Cites." *Heritage of Value, Archaeology of Renown: Reshaping Archaeological Assessment and Significance*, edited by Clay Mathers, Timothy Darvill, and Barbara J. Little, 248–75. Gainesville, FL: University Press of Florida.

Birch, Jennifer. 2010. "Coalescence and Conflict in Iroquoian Ontario." *Archaeological Review From Cambridge* 25(1): 29–48.

– 2012. "Coalescent Communities: Settlement Aggregation and Social Integration in Iroquoian Ontario." *American Antiquity* 77(4): 646–70.

Birch, Jennifer, and Ronald F. Williamson. 2013. *The Mantle Site: An Archaeological History of an Ancestral Huron-Wendat Community*. New York: Altamira Press.

Bird, Louis. 2005. *Telling Our Stories: Omushkego Legends and History from Hudson Bay*. Peterborough, ON: Broadview Press.

– 2007. *The Spirit Lives in the Mind: Omushkego Stories, Lives, and Dreams*. Edited by Susan Elaine Gray. Montreal & Kingston: McGill-Queen's University Press.

Boucher, Pierre. 1883. *Canada in the Seventeenth Century*. Translated by Edward Louis Montizambert. Montreal: George E. Desbarats & Co.

Boyd, M., and C. Surette. 2010. "Northernmost Precontact Maize in North America." *American Antiquity* 75(1): 117–33.

Boyd, M., and C. Surette, and B.A. Nicholson. 2006. "Archaeobotanical Evidence of Prehistoric Maize (Zea Mays) Consumption at the Northern Edge of the Great Plains." *Journal of Archaeological Science* 33: 1129–40.

Boyd, M., T. Varney, C. Surette, and J. Surette. 2008. "Reassessing the Northern Limit of Maize Consumption in North America: Stable Isotope, Plant Microfossil, and Trace Element Content of Carbonized Food Residue." *Journal of Archaeological Science* 35: 2545–56.

Bradley, Bruce A., Michael B. Collins, and Andrew Hemmings. 2010. *Clovis Technology, Archaeological Series 17*. Ann Arbor, MI: International Monographs in Prehistory.

Braun, M., D.C. Cook, and S. Pfeiffer. 1998. "DNA from Mycobacterium Tuberculosis Complex Identified in North American Pre-Columbian Human Skeletal Remains." *Journal of Archaeological Science* 25: 271–7.

Buchanan, Kenneth T. 1992. *The 1991 Spiegel Site Excavation, Archaeological Survey of Laurentian University Report No. 19*. Sudbury, ON: Department of Anthropology, Laurentian University.

Buchner, A.P. 1979. *The 1978 Caribou Lake Project, Including a Summary of the Pre-History of South-Central Manitoba*. Edited by Historic Research Branch *Papers in Manitoba Archaeology Final Report No. 8*. Winnepeg, MB: Manitoba Department of Cultural Affairs and Historical Resources.

Buekens, R.P., L.A. Pavlish, R.G.V. Hancock, R.M. Farquahar, G.C. Wilson, P.J. Julig, and W. Ross. 1992. "Radiocarbon Dating of Copper-Preserved Organics." *Radiocarbon* 34(3): 890–7.

Buikstra, Jane E. 2006. "Repatriation and Bioarchaeology: Challenges and Opportunities." *Bioarchaeology: The Contextual Analysis of Human Remains*, edited by Jane E. Buikstra and L.A. Beck, 389–416. New York: Academic Press.

Bursey, Jeff. 1996. "The Anderson Site (AfGx-54) and the Early and Middle Ontario Iroquoian Occupations of the Lower Grand River." *KEWA* 96(7): 2–20.

– 2006. "The Frog Pond Site (AhGx-359): The Identification of a 17th Century Neutral Iroquoian Medicine Lodge in Southern Ontario." *Canadian Journal of Archaeology* 30(1): 1–39.

Campbell, I.D., and J.H. McAndrews. 1993. "Forest Disequilibrium Caused by Rapid Little Ice Age Cooling." *Nature* 366: 336–8.

Cannon, Aubrey. 1989. "The Historical Dimension in Mortuary Expressions of Status and Sentiment." *Current Anthropology* 30(4): 437–58.

Carr, Christopher. 1995. "Mortuary Practices: Their Social, Philosophical-Religious, Circumstantial, and Physical Determinants." *Journal of Archaeological Method and Theory* 2: 105–200.

Chapdelaine, Claude, and Norman Clermont. 2006. "Adaptation, Continuity and Change in the Middle Ottawa Valley: A View from the Morrison's and Allumette Island Late Archaic Sites." *The Archaic of the Far Northeast*, edited by David Sanger and M.A.P. Renouf, 191–219. Orono, ME: University of Maine Press.

Chapman, L.J., and D.F. Putnam. 1984. *The Physiography of Southern Ontario*. 3rd ed, *Special Volume 2*. Toronto: Ontario Ministry of Natural Resources.

Cleland, Charles E. 1982. "The Inland Shore Fishery of the Northern Great Lakes: Its Development and Importance in Prehistory." *American Antiquity* 47(4): 761–84.

Conway, Julie, and Thor Conway. 1990. *Spirits on Stone: The Agawa Pictographs*. San Luis Obispo, CA: Heritage Discoveries.

Conway, Thor, and Julie Conway. 1989. "Ethno-archaeological Study of Algonkian Rock Art in Northeastern Ontario, Canada." *Ontario Archaeology* 49: 34–59.

Coté, Marc, and Leila Inksetter. 2001. "Ceramics and Chronology of the Late Prehistoric Period: The Abitibi-Témiscamingue Case." Paper read at 33rd Annual Meeting of the Canadian Archaeological Association.

Crawford, Gary W., and David G. Smith. 2003. "Paleoethnobotany in the Northeast." *People and Plants in Ancient Eastern North America*, edited by P. Minnis, 172–257. Washington, DC: Smithsonian Institution Press.

Crawford, Gary W., David G. Smith, J.R. Desloges, and A.M. Davis. 1998. "Floodplains and Agricultural Origins: A Case Study in South-Central Ontario, Canada." *Journal of Field Archaeology* 25: 123–37.

Crawford, Gary W., Della Saunders, and David G. Smith. 2006. "Pre-contact Maize from Ontario, Canada: Context, Chronology, Variation, and Plant Association." *Histories of Maize: Multidisciplinary Approaches to the Prehistory, Biogeography, Domestication, and Evolution of Maize (Zea mays)*, edited by John E. Staller, Robert H. Tykot, and Bruce F. Benz. New York: Academic Press.

Dawson, K.C.A. 1983. "Prehistory of the Interior Forest of Northern Ontario." *Boreal Forest Adaptations: The Northern Algonkians*, edited by A.T. Steegmann Jr, 55–84. New York: Plenum Press.

Day, Gordon M. 1978. "Nipissing." *Northeast, Vol. 15*, edited by Bruce Trigger, 787–91. Washington, DC: Smithsonian Institution.

Day, Gordon M, and Bruce Trigger. 1978. "Algonquin." *Northeast, Vol. 15*, edited by Bruce Trigger, 792–7. Washington, DC: Smithsonian Institution.

Delcourt, Hazel R. 2002. *Forests in Peril: Tracking Deciduous Trees from Ice-Age Refuges Into the Greenhouse World*. Blacksburg, VA: McDonald and Woodword Publishing Company.

Deller, D. Brian, Christopher J. Ellis, and James Keron. 2009. "Understanding Cache Variability: A Deliberately Burned Early Paleoindian Tool Assemblage from the Crowfield Site, Southwestern Ontario, Canada" *American Antiquity* 74(2): 371–97.

Densmore, Frances. 1979 [1929]. *Chippewa [Ojibwa] Customs*. St Paul, MN: Minnesota Historical Society Press.

Dewar, Genevieve, Jamie Ginter, Beth Shook, Neal Ferris, and Heather Henderson. 2010. "A Bioarchaeological Study of a Western Basin Tradition Cemetery on the Detroit River." *Journal of Archaeological Science* 35(9): 2245–54.

Dewdney, Selwyn. 1962. *Indian Rock Paintings of the Great Lakes*. Vol. 4, *Quetico Foundation series*. Toronto: University of Toronto Press.

Dickason, Olive Patricia. 1997. *Canada's First Nations: A History of Founding Peoples from Earliest Times*. 2nd ed. New York: Oxford University Press.

Dodd, Christine. 1984. *Ontario Iroquois Tradition Longhouses, Archaeological Survey of Canada, Mercury Series 124*. Ottawa: National Museum of Man.

Donaldson, William, and Stanley Wortner. 1995. "The Hind Site and the Glacial Kame Burial Complex in Ontario." *Ontario Archaeology* 59: 5–95.

Dougherty, Kathleen. 2003. *Social Organisation and Mortuary Program of the Rice Lake-Trent River Middle Woodland Hopewellian Manifestation at Cameron's Point*. Unpublished MA Thesis, University of Western Ontario, London, ON.

Dupras, T.L. 2003. "The Moatfield Infant and Juvenile Skeletal Remains." *Bones of the Ancestors. The Archaeology and Osteobiography of the Moatfield Ossuary*, edited by Ronald F. Williamson and S Pfeiffer, 295–308. Ottawa: Canadian Museum of Civilization.

Ellis, Christopher J. 1994. "Miniature Early Paleo-Indian Stone Artifacts from the Parkhill, Ontario, Site." *North American Archaeologist* 15: 253–67.

– 2009. "The Crowfield and Caradoc Sites, Ontario: Glimpses of Palaeo-Indian Sacred Ritual and World View." *Painting the Past with a Broad Brush: Papers in Honour of James Valliere Wright*, edited by David L. Keenlyside and Jean-Luc Pilon, 319–52. Gatineau, QC: Canadian Museum of Civilization.

Ellis, Christopher J, and D. Brian Deller. 1990. "Paleo-Indians." *The Archaeology of Southern Ontario to A.D. 1650*, edited by Christopher J. Ellis and Neal Ferris, 37–63. London, ON: London Chapter, Ontario Archaeological Society.

– 2000. *An Early Paleo-Indian Site Near Parkhill, Ontario, Archaeological Survey of Canada, Mercury Series Paper No. 159*. Hull, QC: Canadian Museum of Civilization.

Ellis, Christopher J, Edward Eastaugh, and James Keron. 2010. "A Preliminary Report on a Late Archaic Pithouse from the Davidson Site (AhHk-54)." *KEWA* 10(6–7): 1–12.

Ellis, Christopher J, Ian T. Kenyon, and Michael W. Spence. 1990. "The Archaic." *The Archaeology of Southern Ontario to A.D. 1650*, edited by Christopher J. Ellis and Neal Ferris, 65–124. London, ON: London Chapter, Ontario Archaeological Society.

Ellis, Christopher J, and James Keron. 2011. "A Preliminary Report on a 3000 Year Old 'Wall Trench' Structure from the Davidson Site (AhHk-54)." *KEWA* 11(2): 1–10.

Ellis, Christopher J, Peter A. Timmins, and Holly Martelle. 2009. "At the Crossroads and Periphery: The Archaic Archaeological Record of Southern Ontario." *Archaic Societies: Diversity and Complexity across the Midcontinent*, edited by Thomas E. Emerson, Andrew Fortier, and Dale McElrath, 787–840. Albany, NY: State University of New York Press.

Ethridge, Robbie. 2009. "Introduction." *Mapping the Mississippian Shatter Zone*, edited by Robbie Ethridge and Sheri M. Shuck-Hall, 1–62. Lincoln, NE: University of Nebraska Press.

Eyles, Nick. 2002. *Ontario Rocks*. Markham, ON: Fitzhenry and Whiteside.

Fagan, Brian. 2005. *Ancient North America: The Archaeology of a Continent*. 4th ed. New York: Thames & Hudson.

Feinman, Gary M., and Jill Neitzel. 1984. "Too Many Types: An Overview of Sedentary Prestate Societies in the Americas." *Advances in Archeological Method and Theory*, edited by Michael B. Schiffer, 39–102. New York: Academic Press.

Feit, Harvey. 1973. "The Ethno-ecology of the Waswanipi Cree: Or, How Hunters Can Manage Their Resources." *Cultural Ecology: Readings on the Canadian Indians and Eskimos*, edited by Bruce Cox, 115–25. Toronto: McClelland and Stewart.

– 1986. "Hunting and the Quest for Power: The James Bay Cree." *Native Peoples: The Canadian Experience*, edited by R.B. Morrison and C.R. Wilson, 208–36. Toronto: McClelland and Stewart.

Ferris, Neal. 1989. "A Preliminary Report on the 1987–1988 London Chapter Excavations at the Van Bemmel Site, Kent County, Ontario." *KEWA* 89(6): 2–22.

– 1999. "Telling Tales: Interpretive Trends in Southern Ontario Late Woodland Archaeology." *Ontario Archaeology* 68: 1–62.

– 2003. "Between Colonial and Indigenous Archaeologies: Legal and Extra-legal Ownership of the Archaeological Past in North America." *Canadian Journal of Archaeology* 27(2): 154–90.

– 2007. "Always Fluid: Government Policy Making and Standards of Practice in Ontario Archaeological Resource Management." *Quality Management in Archaeology*, edited by W. Willems and M. van der Dries, 78–99. Oxford, UK: Oxbow Books.

– 2009. *The Archaeology of Native–Lived Colonialism: Challenging History in the Great Lakes*. Tucson, AZ: University of Arizona Press.

Finlayson, William D. 1977. *The Saugeen Culture: A Middle Woodland Manifestation in Southwestern Ontario, Archaeological Survey of Canada Paper 61*. Ottawa: National Museum of Man.

Flannery, Regina, and Mary Elizabeth Chambers. 1985. "Each Man Has His Own Friends: The Role of Dream Visitors in Traditional East Cree Belief and Practice." *Arctic Anthropology* 22(1): 1–22.

Fox, William A. 1980. "The Lakehead Complex: New Insights." *Collected Archaeological*

Papers, edited by David Skene Melvin, 28–49. Toronto: Ontario Ministry of Culture and Recreation.

– 2002. "*Thaniba wakondagi* among the Ontario Iroquois." *Canadian Journal of Archaeology* 26(2): 130–51.

– 2004. "The North-South Copper Axis." *Southeastern Archaeology* 23(1): 85–97.

– 2010. "Exotic Giants." *Arch Notes* 15(5): 5–12.

Fox, William A, and Charles Garrad. 2006. "Hurons in an Algonquian Land." *Ontario Archaeology* 77/78: 121–34.

Fox, William A, R.G.V. Hancock, and L.A. Pavlish. 1995. "Where East Met West: The New Copper Culture." *Wisconsin Archaeologist* 76(3–4): 269–93.

Fox, William A, and Robert J. Pearce, eds. 2005. "Special Edition: Native Symbolic Expression around the Great Lakes and Beyond." *Ontario Archaeology* 79/80.

Gallivan, Martin D. 2007. "Powhatan's Werowocomoco: Constructing Place, Polity, and Personhood in the Chesapeake, CE 1200–CE 1609." *American Anthropologist* 109(1): 85–100.

General, Paul, and Gary Warrick. In press. "The Grand River Sturgeon Fishery." *Ontario Archaeology*.

Granger, Joe. 1978a. "Cache Blades, Chert and Communication: A Reappraisal of Certain Aspects of the Meadowood Phase and the Concept of a Burial Cult in the Northeast." *Essays in Northeastern Anthropology in Memory of Marian E. White*, edited by W.E. Engelbrecht and D.K. Grayson, 96–122.

– 1978b. *Meadowood Phase Settlement Pattern in the Niagara Frontier Region of Western New York State*, *Anthropological Papers No. 65*. Ann Arbor, MI: University of Michigan, Museum of Anthropology.

Grant, W.L., ed. 1907. *Voyages of Samuel de Champlain: 1611–1618*. New York: Charles Scribner's Sons.

Greenman, Emerson F. 1966. "Chronology of Sites at Killarney, Canada." *American Antiquity* 31(4): 540–51.

Greenman, Emerson F., and George M. Stanley. 1941. "Two Post-Nipissing Sites near Killarney, Ontario." *American Antiquity* 6(4): 305–13.

Griffin, J.B., ed. 1961. *Lake Superior Copper and the Indians: Miscellaneous Studies of Great Lakes Prehistory*, *Anthropology Paper No. 17*. Ann Arbor, MI: University of Michigan, Museum of Anthropology.

Hamilton, Scott. 1981. "The Archaeology of the Wenesaga Rapids." *Archaeology Research Report*. Toronto: Archaeology and Heritage Planning Branch, Ontario Ministry of Culture and Recreation.

– 1988. "The Concept of Cultural Edge in Boreal Forest Archaeology." *Boreal Forest and Subarctic Archaeology*, edited by C.S. "Paddy" Reid, 37–71. Toronto.

– 1996. *Pleistocene Landscape Features and Plano Archaeological Sites upon the Kaministiquia River Delta, Thunder Bay District*, *Lakehead University Monographs in Anthropology #1*. Thunder Bay, ON: Department of Anthropology, Lakehead University.

– 2000. "Archaeological Predictive Modelling in the Boreal Forest: No Easy Answers." *Canadian Journal of Archaeology* 24: 41–76.

– 2004. "Early Holocene Human Remains at Wapekeka (FlJj-1), Northern Ontario." *The Late Paleo-Indian Great Lakes: Geological and Archaeological Investigations of Late Pleistocene and Early Holocene Environments* edited by L.J. Jackson and A. Hinshelwood, 337–68. Hull, QC: Canadian Museum of Civilization.

Hamilton, Scott, D. Finch, T. Varney, C. Surette, and C. Matheson. 2011. "Mid-Holocene Human Burial Investigation at the Bug River Mouth, in Collaboration with Kitchenuhmaykoosib Inninuwug First Nation, Big Trout Lake." *44th Annucal Conference of the Canadian Archaeological Association*. Halifax, NS.

Hamilton, Scott, and J.E. Molto. 2006. "A 5,000 Year Old Human Burial at Kitchenuhmaykoosib Inninuwug, Big Trout Lake, Northern Ontario." *39th Annual Canadian Archaeological Association Conference*. Toronto.

Hansen, Brooke, and Jack Rosen. 2007. "Building Bridges through Public Anthropology in the Haudenosaunee Homeland." *Past Meets Present: Archaeologists Partnering with Museum Curators, Teachers, and Community Groups*, edited by John H. Jameson Jr and Sherene Baugher, 127–48. New York: Springer.

Hantman, Jeffrey L. 1990. "Between Powhatan and Quirank: Reconstructing Monacan Culture and History in the Context of Jamestown." *American Anthropologist* 92(3): 676–90.

Hart, John P. 1999. "Dating Roundtop's Domesticates: Implications for Northeast Late Prehistory." *Current Northeast Paleoethnobotany*, edited by John P. Hart, 47–68. Albany, NY: State University of New York.

Hastorf, Christine. 1990. "One Path to the Heights: Negotiating Political Inequality in the Sausa of Peru." *The Evolution of Political Systems: Sociopolitics in Small Scale Sedentary Societies*, edited by Steadman Upham, 146–76. Cambridge: Cambridge University Press.

Hayden, Brian. 1997. "Feasting in Prehistoric and Traditional Societies." *Food and the Status Quest: An Interdisciplinary Perspective*, edited by Polly Wiessner and Wulf Schiefenhovel, 127–48. Oxford, UK: Berghahn Books.

Helm, J., ed. 1981. *Subarctic, Vol. 6*. Edited by William Sturtevant, *Handbook of North American Indians*. Washington, DC: Smithsonian Institution.

Helmuth, Herman. 1993. *The Quackenbush Skeletons: Osteology and Culture, Trent University Occasional Paper in Anthropology 9*. Peterborough, ON: Trent University.

Herman, Mary W. 1956. "The Social Aspect of Huron property." *American Anthropologist* 58(6): 1044–58.

Hickerson, Harold. 1962. *The Southwestern Chippewa, An Ethnohistorical Study, Memoir 92*. Menasha, WI: American Anthropological Association.

– 1970. *The Chippewa and Their Neighbours: A Study in Ethnohistory*. Chicago: Holt, Rinehart, and Winston.

Hinshelwood, Andrew. 2004. "Archaic Reoccupation of Late Palaeo-Indian Sites in North-western Ontario." *The Late Paleo-Indian Great Lakes: Geological and Archaeological*

Investigations of Late Pleistocene and Early Holocene Environments, edited by L.J. Jackson and A. Hinshelwood, 225–50. Hull, QC: Canadian Museum of Civilization.

Holly Jr, D.H. 2002. "Subarctic 'Prehistory' in the Anthropological Imagination." *Arctic Anthropology* 39(1–2): 10–26.

Jackes, M.K. 1983. "Osteological Evidence for Smallpox: A Possible Case from Seventeenth Century Ontario." *American Journal of Physical Anthropology* 60(1): 75–81.

Jackson, L.J. 2000. "New Caribou Fossil Records from Rice Lake, South-Central Ontario: Radiocarbon Evidence and Middle Holocene Climate Change." *Ontario Archaeology* 69: 55–64.

Jackson, L.J., and Andrew Hinshelwood, eds. 2004. *The Late Paleo-Indian Great Lakes: Geological and Archaeological Investigations of Late Pleistocene and Early Holocene Environments* Vol. 165, *Mercury Series Archaeology*. Hull, QC: Canadian Museum of Civilization.

Jackson, L.J., R. Rose, A. Ariss, and C. Theriault. 1992. "A Winter of Discontent: The Charity Site, 1991." *Arch Notes* 92(6): 5–8.

Jameson, Anna. 1838. *Winter Studies and Summer Rambles in Canada*. London: Saunders and Otley.

Jamieson, Susan M. 1992. "Regional Interaction and Ontario Iroquois Evolution." *Canadian Journal of Archaeology* 16: 70–88.

1999. "A Brief History of Aboriginal Social Interactions in Southern Ontario and Their Taxonomic Implications." *Taming the Taxonomy: Toward a New Understanding of Great Lakes Archaeology*, edited by Ronald F. Williamson and Christopher M. Watts, 175–92. Toronto: Eastend Books.

– 2011. "Power and Authority in the Great Lakes-Saint Lawrence Lowlands Region, Eastern Canada." *It's Good to Be King: The Archaeology of Power and Authority*, edited by Shawn Morton and Don Butler, 1–10. Calgary, AB: Archaeological Association of the University of Calgary.

Johnston, Richard B. 1968a. *The Archaeology of Rice Lake, Ontario, Anthropology Papers, No. 19*. Ottawa: National Museum of Canada.

– 1968b. *The Archaeology of the Serpent Mounds Site*. Toronto: Royal Ontario Museum.

–, ed. 1984. *The McIntyre Site: Archaeology, Subsistence and Environment, Archaeological Survey of Canada Paper No. 126, National Museum of Man Mercury Series*. Ottawa: National Museums of Canada.

Johnston, Richard B., and Kenneth A. Cassavoy. 1978. "The Fishweirs at Atherley Narrows, Ontario." *American Antiquity* 43(4): 697–709.

Jordan, Kurt. 2004. "Seneca Iroquois Settlement Pattern, Community Structure and Housing, 1677–1779." *Northeast Anthropology* 67: 23–60.

Julig, Patrick J. 1994. *The Cummins Site Complex and Paleoindian Occupations in the Northwestern Lake Superior Region*. Vol. 2, *Ontario Archaeological Reports*. Toronto: Ontario Heritage Foundation.

– 2002. *The Sheguiandah Site: Archaeological, Geological and Paleobotanical Studies at a*

Paleoindian Site on Manitoulin Island. Vol. Paper 161, *Ontario Mercury Series, Archaeological Survey of Canada*. Hull, QC: Canadian Museum of Civilization.

Julig, Patrick J., and David S. Brose. 2008. "Killarney Bay 1/Spiegel Middle Woodland Site: History of Geoarchaeological Investigations and Site Context." *75th Annual Meeting of the Eastern States Archaeological Federation*. Lockport, NY.

Julig, Patrick J., Alicia Hawkins, and Darrel F.G. Long. 2008. "Sourcing of Chert Artifacts from the Spiegel / Killarney Bay 1 Site, Killarney, Ontario." *75th Annual Meeting of the Eastern States Archaeological Federation*. Lockport, NY.

Julig, Patrick J., J.H. McAndrews, and W.C. Mahaney. 1990. "Geoarchaeology of the Cummins Site on the Beach of Proglacial Lake Minong, Lake Superior Basin, Canada." *Archaeological Geology of North America*, edited by N.P. Lasca and J. Donahue, 21–49. Boulder, CO: Geological Society of America.

Junker-Andersen, C. 1988. "Eel Fisheries of the St Lawrence Iroquoians." *North American Archaeologist* 9(2): 97–121.

Kapches, Mima. 1984. "Cabins on Ontario Iroquois Sites." *North American Archaeologist* 5(1): 63–71.

– 1990. "The Spatial Dynamics of Ontario Iroquoian Longhouses." *American Antiquity* 55(1): 49–67.

– 1992. "'Rude but perfect': A Study of Miniature Pipes in Iroquoia." *Proceedings of the 1989 Smoking Pipe Conference*, 71–81. Rochester, NY: Rochester Museum and Science Center.

– 1994. "The Iroquoian Longhouse: Architectural and Cultural Identity." *Meaningful Architecture: Social Interpretations of Buildings*, edited by M. Locock, 253–70. Brookfield, VT: Avebury.

Karrow, Paul F. 1980. "The Nipissing Transgression around Southern Lake Huron." *Canadian Journal of Earth Sciences* 17: 1271–4.

Karrow, Paul F., and Barry G. Warner. 1990. "The Geological and Biological Environment for Human Occupation in Southern Ontario." *The Archaeology of Southern Ontario to A.D. 1650*, edited by Christopher J. Ellis and Neal Ferris, 5–39. London, ON: London Chapter, Ontario Archaeological Society.

Katzenberg, M.A. 1992. "Changing Diet and Health in Pre- and Protohistoric Ontario." *Health and Lifestyle Change*, edited by R. Huss-Ashmore, J.Schall, and M. Hediger, 23–31. Philadelphia: University of Pennsylvania.

Katzenberg, M.A., H.P. Schwarcz, M. Knyf, and F.J. Melbye. 1995. "Stable Isotope Evidence for Maize Horticulture and Paleodiet in Southern Ontario, Canada." *American Antiquity* 60(2): 335–50.

Kearsley, Ronald Glenn. 1997. *Pinched-Face Human Effigy Pipes: The Social Mechanisms That Conditioned Their Manufacture and Use in Seventeenth-Century Iroquoia*. unpublished MA thesis, Department of Anthropology, Trent University, Peterborough, ON.

Kenyon, Ian. 1988. "Late Woodland Occupations at the Liahn I Site, Kent Co." *KEWA* 88(2): 2–22.

Kenyon, Ian., and Thomas Kenyon. 1986. "Echo the Firekeeper: A Nineteenth Century Iroquois Site." *KEWA* 86(2): 4–27.

Kenyon, Walter A. 1986. *Mounds of the Sacred Earth: Burial Mounds of Ontario*. Toronto: Royal Ontario Museum.

Keron, James. 2010. "The Harrietsville Site (AfHf-10): An Earthwork Surrounded Neutral Village in Middlesex County." *"The Compleat Archaeologist": Papers in Honour of Michael W. Spence*, edited by Christopher J. Ellis, Neal Ferris, P. Timmins, and C. White, 121–36. London: Ontario Archaeological Society.

Kohl, Johann Georg. 1985 [1860]. *Kitchi-Gami: Life among the Lake Superior Ojibway*. St Paul, MN: Minnesota Historical Society Press.

Kuhn, Robert D. 2004. "Reconstructing Patterns of Interaction and Warfare between the Mohawk and Northern Iroquoians during the A.D. 1400–1700 Period." *A Passion for the Past: Papers in Honour of James F. Pendergast*, edited by James V. Wright and Jean-Luc Pilon, 145–66. Gatineau, QC: Canadian Museum of Civilization.

Lake Superior Basin Workshop participants. 1987. "Desperately Seeking Siouans: The Distribution of Sandy Lake Ware." *Arch Notes* 88(3): 9–13.

Landes, Ruth. 1937. *Ojibwa Sociology*. New York: Columbia University Press.

Lee, Gyoung-Ah, Anthony M. Davis, David G. Smith, and John H. McAndrews. 2004. "Identifying Fossil Wild Rice (Zizania) Pollen from Cootes Paradise, Ontario: A New Approach Using Scanning Electron Microscopy." *Journal of Archaeological Science* 31: 411–21.

Lee, Tom. 1958. "The Parker Earthwork, Corunna, Ontario." *Pennsylvania Archaeologist* 29(1): 3–30.

Lennox, Paul. 1984. *The Bogle I and Bogle II Sites: Historic Neutral Hamlets of the Northern Tier, Mercury Series, Archaeological Survey of Canada Paper 121*. Ottawa: National Museum of Man.

– 1995. "The Bradley Ave Site: A Late Prehistoric Neutral Cabin Site, Middlesex County, Ontario." *MTO Contributions to the Archaeology of the Late Woodland Period in Southwestern Ontario: Small Sites Investigations*, edited by Paul Lennox, 77–137. London, ON: London Museum of Archaeology.

– 2000. *The Molson Site: An Early Seventeenth Century First Nations Settlement, Simcoe County, Ontario, Museum of Indian Archaeology Research Bulletin 18*. London, ON: London Museum of Indian Archaeology.

Lennox, Paul., and Christine Dodd. 1991. "The La Salle-Lucier Site: Two Components of the Western Basin Tradition, Essex County, Ontario." *Ontario Archaeology* 52: 17–53.

Lennox, Paul., and William R. Fitzgerald. 1990. "The Culture History and Archaeology of the Neutral Iroquoians " *The Archaeology of Southern Ontario to A.D. 1650*, edited by Christopher J. Ellis and Neal Ferris, 405–56. London, ON: London Chapter, Ontario Archaeological Society.

Lyons, Natasha, Peter Dawson, Matthew Walls, Donald Uluadluak, Louis Angalik, Mark Kalluak, Philip Kigusiutuak, Luke Kiniksi, Joe Karetak, and Luke Suluk. 2010. "Person,

Place, Memory, Thing: How Inuit Elders Are Informing Archaeological Practice in the Canadian North." *Canadian Journal of Archaeology* 34(1): 1–31.

Lytwyn, V. 1986. *The Fur Trade of the Little North*. Winnipeg, MB: Rupert's Land Research Centre, University of Winnipeg.

– 2002. *Muskekowuck Athinuwick: Original People of the Great Swampy Land*. Winnipeg, MB: University of Manitoba Press.

MacDonald, Robert I. 1986. *The Coleman Site (AiHd-7): A Late Prehistoric Iroquoian Village in the Waterloo Region*. unpublished MA thesis, Department of Anthropology, Trent University, Peterborough, ON.

MacDonald, Robert I., and Ronald Williamson. 2001. "Sweat Lodges and Solidarity: The Archaeology of the Hubbert Site." *Ontario Archaeology* 71: 29–78.

Martelle, Holly. 2002. *Huron Potters and Archaeological Constructs: Researching Ceramic Micro-Stylistics*. unpublished PhD dissertation, University of Toronto, Toronto.

– 2004. "Some Thoughts on the Impact of Disease and European Contact on Ceramic Production in Seventeenth Century Huronia." *Ontario Archaeology* 77/78: 22–43.

Mason, R.J. 1970. "Hopewell, Middle Woodland, and the Laurel Culture: A Problem in Archaeological Classification." *American Anthropologist* 72: 805–15.

– 1981. *Great Lakes Archaeology*. Toronto: Academic Press.

McAndrews, J.H. 1984. "Late Quaternary History of Rice Lake, Ontario, and the McIntyre Archaeological Site." *The McIntyre Site: Archaeology, Subsistence and Environment*, edited by Richard B. Johnston, 159–89. Ottawa: National Museums of Canada.

McAndrews, J.H., and C.L. Turton. 2007. "Canada Geese Dispersed Cultigen Pollen Grains from Prehistoric Iroquoian Fields to Crawford Lake, Ontario, Canada." *Palynology* 31: 9–18.

McLeod, Mike. 2004. "Archaeology of the Sydney/Rowdy Lake Narrows Crossing." *Arch Notes* 9(2): 14–19.

Merrett, D.C. 2003. "Maxillary Sinusitis among the Moatfield People." *Bones of the Ancestors. The Archaeology and Osteobiography of the Moatfield Ossuary*, edited by Ronald F. Williamson and S. Pfeiffer, 241–62. Ottawa: Canadian Museum of Civilization.

Merrett, D.C., and S. Pfeiffer. 2000. "Maxillary Sinusitis as an Indicator of Respiratory Health in Past Populations." *American Journal of Physical Anthropology* 111: 301–18.

Merringer, Ian. 2011. "After More than a Century, Atlantic Salmon Return to Credit River." *The Globe and Mail*, 29 July 2011.

Meyer, David, and Scott Hamilton. 1994. "Neighbours to the North in Northern Plains Prehistory." *Plains Indians AD 500–1500: The Archaeological Past of Historic Groups*, edited by Karl H. Schlesier, 71–95. Norman, OK: University of Oklahoma Press.

Mills, William C. 1921. *Certain Mounds and Village Sites in Ohio: Flint Ridge*. Vol. 3. Columbus, OH: F.J. Heer Printing Co.

Molto, J.E. 1979. *Saugeen Osteology: The Evidence of the Second Cemetery at the Donaldson Site, Museum of Indian Archaeology Bulletin 14*. London, ON: Museum of Indian Archaeology at the University of Western Ontario.

Murphy, Carl. 1991. "A Western Basin Winter Cabin from Kent County, Ontario." KEWA 91(1): 3–17.

Murphy, Carl., and Neal Ferris. 1990. "The Late Woodland Western Basin Tradition of Southwestern Ontario." *The Archaeology of Southern Ontario to A.D. 1650*, edited by Christopher J. Ellis and Neal Ferris, 189–278. London, ON: London Chapter, Ontario Archaeological Society.

Nassaney, Michael S., and Kenneth E. Sassaman. 1995. *Native American Interactions: Multiscalar Analayses and Interpretation in the Eastern Woodlands*. Knoxville, TN: University of Tennessee Press.

Needs-Howarth, Suzanne. 1999. *Native Fishing in the Great Lakes: A Multi-disciplinary Approach to Zooarchaeological Remains from Iroquoian Villages Near Lake Simcoe, Ontario*. Groninger Instituut voor Archeologie, University of Groningen, The Netherlands.

Needs-Howarth, Suzanne., and R.I. MacDonald. In press. "The Walleye Fishery at the Peace Bridge Site, Fort Erie, Ontario." *Ontario Archaeology*.

Needs-Howarth, Suzanne., and S.C. Thomas. 1998. "Seasonal Variation in Fishing Strategies at Two Iroquoian Village Sites Near Lake Simcoe, Ontario." *Environmental Archaeology* 3: 109–20.

Needs-Howarth, Suzanne., and Ronald F. Williamson. 2010. "Feeding and Clothing the Masses: The Role of White-Tailed Deer in Community Planning in Sixteenth Century Ontario." *11th Conference of the International Council for Archaeozoology*. Paris.

Newman, M., and Patrick J. Julig. 1989. "The Identification of Protein Residues on Lithic Artifacts from a Stratified Boreal Forest Site." *Canadian Journal of Archaeology* 13: 119–32.

Noble, William C. 1984. "Historic Neutral Settlement Patterns." *Canadian Journal of Archaeology* 8(1): 1–28.

– 1985. "Tsouharissen's Chiefdom: An Early Historic 17th Century Neutral Iroquoian Ranked Society." *Canadian Journal of Archaeology* 9(2): 131–46.

Oka, Rahul, and Chapurukha M. Kusimba. 2008. "The Archaeology of Trading Systems, Part I: Towards a New Trade Synthesis." *Journal of Archaeological Research* 16: 339–95.

O'Shea, J.M., and G.A.Meadows. 2009. "Evidence for Early Hunters beneath the Great Lakes." *PNAS* 106: 10, 120–3.

Ossenberg, N.S. 1969. *Osteology of the Miller Site, Royal Ontario Museum Art and Archaeology Occasional Paper 18*. Toronto: Royal Ontario Museum.

Pearce, R. 1996. *Mapping Middleport: A Case Study in Societal Archaeology, Research Report 25*. London, ON: London Museum of Archaeology.

Pearsall, Deborah M. 1989. *Paleoethnobotany: A Handbook of Procedures*. San Diego, CA: Academic Press.

Pettipas, L. 1983. *Introducing Manitoba Prehistory, Papers in Manitoba Archaeology, Popular Series No. 4*. Winnipeg, MB: Manitoba Department of Culture, Heritage and Recreation.

Pfeiffer, S. 1984. "Palaeopathology in an Iroquoian Ossuary, with Special Reference to Tuberculosis." *American Journal of Physical Anthropology* 62(2): 181–9.

Pihl, Robert H., Stephen G. Monckton, David A. Robertson, and Ronald F. Williamson. 2008. "Settlement and Subsistence Change at the Turn of the First Millennium: The View from the Holmedale Site, Brantford, Ontario." *Current Northeast Paleoethnobotany* 2: 151–72.

Pilon, Jean-Luc, and Luke Dalla Bona. 2004. "Insights into the Early Peopling of Northwestern Ontario as Documented at the Allen Site (EcJs-1), Sioux Lookout District, Ontario." *The Late Paleo-Indian Great Lakes: Geological and Archaeological Investigations of Late Pleistocene and Early Holocene Environments*, edited by L.J. Jackson and A. Hinshelwood, 315–36. Hull, QC: Canadian Museum of Civilization.

Potter, Stephen R. 1993. *Commoners, Tribute, and Chiefs: The Development of Algonquian Culture in the Potomac Valley*. Charlottesville, VA: University of Virginia Press.

Prevec, R. 1985. "Archaeological Evidence of the Carolina Parakeet in Ontario." *Ontario Birds* 3(1): 24–8.

Prevec, Rosemary, and William C. Noble. 1983. "Historic Neutral Iroquois Faunal Utilization." *Ontario Archaeology* 39: 41–56.

Prowse, S.L. 2008–09. "Much Ado about Netsinkers: An Examination of Pre-contact Aboriginal Netsinker Manufacture and Use Patterns at Five Woodland Period Archaeological Sites within Southern Ontario." *Ontario Archaeology* 85–8: 69–96.

Rajnovich, Grace. 1980. "The Ballysadare Site (DkKp-10): A Laurel-Blackduck Site at the Source of the Winnipeg River." *Ontario Archaeology* 33: 37–58.

– 1994. *Reading Rock Art: Interpreting the Indian Rock Paintings of the Canadian Shield*. Toronto: Natural Heritage/Natural History Inc.

Ramsden, Peter. 1990. "St Lawrence Iroquoians in the Upper Trent River Valley." *Man in the Northeast* 39: 87–95.

– 1991. "Death in winter: Changing Symbolic Patterns in Southern Ontario Prehistory." *Anthropologica* 32: 167–81.

Ray, A.J. 1974. *Indians in the Fur Trade: Their Role as Trappers, Hunters, and Middlemen in the Lands Southwest of Hudson's Bay 1660–1870*. Toronto: University of Toronto Press.

Reid, C.S. "Paddy", ed. 1988a. *Boreal Forest and Subarctic Archaeology*. Vol. 6, *Occasional Publications of the London Chapter, Ontario Archaeological Society*. Toronto.

– 1988b. "Some Ideas Concerning the Formulation of Research Designs and Excavation Methodologies on Boreal Forest Habitation Sites." *Midcontinental Journal of Archaeology* 13(2): 187–221.

Reid, C.S. "Paddy", and Grace Rajnovich. 1991. "Laurel: A Re-evaluation of the Spatial, Social and Temporal Paradigms." *Canadian Journal of Archaeology* 15: 193–234.

Rice, Prudence. 1987. *Pottery Analysis*. Chicago: University of Chicago Press.

Ringer, R. James. 2006. "Atherley Narrows Fish Weirs." *Underwater Cultural Heritage at*

Risk: Managing Natural and Human Impacts, edited by R. Grenier, D. Nutley, and I. Cochran, 44–5. Paris: International Council on Monuments and Sites.

Ritchie, William A. 1932. "The Lamoka Site: The Type Site of the Archaic Algonkian Period in New York." *New York State Archaeological Association Researches and Transactions* 7(4): 79–134.

– 1973. "The Roundtop Site (Apl.1)." *Aboriginal Settlement Patterns in the Northeast*, edited by William A. Ritchie and R.E. Funk, 179–94. Albany, NY: State University of New York.

Rogers, Edward. 1962. *The Round Lake Ojibwa*. Toronto: Ontario Department of Lands and Forests for the Royal Ontario Museum

– 1969. "Band Organization among the Indians of Eastern Subarctic Canada." *National Museums of Canada Bulletin 228*, 21–50. Ottawa: National Museums of Canada.

– 1978. "Southeastern Ojibwa." *Northeast, Vol. 15*, edited by Bruce Trigger, 760–71. Washington, DC: Smithsonian Institution.

– 1988. "The Mistassini Cree." *Hunters and Gatherers Today* edited by M.G. Bicchieri. Prospect Heights: Waveland Press.

Rogers, Edward., and Donald Smith, eds. 1994a. *Aboriginal Ontario*. Toronto: Dundurn Press.

– eds. 1994b. *Aboriginal Ontario: Historical Perspectives on the First Nations of Ontario, Historical Studies Series*. Toronto: Dundurn Press.

Rosenswig, Robert M. 1997. "Ethics in Canadian Archaeology: An International Comparative Analysis." *Canadian Journal of Archaeology* 21(2): 99–114.

Ross, W.I. 1997. "The Interlakes Composite: A Re-definition of the Initial Settlement of the Agassiz-Minong Peninsula." *Wisconsin Archaeologist* 76(3–4): 244–68.

Sagard, G. 1939. *The Long Journey to the Country of the Hurons*. Edited by George M. Wrong. Toronto: Champlain Society.

Sahlins, Marshall D. 1968. *Tribesmen*. Englewood Cliffs, NJ: Prentice-Hall.

Saunders, S.R., P.G. Ramsden, and D.A. Herring. 1992. "Transformation and Disease: Precontact Ontario Iroquoians." *Disease and Demography in the Americas*, edited by D.H. Ubelaker, 117–25. Washington, DC: Smithsonian Institution Press.

Sioui, Georges E. 1999. *Huron-Wendat: The Heritage of the Circle*. Toronto: University of British Columbia Press.

Smith, David G., and Gary W. Crawford. 1997. "Recent developments in the Archaeology of the Princess Point Complex in Southern Ontario." *Canadian Journal of Archaeology* 21: 9–32.

Smith, Donald B. 1987. *Sacred Feathers: The Reverend Peter Jones (Kahkewaquonaby) and the Mississauga Indians*. Toronto: University of Toronto Press.

Snow, Dean. 1995. "Migration in Prehistory: The Northern Iroquoian Case." *American Antiquity* 60: 59–79.

Speck, F.G. 1913. *Family Hunting Territories and Social Life of Various Algonkian Bands of the Ottawa Valley, Memoir 70, No. 8, Anthropological Series 1915.* Ottawa: Geological Survey of Canada.

– 1915. *Myths and Folk-lore of the Timiskaming Algonguin and Timagami Ojibwa, Memoir 71, No. 9, Anthropological Series 1915.* Ottawa: Geological Survey, Canada Department of Mines.

Spence, Michael W. 1967. *Middle Woodland Burial Complex in the St Lawrence Valley, Anthropological Paper No. 14.* Ottawa: National Museum of Canada.

– 1986. "Band Structure and Interaction in Early Southern Ontario." *Canadian Journal of Anthropology* 5(2): 83–95.

– 1994. "Mortuary Programmes of the Early Ontario Iroquoians." *Ontario Archaeology* 58: 7–27.

Spence, Michael W., William D. Finlayson, and Robert H. Pihl. 1979. "Hopewellian Influence on Middle Woodland Cultures in Southern Ontario." *Hopewell Archaeology: The Chillicothe Conference*, edited by David Brose and N'omi Greber, 115–21. Kent, OH: Kent State University Press.

Spence, Michael W., and William A. Fox. 1986. "The Early Woodland Occupations of Southern Ontario." *Early Woodland Archaeology*, edited by K.B. Farnsworth and T.E. Emerson, 4–46. Kampsville, IL: Centre for American Archaeology Press.

Spence, Michael W., and J. Russell Harper. 1968. *The Cameron's Point Site, Art and Archaeology Occasional Paper 12.* Toronto: Royal Ontario Museum.

Spence, Michael W., Robert Pihl, and J.E. Molto. 1984. "Hunter-Gatherer Social Group Identification: A Case Study from Middle Woodland Southern Ontario." *Exploring the Limits: Frontiers and Boundaries in Prehistory*, edited by Suzanne P. deAtley and Frank J. Findlow, 117–42. Oxford: British Archaeological Reports.

Spence, Michael W., Robert H. Pihl, and Carl R. Murphy. 1990. "Cultural Complexes of the Early and Middle Woodland Periods." *The Archaeology of Southern Ontario to A.D. 1650*, edited by Christopher J. Ellis and Neal Ferris, 125–69. London: London Chapter, Ontario Archaeological Society.

Spence, Michael W., Ronald F. Williamson, and J.H. Dawkins. 1978. "The Bruce Boyd Site: An Early Woodland Component in Southwestern Ontario." *Ontario Archaeology* 29: 33–46.

Spielmann, Katherine A. 2002. "Feasting, Craft Specialization, and the Ritual Mode of Production in Small-Scale Societies." *American Anthropologist* 104(1): 195–207.

St Denis, Guy 2005. *Tecumseh's Bones.* Montreal & Kingston: McGill-Queen's University Press.

Steckley, John L. 2007. *Words of the Huron.* Waterloo, ON: Wilfrid Laurier University Press.

Stewart, F.L. 2000. "Variability in Neutral Iroquoian Subsistence: A.D. 1540–1651." *Ontario Archaeology* 69: 92–117.

Storck, Peter L. 2004. *Journey to the Ice Age: Discovering an Ancient World.* Vancouver, BC: University of British Columbia Press.

– 1997. *The Fisher Site: Archaeological, Geological, and Paleobotanical Studies at an Early Paleo-Indian Site in Southern Ontario, Canada.* Memoir 30. Ann Arbor, MI: University of Michigan, Museum of Anthropology.

Storck, Peter L., and Arthur E. Spiess. 1994. "The Significance of New Faunal Identifications Attributed to an Early Paleoindian (Gainey Complex) Occupation at the Udora Site, Ontario." *American Antiquity* 59: 121–42.

Taché, Karine. 2011a. "New Perspectives on Meadowood Trade Items." *American Antiquity* 76(1): 41–80.

– 2011b. *Structure and Regional Diversity and of the Meadowood Interaction Sphere, Memoir 48.* Ann Arbor, MI: University of Michigan, Museum of Anthropology.

Tanner, Adrian. 1979. *Bringing Home Animals: Religious Ideology and Mode of Production of the Mistassini Cree Hunters, Social and Economic Studies No. 23.* St John's, NL: Institute of Social and Economic Research, Memorial University.

Taylor-Hollings, Jill. 1999. *The Northwestern Extent of Sandy Lake Ware: A Canadian Perspective.* Unpublished MA thesis, Department of Anthropology and Archaeology, University of Saskatchewan, Saskatoon, SK.

Thomas, S.C. 1988. "The Muskrat: A Lean-Season Resource in the Late Archaic of Southwestern Ontario." *Diet and Subsistence: Current Archaeological Perspectives*, edited by B.V. Kennedy and G.M. LeMoine, 349–54. Calgary, AB: Chacmool, The Archaeological Association of the University of Calgary.

Thor, Kristin. 2006. *The Schlegel Site Report, BfGw-6.* Unpublished BA thesis, Department of Anthropology, Laurentian University, Sudbury, ON.

Thwaites, R.G., ed. 1896–1901. *The Jesuit Relations and Allied Documents: Travels and Explorations of the Jesuit Missionaries in New France, 1610–1791.* 73 vols. Cleveland, OH: Burrows Brothers Company.

Timmins, Peter. 1997. *The Calvert Site: An Interpretive Framework for the Early Iroquoian Village, Mercury Series, Archaeological Survey of Canada, Paper 156.* Ottawa: Canadian Museum of Civilization.

Tobias, Terry. 2000. *Chief Kerry's Moose: A Guidebook to Land Use and Occupancy Mapping, Research Design and Data Collection.* Vancouver, BC: Union of British Columbia Indian Chiefs and Ecotrust Canada.

– 2009. *Living Proof: The Essential Data-Collection Guide for Indigenous Use-and-Occupancy Map Surveys.* Vancouver, BC: Ecotrust Canada.

Tooker, Elisabeth. 1967. *An Ethnography of the Huron Indians, 1615–1649.* Washington, DC: Smithsonian Institution.

Trigger, Bruce. 1976. *The Children of Aataentsic, Vols. I and II.* Montreal & Kingston: McGill-Queen's University Press.

– 1985. *Natives and Newcomers: Canada's "Heroic Age" Reconsidered.* Montreal & Kingston: McGill-Queen's University Press.

– 1990a. *The Huron Farmers of the North.* 2nd ed. Chicago: Holt, Rinehart and Winston.

– 1990b. "Maintaining Economic Equality in Opposition to Complexity: A Iroquoian Case

Study." *The Evolution of Political Systems: Sociopolitics in Small Scale Sedentary Societies*, edited by Steadman Upham, 119–45. Cambridge: Cambridge University Press.

– 2003. "All People Are [Not] Good." *Anthropologica* 45: 39–44.

Trigger, Bruce., and Gordon M. Day. 1994. "Southern Algonquian Middlemen: Algonquin, Nipissing, and Ottawa, 1550–1780." *Aboriginal Ontario: Historical Perspectives on the First Nations*, edited by Edward S. Rogers and Donald B. Smith, 64–78. Toronto: Dundurn Press.

Vastokas, Joan M., and Romas K. Vastokas. 1973. *Sacred Art of the Algonkians: A Study of the Peterborough Petroglyphs*. Peterborough, ON: Mansard Press.

Verano, J.W., and D.H. Ubelaker. 1992. *Disease and Demography in the Americas*. Washington, DC: Smithsonian Institution Press.

von Gernet, A., and P. Timmins. 1987. "Pipes and Parakeets: Reconstructing Meaning in an Early Iroquoian Context." *Archaeology as Long-Term History*, edited by Ian Hodder, 31–42. Cambridge: Cambridge University Press.

Wagner, Norman E., Lawrence E. Toombs, and Eduard R. Riegert. 1973. *The Moyer Site: A Prehistoric Village in Waterloo County*. Waterloo, ON: Wilfrid Laurier University.

Walker, P.L. 2008. "Bioarchaeological Ethics: A Historical Perspective on the Value of Human Remains." *Biological Anthropology of the Human Skeleton*, edited by M.A. Katzenberg and S.R. Saunders, 3–40. Toronto: Wiley-Liss.

Warrick, Gary. 1996. "Evolution of the Iroquoian Longhouse." *People Who Lived in Big Houses: Archaeological Perspectives on Large Domestic Structures*, edited by Gary Coupland and E.B. Banning, 11–26. Madison: Prehistory Press.

– 2000. "Precontact Iroquoian Occupation of Southern Ontario." *Journal of World Prehistory* 14(4): 415–66.

– 2003. "European Infectious Disease and Depopulation of the Wendat-Tionontate (Huron-Petun)." *World Archaeology* 35(2): 258–75.

– 2006. "Davisville 2 Site: Archaeological Test Excavation of an Early 19th Century Mohawk Cabin on the Grand River." *Annual Archaeological Report, Ontario* 13: 53–7.

– 2008. *A Population History of the Huron-Petun, A.D. 500–1650*. Cambridge: Cambridge University Press.

Watkins, Joe. 2003. "Beyond the Margin: American Indians, First Nations, and Archaeology in North America." *American Antiquity* 62: 273–85.

Williamson, Ronald F. 1983. *The Robin Hood Site: A Study in Functional Variability in Late Iroquoian Settlement Patterns*. Edited by Richard B. Johnston, *Monographs in Ontario Archaeology 1*. Toronto: Ontario Archaeological Society.

– 1990. "The Early Iroquoian Period of Southern Ontario." *The Archaeology of Southern Ontario to A.D. 1650*, edited by Christopher J. Ellis and Neal Ferris, 291–320. London, ON: London Chapter, Ontario Archaeological Society.

– 1996. "Sacred Stone: The Archaeology of Caches." *Annual Meeting of the Ontario Archaeological Society*.

Williamson, Ronald F., ed. 1998. *The Myers Road Site: Archaeology of the Early to Middle*

Iroquoian Transition, Occasional Publication of the Ontario Archaeological Society, 7. London, ON: London Chapter, Ontario Archaeological Society.

Williamson, Ronald F., and R.I. MacDonald. 1998. *Legacy of Stone: Ancient Life on the Niagara Frontier.* Toronto: eastendbooks.

Williamson, Ronald F., and S. Pfeiffer, eds. 2003. *Bones of the Ancestors. The Archaeology and Osteobiography of the Moatfield Ossuary, Mercury Series Archaeology Paper 163.* Ottawa: Canadian Museum of Civilization.

Williamson, Ronald F., and R.H. Pihl. 2002. "Foragers and Fishers on the Credit River: The Scott-O'Brien Site." *Mississauga: The First Ten Thousand Years*, edited by Frank Dieterman, 88–9. Toronto: eastendbooks.

Wintemberg, William J. 1928. *Uren Prehistoric Village Site, Oxford County, Ontario, National Museum of Canada Bulletin 51.* Ottawa: Canada Department of Mines and Resources.

– 1939. *Lawson Prehistoric Village Site, Middlesex County, Ontario, Bulletin 94.* Ottawa: National Museum of Canada.

– 1948. *The Middleport Prehistoric Village Site, National Museum of Canada Bulletin 109.* Ottawa: Canada Department of Mines and Resources.

Winterhalder, Bruce. 1983a. "Boreal Foraging Strategies." *Boreal Forest Adaptations: The Northern Algonkians*, edited by A.T. Steegmann Jr, 201–41. New York: Plenum Press.

– 1983b. "History and Ecology of the Boreal Zone of Northern Ontario." *Boreal Forest Adaptations: The Northern Algonkians*, edited by A.T. Steegmann Jr, 9–54. New York: Plenum Press.

Wormington, H.M. 1957. *Ancient Man in North America.* Vol. 4, *Popular Series.* Denver, CO: Denver Museum of Natural History.

Wright, James V. 1967. *The Laurel Tradition and the Middle Woodland Period, National Museum of Canada Bulletin 217.* Ottawa: Department of the Secretary of State.

– 1968. *The Michipicoten Site, Ontario, National Museum of Canada, Bulletin 224.* Ottawa: National Museum of Canada.

– 1972a. *Ontario Prehistory: An Eleven-Thousand-Year Archaeological Outline.* Ottawa: National Museum of Man.

– 1972b. *The Shield Archaic, National Museum of Man, Publications in Archaeology, No. 3.* Ottawa: National Museum of Man.

– 1981. "Prehistory of the Canadian Shield." *Subarctic, Vol. 6*, edited by J. Helm, 86–96. Washington, DC: Smithsonian Institution.

– 1995a. *A History of the Native People of Canada Vol. 1 (10,000–1,000 BC).* Hull, QC: Canadian Museum of Civilization.

– 1995b. "Three Dimensional Reconstructions of Iroquoian Longhouses: A Comment." *Archaeology of Eastern North America* 23: 9–21.

– 2004. *A History of the Native People of Canada Vol. III (AD500–European Contact).* Hull, QC: Canadian Museum of Civilization.

Wright, James V., and J.E. Anderson. 1963. *The Donaldson Site, National Museum of Canada Bulletin 184*. Ottawa: Department of Northern Affairs and National Resources.

Wright, Milt. 1986. *The Uren Site AfHd-3: An Analysis and Reappraisal of the Uren Substage Type Site, Monographs in Ontario Archaeology 2*. Toronto: Ontario Archaeological Society.

Wylie, Alison. 1997. "Contextualizing Ethics: Comments on 'Ethics in Canadian Archaeology' by Robert Rosenswig." *Canadian Journal of Archaeology* 21(2): 115–20.

Yellowhorn, Eldon. 1996. "Indians, Archaeology and the Changing World." *Native Studies Review* 11(2): 23–50.

Yu, Z. 2000. "Ecosystem Response to Late Glacial and Early Holocene Climate Oscillations in the Great Lakes Region of North America " *Quaternary Science Reviews* 19: 1723–47.

Index

forests, 25, 33–4, 114, 116; evolution of, 27–8, 84, 118, 132–3. *See also* boreal forest

Founding First Nations Circle, 208–9

frog, 119, 123

fruits, 54, 82, 125, 127, 128

fur trade, 63, 79, 94. *See also* trapping

galena, 42, 159, 164

gathering, 33–4, 92, 119, 126, 127–30; as complement to farming, 33–4, 55, 126. *See also* hunting and gathering

generosity, 166–9, 170, 173, 189

Georgian Bay, 25–7, 28–30

gifting, 170, 175; and leadership, 167–8, 189–90; and obligation, 167; and sociopolitical organization, 149

glacial lakes, 25–7; Agassiz, 84, 85, 87; Algonquin, 25–8; Iroquois, 25, 26; Minong, 84, 85

glaciation, 25–9, 77–9, 83–4, 85, 87; and distribution of tool stone, 88, 138; effects on landscape, 25–8, 87; features created by, 154, 164; and location of archaeological sites, 27, 44, 81, 84. *See also* strandline

Glen Williams ossuary, 184

goose, 29, 119, 158

goosefoot. *See* chenopod

gorgets, 42, 43, 49, 192, 193

Great Lakes. *See* Lake Erie; Lake Huron; Lake Ontario; Lake Superior; Nipissing phase

Grimsby Site, 170

ground stone tools. *See* stone tools, ground

hamlet, 78, 79, 107

Harris lines, 180, 185, 186

Haudenosaunee, 62–3, 74

health, 58, 177–87; dental, 58, 182; effect of age on, 180; effect of European contact on, 60, 62, 183, 186–7; effect of living conditions on, 58, 177; of individuals, 199–200. *See also* cavities; diet; injuries; violence

hemlock, 28

heritage. *See* cultural heritage

Hind Site, 32

historic records: as source of information, 9–10, 102, 144, 165, 204

Holmedale Site, 55, 56

Honey Harbour Site, 91

Hopewell culture, 164; influence of, 91, 92; and trade, 139–40

horticulture. *See* farming

houses, 99–100; Archaic period, 45–6. *See also* cabins; huts; longhouses; wigwams

human remains, 178–87; aging and sexing of, 178; chemical analyses of, 183, 185; and contemporary First Nations, 200, 209–10. *See also* burials

hunter-gatherers, 46–7, 147, 184; stereotyped views of, 81

hunting, 36, 82–3, 114–18; camps, 49, 55, 106; and ritual, 160, 191; strategies, 33, 114

hunting and gathering, 48–9, 57, 62, 82–3, 92

Huron/Wendat, 8, 121, 140, 141, 143, 151, 189–90, 208; burial practices, 197–8; ceremonies, 169, 173; health of, 183, 186; history, 55, 60, 63, 69, 70, 71–4, 186, 187; identity, 10, 67; style pottery, 145–6

huts, 107, 108–9

Ice Age, 25–7, 37. *See also* glaciation

identity, 10–11, 49, 52; clan, 61; and trade, 67

infants: burial of, 198, 199

injuries, 180–1, 185

Interlakes Composite. *See* Lakehead Complex

McLeod Site, 38–9

Meadowood: bifaces, 49, 52–3, 191–2; cemeteries, 190–1; culture, 49, 52

medicine, 60, 106, 128, 129, 158–9, 181

Mesquakie. *See* Fire Nation/Assistaeronon

Michipicoten, 67

microbotanical remains, 125. *See also* pollen

middens, 46, 63, 106–8, 128, 195

Middle Woodland, 12, 13, 48; in northern Ontario, 89–92

Miller Site, 185

minerals, 159. *See also* galena; iron pyrite; ochre

mink, 116, 123

Mishipizhiw, 30, 155–6, 158, 161, 162

Mississauga, 60–1, 62–3, 67, 74, 151

Mnjikaning Fish Weirs, 42, 120

Moatfield ossuary, 57–8, 179–80, 184–5, 196–7, 198

mobility, 35, 37, 82–3, 108–11, 190; and effect on archaeological visibility, 11, 65–7, 74

Mohawk Village Site, 74–5

moiety, 167

Molson Site, 66, 67

moose, 84, 113, 114, 156

mortuary practices. *See* burial practices

mounds, 172–4; as imitation of natural features, 154, 164. *See also* burial mounds; Cameron's Point Mounds; East Sugar Island Mounds; Serpent Mounds Site

Moyer site, 70

muskrat, 114, 116

Nation. *See* First Nations

near north, 77, 78

Neutral, 63; history, 60, 63, 65, 69–74, 186, 187; Nation, 8, 56, 60, 168; style pottery, 145; trade, 140, 141

Nipissing (people), 63, 67, 73

Nipissing phase, 29, 31

Nipissirini. *See* Nipissing (people)

northern Ontario: current conditions in, 78, 83, 207–8; as distinct region, 94–5; history of, 77–9, 83–95; and relationship with south, 77, 79, 92; stereotyped views of, 77, 81–2; working in, 80–2. *See also* boreal forest; Canadian Shield

nuts, 130

ochre, 49, 50, 136, 159, 160, 191; as pigment, 161; symbolism of, 49, 136, 164

Odawa, 63, 67, 73, 141

offerings, 40, 156, 158–9, 160, 191. *See also* burial offerings

Ojibwa, 25, 67, 77, 82; and Blackduck pottery style, 70–1; history of, 62–3, 64, 74

Old Copper Complex, 88, 89

Onondaga chert, 138–40

Ontario Cemeteries Act. *See* Cemeteries Act

Ontario Heritage Act, 18, 63

oral history, 6, 68, 72

ossuaries, 57, 169, 178–80, 196. *See also* Fairty ossuary; Glen Williams ossuary; Moatfield ossuary; Teston ossuary; Uxbridge ossuary

Ottawa (people), 63, 67, 73

Ottawa River, 28–9, 31, 72

paleoethnobotany, 124

Paleoindian, 35–40, 77, 83–5; colonization of Ontario, 26–7, 83–4, 85, 205–6; and hunting, 36, 84, 114 ; and ritual, 38, 40; sites, 35–7, 84; time period, 13, 35; tools of, 27, 37–40, 84–6, 135–6

palisades, 55, 59, 62, 101–2, 105–6, 110, 198–9; and defense, 68, 106, 187; as defining space, 105, 106–7; remodelling of, 68, 70, 106

panpipes, 172–3, 194

Parkhill Site, 38–9